# HEROES KNEEL

ALEX W. FOLEY

# HEROES
# KNEEL

An Old Testament Quest for
the Source of Honor and Love

*"The greatest among you
must be **a servant**."*
MATTHEW 23:11 (NLT)

✦

*"Whoever wants to be first
must take last place
and be **the servant**
of everyone else."*
MARK 9:35 (NLT)

✦

*"You see, we don't go around
preaching about ourselves.
We preach that Jesus Christ is Lord,
and we ourselves are **your
servants** for Jesus' sake."*
2 CORINTHIANS 4:5 (NLT)

# CONTENTS

## PART I:
## The Ancient Greats and How They Knelt

## PART II:
## Love Despite Adultery in the Life of Hosea

✦

*"Oh come, let us worship
and bow down:
**let us kneel** before
the LORD our maker."*
Psalm 95:6 (KJV)

# A WORD FROM THE AUTHOR

## by Alex W. Foley

THIS BOOK IS NOT ABOUT me, but for a very long time, I thought everything was.

Growing up in small-town Illinois, I was your classic '90s kid. Life started simple: excel in school, win at sports, and if there's time left over, play Nintendo. Quickly, I rose to little-kid stardom, winning trophies and posting straight As. Down deep, however, things were not so shiny, as my heart kept chasing the same poisonous whisper: *Be more impressive.*

Meanwhile, I attended a Catholic school and a Baptist church. Talk about confusing. The Catholics insisted I should be baptized to avoid hell, so I was. The Baptists told me I had to ask Jesus into my heart, so I did—like a hundred times. Still, I never felt sure about salvation, always questioning how much doubt was allowed before faith was just wishful thinking.

When high school hit, the whispers got more intense. Everything became about eclipsing my peers, from math club to Xbox to tennis. The more accolades I amassed, the deeper I could bury my concerns about eternity. After all, I was the king of my little jungle.

Then one day, it burnt down.

A few days before Christmas 2006, my sister and I received the last news any child wants to hear: our parents were divorcing. Suddenly, the main stabilizing force in my life was ripped away, so I looked for replacements. First, it was a few gulps of alcohol. Before long, it was party or bust. This goose chase for satisfaction continued through college, where I got a bachelor's in astrophysics while laughing off God—all to make the world say, "Wow."

Then, reality punched back. Like a good millennial, I was jobless upon graduation and subsequently moved home with my dad. Most of my friends were landing careers and spouses, but not me. I was sour and single, slinging tapes at Family Video for minimum wage.

"Aren't you that Foley kid?" strangers would ask as they rented their movies. "You were valedictorian! What are you doing here?"

I could only laugh off that question so many times. So instead, I wrote poetry. This was my first attempt:

> Like curdled milk, a crippled mind
> corrupts a nearby neighbor.
> A sickening stench, a thirst unquenched,
> no nourishment left to savor.
>
> Rotting cores from gifts ignored
> plague those some once deemed blessed.
> Squandered talents as hopeful parents
> reach out from an empty nest.
>
> Compounding fear of a looming career
> swiftly whittles away resolve.
> Failure, the fright, delaying delight
> as doors close, decisions devolve.
>
> Still clinging to the memories,
> few could grasp the meaningful fodder.
> 'Twas difficult to discern the two
> for the clay does not mold the potter.
>
> Festering thoughts of the time it costs
> when falling for fool's gold.
> Fascination of fun, no prize to be won,
> eternal questions of the life untold.

One by one, every impressive aspect of my life was peeled back like wrapping paper. The last to go was my athleticism. While weight training to windmill-dunk a basketball, my right hamstring decided it didn't want to stay attached to my pelvis anymore. And just like that, I couldn't walk or run from anything—including God.

Over the next few days, as I laid in my bed, I decided to do the unthinkable: read the New Testament. All my life, people had been telling me what to believe. Some demanded I trust the Bible; others declared religion a joke. Why not actually decide for myself?

So I did.

For years, I had bounced around in the Bible—in church and youth group and religion class—but this was different. The gloves were on, and I was sparring with God. The days of memorizing Bible verses for candy or a quiz were long gone. Now, I was searching for answers, or contradictions, but the key was I was *searching*.

I hated reading, and yet I was captivated. Within a week, I had read from Matthew to Revelation, filling the margins with my curious thoughts. I then took all my questions to a local pastor in a six-hour attempt to stump him. Each stab I took, however, seemed to cut me in return. It wasn't the pastor's answers that kept wounding me; it was hearing myself scrounge for excuses to stay on the throne of my life.

So that evening, I waited until I had the house to myself. And then, for the very first time, my heart truly knelt. No hell-haggling, no self-pity; just a cry for mercy and a readiness to serve.

That day in the fall of 2014 wasn't some magical wand-waving where all my flaws and addictions disappeared. It wasn't as much an *end* as it was a *beginning*—the beginning of a relationship, of a passion, of a quest.

Before long, I found myself getting a master's in theological studies, memorizing chapters of the Bible, and growing children's ministries. At one point, I substitute-taught kindergartners; at another, I lived in South Asia helping the persecuted church. Little did I know, all these adventures were preparing me for what was to come.

In January 2020, my pastor at the time connected me with a nonprofit in Iowa called Developing Great Relationships (DGR). He said they were looking for someone to write books about the Bible, and I (of all people) would be perfect. One call, one visit to the quaint Dutch town of Pella, Iowa, and I was a bona fide writer.

It gets better.

DGR, for over fifteen years, has been organizing biblical retreats to fortify marriages. Our mission at DGR is to help couples realize that the best marriages are built by cheerfully serving your spouse ahead of yourself. So now, as part of the DGR team, I get to help families grow together and avoid the implosion that mine underwent. Every day at DGR is a chance not only to dig deeper into the Word of God, but also an opportunity to flip the script of my parents' marriage by blessing the couples we serve. After all, as good ol' Teddy Roosevelt put it, "People don't care how much you know until they know how much you care."[1]

That's why this book exists. *Heroes Kneel* isn't some theological treatise with fancy words and obscure arguments. It's a down-to-earth quest to better know Jesus and cheerfully serve just like Him. Because the closer we draw to Him, the less selfish we become.

I hope you enjoy the pages ahead of you. I pray the Old Testament comes alive like you've never experienced before. And if that happens, I ask that you give all glory to God. He surely deserves it, and I surely do not.

For twenty-three long years, I thought a hero was someone who conquers, who wins, who *impresses*. Thankfully, the Bible changed my outlook.

Perhaps it will change yours too.

---

1    Fun fact: President Theodore "Teddy" Roosevelt was the first American to ever win a Nobel Prize, capturing the 1906 Nobel Peace Prize for brokering the end of the Russo-Japanese War. Thus, "good ol" is historically warranted.

# INTRODUCTION

## *What Gives?*

O UR WORLD IS BUILT ON giving.

The sun sends heat to an otherwise frozen earth. Plants afford creatures their precious oxygen.[1] One lifeform breathes its last, and decomposition brings nutrients to another. The planet pulses with giving at every turn, yet mankind struggles to cheerfully follow suit.

Still, the giving of self is not optional. It's not the tip jar in case we're feeling generous that day. Every moment, the heart decides the object of its affection, the mind its attention, the hand its service. The issue is not our lack of giving, but rather our inability to choose the right recipient.

Some let life choose for them, deferring to a daily Secret Santa of sorts, but all is allocated nonetheless. As the years pass, hearts place their bets on what they think will satisfy. Many stack their chips on pleasure jolts, only to see them swept away. No one gets blackjack, and yet we can't stop hitting. But the answer is not self-control—the game we've picked is rigged to rob us.

The losses are stacking up. Just watch the news. Global horrors have become a staple, flagrant greed the norm. All the while, depression skyrockets as media outlets sell the pursuit of happiness on interest.

---

1   Ninety-eight percent of Earth's atmospheric oxygen comes from plants, namely oceanic phytoplankton (70 percent) and Earth's three trillion trees (28 percent), though deforestation is steadily changing that number. At the current rate, by the year 2100, there will be no more rainforests on planet Earth, and by 2325, no trees whatsoever. Indeed, the Earth loves to give, but not as much as humans love to take.

"Serve the self and gain the world!" they say. But in reality, it's just the opposite.[2] In the timeless words of C.S. Lewis, "There must be a real giving up of the self . . . Look for yourself, and you will find in the long run only hatred, loneliness, despair, rage, ruin, and decay. But look for Christ and you will find Him, and with Him, everything else thrown in."

The solution to selfishness lies not in rejecting pleasure but in pursuing its perfect Source. John Piper echoes this sentiment, preaching, "The problem with the world is not hedonism; it's the failure of hedonism to go for what's truly satisfying." Yet this is hardly new. Aristotle spoke of our misguided pleasure quest some 2,300 years ago: "The problem is not that we aim too high and miss, but that we aim too low and hit." In short, contentment isn't found at the casino. It's high time to cash out.

But where to go? **In a world so bent on division, the need for unity is ever-glaring.** Such compassionate togetherness is both God's endgame and Satan's nemesis.[3] While the devil may be in the details, his grand mission has always been to focus our attention inward. Indeed, all relational conflicts—whether at the office, in the community, on the playground, or at home—are the tumors of this disease: We are wildly addicted to ourselves.[4]

It is no surprise that the devil leverages our selfish thoughts to spread destruction. C.S. Lewis went so far as to describe hell as "the ruthless, sleepless, unsmiling concentration upon self . . . where everyone is perpetually concerned about his own dignity and advancement."

In Western society, this mentality is sold to us at every turn. Listen to the Billboard top songs and tally how many promote sacrificial generosity versus lustful greed.[5] Search for a news station that blesses its opposition rather than mocking it. Whether it's food or power or money or romance, the thirsty soon thirst again. As one restaurant sign put it, "The gap between

---

2   In a real sense, followers of Jesus *gain* the self and *serve* the world. Colossians 3:8-9 details the new self that is gained through faith in Christ alone. Galatians 5:13 and 6:10 describe how this spiritual freedom from selfishness is purposed for the sake of serving the world.

3   Compassionate togetherness as God's endgame is a reference to Ephesians 1:10. Regarding such unity being Satan's nemesis, the claim is a combination of Proverbs 6:19 and John 10:10.

4   Adam and Eve, before sin entered into the world, were not addicted to themselves, but all humans since have been. This proclivity to selfishness is passed, at least in a spiritual way, through the man's "seed" as seen in Psalm 51:5 and Romans 5:12. Importantly, this separates Christ from such addiction to self through His virgin birth, though He surely still wrestled temptation.

5   Enter at your own risk. Reading the lyrics online may prove more palatable.

more and enough never closes."[6] In a word, selfishness and serving God don't mix. It's like hugging yourself and trying to swim.

Thankfully, our Creator doesn't expect us to fix ourselves. Rather, He gave us His Son and simply calls us to seek Him. It is in this seeking that we find the Satisfier of our souls. Nothing else will do. No textbook or talk show can free a human heart. No food or fancy can content it. They may massage our minds for a season, but they all pass away in the end. Even our loved ones can be taken from us. To whom will we turn then? In the face of death, durable hope can only be found in a Love that lasts forever:

> As the Scriptures say, "People are like grass; their beauty is like a flower in the field. The grass withers and the flower fades. But the word of the Lord remains forever." And that word is the Good News that was preached to you,[7] good news of peace through Jesus Christ, who is Lord of all.[8] And now we are here to bring you this Good News.[9] Christ died for our sins, just as the Scriptures said. He was buried, and he was raised from the dead on the third day, just as the Scriptures said.[10]

It's the greatest story ever told, and it's true. Jesus Christ, King of the Universe, became nothing to give us everything.[11] His love is from everlasting to everlasting. Only in Him can the thirsty find their fill and the weary their rest. The best news in history is officially at our fingertips. Just imagine the headline:

### Royal Heir Accepts Torture to Save a World of Villains—from Themselves!

---

6   A sign on the wall at Jimmy John's sandwich shop in Clinton, Iowa.

7   1 Peter 1:24-25 (NLT). The paragraph is made of separate verses pieced together, much like Romans 3:10-18.

8   Acts 10:36b (NIV).

9   Acts 13:32a (NLT).

10  1 Corinthians 15:3b-4 (NLT).

11  "Nothing" is a reference to Philippians 2:7 (NIV). "Everything" is a reference to Ephesians 1:4, 2 Peter 1:3, and Romans 8:32. To be clear, Paul's phrasing that Jesus became nothing was intended to accentuate the servanthood Christ took on—that He sacrificed all reputation and rank. It was not meant derogatorily by Paul, nor is it above.

All through the Bible, Jesus leads the charge of self-giving service. The Old Testament foreshadows His coming, the gospels record His fulfillment, and the epistles connect the dots. All passages point to either the *need for* or *nature of* Jesus, the Leading Servant.[12] Surely, if Christ came to serve, there is no better bull's-eye to aim for.

## THE NATURE OF THIS BOOK

In the pages to come, you'll find a series of Old Testament stories coming to life, from the familiar to the peculiar, all pointing to heaven's definition of a true hero. One by one, God's servants go under the microscope, revealing our desperate need for cheerful service and how the Savior fulfills it all.

Part I invites you on a short journey through Scripture's ancient greats, those called "My servant" by God Himself. Then, Part II explores what may be the juiciest earthly drama in history: love despite adultery in the life of Hosea. Along the way, every chapter centers upon the same threefold quest:

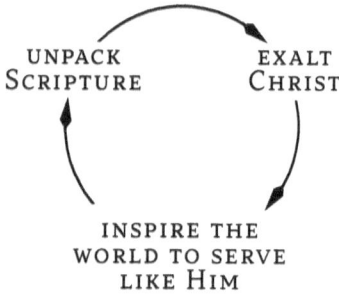

UNPACK SCRIPTURE

EXALT CHRIST

INSPIRE THE WORLD TO SERVE LIKE HIM

Also awaiting you at the end of each chapter are three key resources built to help you move the material from the mind to the heart. First, you'll find a single-page summary of all the connections to Christ buried in the chapter—a little cheat sheet called **Hidden Gems**. Then, the

---

12  Countless volumes have been written on *servant leadership*—some seminaries even require "biblical servant leadership" courses—but the reversed wording begs the wrong question. Servant leadership asks, "What type of leader should I be?", answering with "like a servant—one who exudes charitable humility." This identifies us as leaders who merely need a change of style. On the other hand, leading servanthood asks, "What type of servant should I be?" with the response "like a leader—one who exudes wise charisma." This identifies us as servants who should be the first to sacrifice for others. It may seem nuanced, but the difference is massive. Assuming leadership steers the heart toward arrogance. Assuming servanthood steers the heart toward the gospel.

**Wrap Up** compiles the main takeaways for modern society. And finally, the **Engage Page** is a study guide designed to help readers be doers of the Word, putting truth to work.

Consequently, *Heroes Kneel* is perfect for group Bible studies as well as personal exploration. No matter the setting, the steps are the same: learn, love, become. So whether you've read the Bible for decades or you're just starting to seek the truth, if your goal is to know Christ better, you're in the right place.

## FINAL THOUGHTS

The world seeks answers from the attractive and strong, but the antidote to our addiction is not gorgeous at first glance. The Lord's life was lowly, and His teaching was meek. Instead of mixed drinks and money, He hands us a mop. But there's no drudgery here, no chore to be checked off. It's all infused with thankfulness. Serving becomes the highest pleasure when the Savior becomes the choicest gift.

Humanity desperately needs to recover the giving of self as seen in the person of Christ. Developing great relationships will come no other way. In the words of pastor Rich Wilkerson Jr., "You can always give without loving, but you cannot love without giving." Pure, cheerful service comes only through the embrace of divine love. If marriages are to be healed, workplaces optimized, friendships mended, wars stopped, then Jesus must be followed as the Lord and Leading Servant from whom all life flows.[13]

So, get excited. The journey ahead may change your life. It's time to resurrect passion for God's Word and zeal for selfless service. Come get to know Jesus the same way He revealed Himself to the disciples—through the Old Testament!

We shall start at the very beginning, a *very good* place to start: Eden.

---

13  A reference to various verses about Christ as the Source of life such as John 11:25-26, Romans 6:23, Colossians 1:16, and 1 John 3:16. All point to the same truth: Lovingly, life has been given to be lovingly given away.

# PART I

## THE ANCIENT GREATS AND HOW THEY KNELT

*An Old Testament Walk-through*

# 1

# FROM EDEN TO EXODUS

*Remember His wonders which He has done . . .*
*You descendants of Abraham, His servant . . .*
*He is the LORD our God . . .*
*He has remembered His covenant forever.*
—PSALM 105:5-8A (NASB)

W<small>E WANT TO BE LIKE</small> God, and it's killing us.

This is nothing new. From Eden to Exodus to Earth as we know it, mankind has battled this fatal infection: the desire to crown ourselves king, to be our own Most High.[1] It grows with each new injustice, but the root is with us at birth—the whisper that says, *I know best.*[2] Any parent can testify to this. Pleasure restrictions stir up fuss tornadoes. As we age, our defiance moves from bedtimes and vegetables to speed limits and taxes, but it's all the same rebellion. Sin's venom is in our veins, leeching away our love, our peace, and eventually our lives.

---

1   This, recorded in Isaiah 14:14, was the precise thought of Satan that brought him to fall.
2   The summary of such a deception is brought to life by Paul in Galatians 6:3 and 1 Corinthians 3:18.

Fortunately, there is an antidote.

To find it, we best locate our original snakebite. After all, if your ceiling develops water stains, paint is not the remedy. A hole must be cut, the leak traced, and the roof repaired. Anything less, and eventually, the ceiling will collapse.[3]

In other words, tumors need surgery, not Tums. The same is true spiritually. If we wish to root out the devastating plague of selfishness, we must begin by studying how it started. This makes the book of Genesis a vital crime scene to investigate. Each main character mentioned points directly to our much-needed cure. For every story and struggle inscribed, there are millions who can relate. Together, these narrative accounts unpack the origin of sin, how it spreads, and who we must look to for help.

# ADAM AND "EVEN"

When Adam and Eve first walked the Earth, the Lord walked with them.

Take in the scene. The Garden hums with life: every sound its own symphony, every surface hand-painted by heaven. Dewdrops on a thousand fresh flowers send starlight back to the skies. Creatures of all kinds roam with grace, a certain softness in every step. And there, amid such perfection, mankind communes with the Almighty.

Of course, the flawless world wouldn't last. The serpent sold it well: "Eat from the Tree of Knowledge, and you will be like God," he told Eve.[4] Surrounded by glory, she was given a choice: serve the Lord or be the boss.[5] She took a bite of the forbidden fruit, and the rest is history.

One quick look at the modern world, and it's clear the route that Eve took, followed by Adam. Though God fashioned a paradise, they doubted

---

3  Unfortunately, this I know from experience. In college, a neglected water stain on my ceiling soon became a wet pile of tile all over my desk. Bye-bye iPod Touch.

4  A paraphrase of Genesis 3:5. The use of "us" serves as a connection point to Paul's assertion in 1 Corinthians 15:22 that all humans were once "in Adam."

5  In reality, no human is ever "the boss." Regardless of faith or circumstance, God sovereignly owns and rules the world (see Psalm 22:28).

their Creator's credentials.[6]

This event may seem antiquated, insignificant, or even fictitious. It isn't. All wars, all feuds, all divorces—every modern conflict can be traced back to the moment we decided self knows best. Our control issue is not the fault of our neighbor or our Creator. The desire to go our own way is nestled deep in the heart of every human on Earth:

*Explore the forbidden.*
*It's worth the rush.*
*How else will I know what's best?*
*I must see for myself.*

The problem is, we don't grow out of this. In fact, the need for control is a parasite; it grows out of us.

**Adam desired to get even with God and wound up in a leaf suit of fear.** When we roost our caboose on the throne of our lives, things get ugly quickly. Just imagine a sport where the team in the lead can change all the rules they want. Soon, those in power do whatever it takes to never lose again. This is the recipe for tyranny, and it's what happens when hearts reject God.

Unrestricted choice is the fount of chaos, not freedom. Is a runaway child really freer than one in a healthy home? Of course not. Toddlers need parents the way humans need God—for everything. What

> Unrestricted choice is the fount of chaos, not freedom.

begins as a rush of brazen defiance soon becomes guilt-ridden guesswork. Throwing out the Rulebook doesn't make a conscience quieter. It makes us repeatedly burn our hands on the stove and fear returning home.

**Yet God sought to get even with us by becoming a servant to save, as it is written:**

You see, at just the right time, when we were still powerless,

---

6   God is, in a sense, currently building a paradise to join us within it in heaven as well (see John 14:2). His "credentials" can be best seen in Job 38-41.

Christ died for the ungodly.[7] He made himself nothing by taking the very nature of a servant, being made in human likeness.[8] There was nothing beautiful or majestic about his appearance, nothing to attract us to him[9]—one who was tempted in every way, yet without sin.[10] God made him who had no sin to be sin for us, so that in him we might become the righteousness of God.[11]

# CAIN AND UNABLE

After Adam and Eve were banished from the Garden, they had two famous sons: Cain and Abel. Little is known of their upbringings or lifestyles except that Abel became a shepherd and Cain tilled the ground.[12]

One day, both brothers made an offering to the Lord. Cain gave a selection of fruit, Abel his firstborn sheep.[13] Immediately, the Lord rejected Cain's offering, but He accepted Abel's.

This infuriated Cain. His whole life was filled with backbreaking labor while his little brother waltzed with some wool. Over the years, all the anger and envy had built up like a dormant volcano. Now, it was time to erupt. He had offered the literal fruit of his labor and got spurned for the sheep he despised. Unacceptable.

Immediately, the Lord offered words of compassionate wisdom, but Cain's mind was already set. If life wasn't going to be fair for him, then his brother's life shouldn't be either. Inviting Abel out into the field, the death march began.[14] You have to wonder what they talked about until it was time. Regardless, there in broad daylight, Cain

---

7   Romans 5:6 (NIV). The paragraph is made of separate verses pieced together, much like Romans 3:10-18.

8   Philippians 2:7 (NIV).

9   Isaiah 53:2 (NLT).

10   Hebrews 4:15 (BSB).

11   2 Corinthians 5:21 (NIV).

12   Cain's story is unknown, so all statements about what caused his anger are conjecture to some degree.

13   Abel also gave the fat portions of these animals, further cementing his love for the Lord, going above and beyond for his King.

14   Why does the Bible include seemingly insignificant details like the first half of Genesis 4:8? Could it be because Christ's jealous murderers, the Pharisees, also spoke with Jesus before taking him "outside the gate" to be killed in the "field"? See Hebrews 13:12 for further study.

gruesomely murdered his brother.

Careful now. We can be so quick to distance ourselves from accounts of heinous crimes[15] with thoughts of "How despicable! What a monster!" But are we really so different?

The cause of Cain's eruption has its teeth in every one of us: toxic comparisons. When others have what we desire, the lava churns within us. The Bible calls these our passions. And without God's Spirit, there's no stopping them.

**Cain, unable to impress the Lord, killed for his own self-image.** Just like his father, Cain's desires got the best of him. Adam likely taught him of such dangers, saying something like, "Listen, envy bites back. Just keep your head down, trust the Lord, and work hard."

And that's just what Cain did. He had the world's greatest garden and was peacock-proud of it.[16] Every look at Abel's dim-witted sheep affirmed his garden's splendor. *Surely, God would be proud.* After all, Cain spent his days growing a masterpiece while his brother befriended animals. Yet God wasn't impressed—He was grieved, for Cain's heart was set on self.[17]

Both Adam and Cain chose fruit over God, but for Cain, it was all about self-image. When work is king, affirmation is mandatory. Cain built his life on pride, attempting to manage his anger, but managing sin just makes things worse. It's like having appendicitis: you don't manage it. You get it out, or the toxins will kill you. The same is true with envy. If inside you scream, "I'd kill to be favored!" watch out. It runs in the family.

**Yet the Good Shepherd let Himself be killed so our image might be restored, as it is written:**

---

15 Which is more shocking, a firefighter's rescue or a mobster's whacking? The world feeds us almost exclusive negative news because it produces better ratings. We look at a murder and think, "How terrible! What kind of wretched soul would do that?!" Somehow, we all think we are closer to a firefighter than a felon in spirit, but the Bible suggests otherwise.

16 This belief comes from Genesis 4:12. Before Cain killed Abel, the ground was yielding "its strength." Also, for all we know, Cain was the only gardener on Earth, so calling his garden the "world's greatest" is a fairly sure bet.

17 The Bible doesn't record the state of Cain's heart during his offering, but it does give an ominous clue. Whereas Abel's offering is specifically described as a sacrifice "of the firstborn of his flock and of their fat portions" (Genesis 4:4 ESV), Cain's offering has no indication of bringing his first or best to God—just some random "fruit of the ground" (Genesis 4:3 ESV). Many scholars infer that Cain served himself first and then tossed God some leftovers—the way people treat their dogs.

The good shepherd gives His life for the sheep.[18] He humbled Himself by becoming obedient to the point of death, even death on a cross,[19] that we might die to sin and live to righteousness.[20] He is the image of the invisible God, the firstborn of all creation.[21] And the Lord—who is the Spirit—makes us more and more like him as we are changed into his glorious image.[22]

# NOAH'S ARC

Generations passed, and the evil only got worse. By the time we meet Noah, the Earth had become so utterly corrupt that God chose to wipe it clean,[23] thus having Noah build a massive ship. Standing seven stories high and spanning one-and-a-half football fields, this ark was to fit representatives from every animal kind,[24] along with Noah's family of eight. The enormous wooden vessel did so easily,[25] saving all on board. Eventually, the waters receded, the animals dispersed, and Noah resettled in the land. Then, the Lord placed a rainbow in the sky, promising never to flood the Earth again. This is where most Noah narrations stop, but it's not how his story ends.

After the rainbow, Noah took to the soil and planted a vineyard. One thing led to another, and soon heroic Noah—the man who was blameless before the Lord, the godly individual who spent decades building an ark

---

18  An excerpt from John 10:11 (NASB95), which is a direct quote from the mouth of Jesus. The paragraph is made of separate verses pieced together.

19  An excerpt from Philippians 2:8 (ESV).

20  An excerpt from 1 Peter 2:24 (ESV).

21  Colossians 1:15 (ESV).

22  An excerpt from 2 Corinthians 3:18 (NLT).

23  We may think it's bad now but imagine if "every inclination of the thoughts of the human heart was only evil all the time" (Genesis 6:5, NIV). That was Noah's world.

24  It's important to remember that each *kind* does not mean each *species* we see today. A *kind* would most closely translate to the *family* category in taxonomy. Recent studies estimate a maximum of 7,000 animals on the ark, which is entirely realistic for the size of Noah's vessel, being 510 feet long with more than three million board feet of timber.

25  The Western church at large has done little to equip young people with teaching on the historicity of Old Testament records. Whimsical cartoon images of Noah's ark have only worsened the situation. If you find yourself asking questions like "How did the dinosaurs fit?" or "Where did all the excrement go?", then you are strongly encouraged to visit the Ark Encounter in Williamstown, Kentucky. It is not childish to believe in Noah's Ark.

while everyone else partied—was found passed out, naked and drunk. Sadly, this is the last we hear of Noah, cursing the son who found him.[26] What happened to our hero?

**Noah found ease and began treating himself, sipping on self-indulgence.** When the world was throwing keggers, Noah stood firm in faith. For decades, he obeyed the Lord, building a humongous boat while everyone else played. Why then—directly after being miraculously saved and blessed with a promise—did Noah turn inward?

The answer is simple, and we know it all too well: ease produces indulgence.[27] Besides, after some seventy years of grueling labor and five months at sea, what's wrong with a little celebration?

This mentality of earned ease reigns supreme in the Western world. It's all about get-rich-quick schemes, planning the next vacation, and early-retirement goals. The '80s hit song by the rock band Loverboy says it well: "Everybody's working for the weekend . . . everybody's going off the deep end."

> The answer is simple, and we know it all too well: ease produces indulgence.

This carrot-chasing, if left unchecked, becomes generational. Noah, just like his forefathers, fell to the worship of fruit. For Adam, it was desiring the forbidden; for Cain, the pride of his labor; for Noah, it was prioritizing pleasure over everything.

Considering Noah's full story arc, there's a serious warning against living for such ease. Clearly, though, Western culture refuses to care. All throughout childhood, we're asked, "What do you want to *be* when you grow up?" as if vocation and identity are synonymous. Soon, what we think we've earned becomes *who* we think we are.

What's worse, the media does whatever it can to reinforce such

---

26  His last words also include blessings upon his other two sons, but these blessings include them ruling over Ham, which is virtually identical to the curse he spoke over Ham.

27  To be clear, the Scriptures don't tell us why he got drunk. He could've done so as a coping mechanism for the horrible sounds of death he heard while in the ark. He could've even gotten drunk by complete accident. However, the way the Scriptures record his story makes the drunkenness out of moral laxity most likely. For more on ease producing rebellion, see Proverbs 30:9.

entitlement. In the words of the carmaker Nissan, "You deserve a car that thrills you."[28] These greedy whispers are more than just in our heads. They are in our homes, our hearts, our blood.

**Yet Jesus gave up ease to drink the cup of wrath so that all may be satisfied in Him, as it is written:**

> You know the generous grace of our Lord Jesus Christ. Though he was rich, yet for your sakes he became poor, so that by his poverty he could make you rich.[29] He emptied Himself[30] saying, "This cup that is poured out for you is the new covenant in my blood."[31] He was pierced for our rebellion, crushed for our sins. He was beaten so we could be whole.[32] For he satisfies the longing soul, and the hungry soul he fills with good things.[33]

## ABRAHAM AND I SICK

Then there's Abraham, one of the most foundational figures in history,[34] often remembered for his incredible faith. His journey starts soon after his father dies when Abraham[35] receives a call from the Lord to leave all he knows in pursuit of an unspecified land.[36] He's told no details, and yet he does not hesitate.

At the ripe old age of one hundred, God gifts him a son, only to later demand the child be sacrificed. Abraham obeyed even this

---

28  This disturbing tagline comes from a Nissan television advertisement in April 2021.

29  2 Corinthians 8:9 (NLT). The paragraph is made of separate verses pieced together.

30  An excerpt of Philippians 2:7 (HCSB).

31  Luke 22:20 (NET).

32  An excerpt of Isaiah 53:5 (NLT).

33  Psalm 107:9 (ESV).

34  More than just in the Bible, the story of Abram is also a pivotal component of Islam. Thus, while Muslims differ in their beliefs about certain events in Abram's life, he is a key player in both Christianity and Islam, which together represent over half of the current world population.

35  Technically, his name was Abram at this point. God would later change it to Abraham.

36  This powerfully resonates with Christ's call to "denounce" (Greek *apotassō*, meaning "to bid adieu") all that we have in pursuit of Him, as well as Paul's profession to live "forgetting what lies behind and straining toward what lies ahead, I press on toward the goal for the prize of the upward call of God in Christ Jesus" (Luke 14:33, Philippians 2:13-14).

command, believing God would raise his son from the dead.[37]

The pointers to Christ in these historical nuggets are undoubtedly profound, and many a sermon has headlined them. Rarely, however, since we admire Abraham's faith, does a teaching ever study his selfishness. This is indeed a great shame, for even in his shortcomings, we find not only a warning to heed but a glimpse of our need for Christ.

Though a godly man of incredible faith, Abraham was far from perfect. On multiple occasions, he told those in power that his wife Sarah was merely his sister, fearing they'd kill him to take her. Abraham's goal was self-preservation, and it almost got people killed.

Then years later, Abraham's son did the very same thing to his wife, even though these men had received numerous promises from the audible voice of God! Heaven's promise was heard, but God didn't seem good for it. What went wrong? One word: fear.

**Abraham threw others under the bus, deceiving them to save his own skin.** Despite the many promises declared by the Lord, fear can override them all. By no means can it stop these promises from coming true; it merely stops us from trusting them.[38] Fear is a serious sickness, and we all have it. Relationally, it is deadly. Trust is the bedrock of all great relationships, and fear is Satan's jackhammer.

Trust is the bedrock of all great relationships, and fear is Satan's jackhammer.

There's a reason why perfect love casts out fear: they cannot coexist. The fear of death drowns hope with worry until selflessness is impossible. In other words, when we're focused on our survival, others get left behind. It's like outrunning your friend so the bear doesn't eat you. Only by treasuring Christ's sacrificial service can the shackles of

---

37 Famously, after Abraham made all the preparations and readied himself with the knife, God halted him, providing a ram instead.

38 Romans 4:20-21 states that no mistrust made Abraham waiver. However, this is a general statement regarding Abraham's key moments of obedience. It does not mean Abraham's faith and trust were always perfect.

fear be broken for good.[39]

**Yet Christ elected Himself to be crushed, preaching truth whatever the cost, as it is written:**

> "No one takes my life from me. I sacrifice it voluntarily.[40] The Son of Man is going to be handed over to men; they will kill him, and He will be raised on the third day.[41] I have not spoken on My own, but the Father who sent Me has commanded Me what to say and how to say it,[42] and yet they have hated both me and my Father.[43] If the world hates you, keep in mind that it hated me first."[44]

# JACOB'S LADDER

Fast forward a few decades, and Isaac also became a father. Little did he know, he'd be parenting the most famous twins in history. His firstborn, Esau, grew into a master hunter and man of the field. The younger, Jacob, became the first true homeboy, preferring to lounge in the shade of his tent. As you can imagine, these twins weren't the best of friends.

One day, after an exhausting hunting trip, Esau got suckered into the worst deal of his life. Desperately faint, he begged Jacob for food but heard from his brother only this: "Sell me your birthright now."[45] Sadly, the demand worked. Jacob saw weakness, and he pounced. Finally, *he* was the hunter, and yet, even with the birthright in his hands, Jacob was hungry for more.[46]

Years later, when Isaac was advanced in years, he sent Esau to hunt him down a meal. Isaac planned to bestow the familial blessing on Esau when his beloved hunter returned, but Isaac's wife, Rebekah, had other ideas.

---

39  For more on this, check out Hebrews 2:9-18 where Paul explains how the suffering of Christ delivers "the offspring of Abraham" from the enslaving fear of death.

40  An excerpt of John 10:18 (NLT). The paragraph is made of separate verses pieced together.

41  An excerpt of Matthew 17:22-23 (NASB95).

42  John 12:49-50 (BLB).

43  An excerpt of John 15:24 (NIV).

44  John 15:18 (NIV).

45  An excerpt of Genesis 25:31 (ESV).

46  God is the only One who will ever be "enough," and He is not an *it*.

Swiftly, Rebekah conspired to deceive her blind husband, instructing Jacob to pretend to be the firstborn and snag the coveted blessing. This put Jacob in a hairy situation, but greed overtook him, and he capitulated. Betraying his father three times with lies, the wolfish plan worked.[47] The blessing was given to Jacob, undercutting Esau once more. Bitterness followed, and the family imploded. Many families can relate.

**Jacob exploited the weaknesses of others, swindling his family for earthly gain.** When selfishness rears its ugly head, whoever stands in the way gets rhinoed—kin or not.

According to *National Geographic*, rhinos charge at 30 mph but struggle to see even fifteen feet in front of them. Naval-gazers are no different. Just imagine a world of people staring at their stomachs, running around at full speed. There's a reason a group of rhinos is called a *crash*.

> Just imagine a world of people staring at their stomachs, running around at full speed.

Truth be told, we have more in common with Jacob the Cheat[48] than we realize. Exploiting the weak sounds unthinkable, and yet it's taught as the way we "evolved." Remember, *survival of the fittest* implies *elimination of the weak*. So, which is it? Do we thank our ancestors for dominating their neighbors, or do we preach compassion for all? Pushing both is not an option: it's hypocrisy. We all have a dog in this fight—ourselves!—and it's high time we stop returning to our vomit.

The world may teach dog-eat-dog, but the gospel is man's best friend. Still, we can easily revert to climbing over others on our race up the ladder.

**Yet Jesus took on the weakness of man, saving His enemies for eternal life, as it is written:**

---

47  A reference to Genesis 27:19, 27:20, and 27:24, much like Peter's three denials of Christ.

48  The name Jacob in Hebrew means "supplanter" or "he cheats." Curiously, from 1999 to 2013—for fourteen straight years—the most popular name of American baby boys was Jacob. Thankfully, names often don't carry the same meanings they used to.

Surely he took up our pain and bore our suffering.[49] The author of eternal salvation[50] understands our weaknesses, for he faced all of the same testings we do, yet he did not sin.[51] Christ died for us so that, whether we are dead or alive when he returns, we can live with him forever.[52] For if, while we were God's enemies, we were reconciled to him through the death of his Son, how much more, having been reconciled, shall we be saved through his life![53]

## THE PRIME MINISTER

Finally, we come to Jacob's son, Joseph, the last main character of Genesis. No historical figure is allotted more chapters in Genesis than he is, and for good reason.[54] Not only is Joseph's life story remarkable, it's decidedly unique. Even Broadway couldn't resist putting his name in lights for over a decade, albeit comedically.[55]

Unfortunately, with so great a focus placed on his "amazing technicolor" coat, much of his life gets lost in the mix.[56] For many, Joseph becomes *that guy with the fancy robe who goes to Egypt and stuff.* This is a tragedy. **Of all the individuals in Genesis, Joseph points us most vividly to Christ.**

Being the firstborn of Rachel and miraculously conceived, Joseph was his father's beloved son. Early on, while working in the fields with his brothers, Joseph dreams that his family—and even the heavens—would

---

49   An excerpt of Isaiah 53:4 (NIV). The paragraph is made of separate verses pieced together.

50   An excerpt of Hebrews 5:9 (KJV).

51   An excerpt of Hebrews 4:15 (NLT).

52   1 Thessalonians 5:10 (NLT).

53   Romans 5:10 (NIV).

54   Whenever the Bible lingers on a person or topic, it's a strong indicator that God is particularly interested in our learning on the subject. For Joseph to be allocated 13 chapters (37, 39-50) should be a tornado siren to study his story.

55   From 1974 to 1984, "Joseph and the Amazing Technicolored Dreamcoat" played on Broadway, a wildly famous musical comedy seen by over thirty million people around the world.

56   Ironically, though Joseph's coat gets most of the press, the Hebrew word famously translated "technicolor" is actually unclear. If read literally, it simply means "a long tunic with sleeves." Biblically, the only other garment described in this manner is Tamar's "long-sleeved robe" in the tragic story surrounding 2 Samuel 13:18.

one day bow down to him. This infuriates his brothers so much that they plot his demise.

Sadly, it wouldn't be long before Joseph, sent by his father on a mission to his brothers, experienced this fury in full. Drunk with envy, Joseph's brothers attack like a mob and sell him as a slave. In the process, his robe is ripped off and dipped in blood—a cover-up story of his death for their guilt. Joseph is then marched off to Egypt, given to the captain of the guard, and falsely accused.

Wrongfully convicted, he goes to prison, where he ministers to all the inmates. Then one day, a dramatic reversal takes place: Pharaoh, the king of the land, raises Joseph from the pit[57] and seats him beside the throne as the royal prime minister, placing Joseph in charge of all things. Soon after, amid a great famine, Joseph's brothers come before him, seeking food. They are tested for genuineness and ultimately find reconciliation. At last, the family unites in peace, dwelling permanently in the best of the land.

*Ring any bells?* The account of Joseph in Genesis offers immense wisdom and life lessons, but it's far more than an inspiring biography. It foreshadows Christ! Did you spot the connections? Every sentence of the story has multiple New Testament touchpoints.[58]

Jesus was the beloved Son of the Father sent on a mission to His brothers. Jesus was sold as a slave, falsely accused, and raised to the right hand of the Most High. Only through Jesus do we find reconciliation, unity, and peace as we head for the best land of all.

It's a lot to take in, yet these connections are just a sliver of the pie. Of all these pointers to Christ, though, here's the real kicker: Scripture has no record of Joseph sinning.

---

57  "The pit" was a common name for prison in those times, as seen in Genesis 40:15 (ESV). Interestingly, this prison holding Joseph was actually part of the house of the man (Potiphar) who sent him there (see Genesis 39:1 and 40:3). On top of that, Potiphar was the one who put Joseph in charge of the inmates (Genesis 40:4). Still, the Egyptian Pharoah had authority over all and personally liberated Joseph because the young man interpreted Pharoah's dreams.

58  Try reading back through the summary of Joseph's story, replacing his name with "Jesus." Consider who the other characters in the story might foreshadow too. See how many details match the life, death, and Resurrection of Christ. Keep in mind, Genesis was written around 1,400 years before Jesus walked the earth!

# FINISHING THOUGHTS

Throughout this chapter, we've walked amongst the "stars" of Genesis and seen how their selfish acts illuminate our Savior's sufficiency. This trail, however, dead ends at Joseph. The harder we look, the less fault we find in him.

Sure, Joseph sinned—we all do. Of this, Scripture is clear.[59] The Spirit simply chose not to include Joseph's sin in the Bible.[60] It is as if, after exposing the different brands of selfishness through previous patriarchs,[61] God decided to end the book of Genesis with an account so rich in gospel connections that His sovereignty becomes undeniable, His Son irresistible. In a similar fashion, each chapter of *Heroes Kneel* will close with a highlight reel of the gospel fingerprints that magnify our Perfect Prime Minister, Jesus Christ.

So, while our stroll through Genesis may be at a close, our quest has only begun. Next up, we meet a servant of the Lord known for everything from murder to humility: Moses.

---

59  This is easily confirmed by a vast array of verses, most demonstrably Isaiah 53:6 and Romans 3:23.

60  Some have argued that Joseph was arrogant or harsh to his brothers, but a careful look at the text reveals nothing of the sort. Others accuse him of deceiving his brothers by testing them, but multiple biblical characters like Rahab are commended in Scripture for certain acts done with the right motives. Genesis 43:34 also appears to say that Joseph may have gotten drunk with his brothers, but closer inspection shows that the text most closely says he "drank freely," as in the NASB. This is but another touch point to Christ as seen in Revelation 22:17 (BSB).

61  Abel also has no explicit sin mentioned in Scripture. However, since only seven verses are dedicated to his life, for the purposes of this book, he is not considered a "main character" or "patriarch" of Genesis.

#  HIDDEN GEMS

Below are buried treasures from the chapter that connect biblical characters to Christ. At their best, these famous ancients were only shadows of the One to come (Colossians 2:17). At their worst, they reveal our deep need for Him. Jesus said He came to fulfill the Old Testament (Matthew 5:17), and that's exactly what He did.

## JESUS: OUR PRIME MINISTER

Adam rebelled for self-exaltation, hoping to get even with God. *(Genesis 3:5, Isaiah 14:14)* → Jesus obeyed through humiliation, even though He was equal with God. *(Acts 8:33, Philippians 2:6)*

Cain killed for his self-image, hating others in toxic comparisons. *(James 4:2, 1 John 3:12-16)* → Jesus died for our self-image, loving others incomparably. *(John 15:13, Romans 5:8)*

Noah imbibed for self-indulgence, using grace as a chance for debauchery. *(Isaiah 17:10, Galatians 5:13)* → Jesus drank the cup of wrath, offering grace as the path to virtue. *(Luke 22:42, Titus 2:11-15)*

Abraham deceived for self-preservation, manipulating others in fear of death. *(Hebrews 2:15, 1 John 4:18)* → Jesus spoke truth at highest cost, serving others in boldness unto death. *(John 8:58-59, John 18:8)*

Jacob defrauded for self-advancement, climbing over others to exalt himself. *(Proverbs 14:30, 1 Samuel 8:3)* → Jesus loved by self-sacrifice, coming down to lift others up. *(John 6:51, Luke 19:10)*

Joseph has no recorded wrongdoing, showing mercy amid injustice. *(Ephesians 5:3, Luke 6:35)* → Jesus has no wrongdoing at all, showing mercy amid injustice. *(1 John 3:5, Luke 23:34)*

### Bottom Line

Jesus Christ is the soul cure to our selfishness! *(Philippians 2:3-5)*

# WRAP UP: Join the Club?

While the patriarchs did much that pleased God, their lives also expose our main weakness: rather than obey God, we prefer to search for a *better* way.

But there isn't one.

Time and again, we fall for different fruits, whether forbidden or grown or fermented. If you're sick of getting tricked, join the club. Still, despite our stumblings, God keeps His promises. The question, therefore, is not "Will He provide?" but "Will we believe?"

**To be clear though, believing in Jesus is not like joining a club.** Whereas health clubs focus on improvement, this is a call to surrender. Chess clubs may refine mental acumen, but faith isn't up to our wisdom. The body of Christ is so much more than all that. It's a family, a kingdom, a battalion, a band. No earthly institution compares. And while the church has had its fair share of conflict through the centuries, the gospel of Jesus Christ is *not* like some top-secret fight club—we get to talk about it!

When we're convinced God is for us, our service is unstoppable. There's no ask too great, no command too costly. Often, however, we doubt He knows best. Our hearts are desperately sick, the Bible even calling them "more deceitful than anything else."[62] We tell ourselves *harder, better, faster, stronger,* but nothing we try ever fixes our world—because we aren't the solution.

Rather, lasting peace requires surrendering ourselves to *the One who is,* "for where jealousy and selfish ambition exist, there will be disorder and every vile practice," as the apostle James wrote.[63] Overcoming selfishness isn't about willpower; it's about renewal. This is the gospel, and it works.

In essence, every human heart chases the maximization of its treasure. Some seek fruit to satisfy the heart and end up living with sour grapes. Others seek the Vine.[64] It all comes down to where your treasure is found.

Location, location, location.

---

62  An excerpt of Jeremiah 17:9 (CSB).

63  James 3:16 (ESV). "The One who is" serves as a double reference to Jesus, for "He Himself is our peace" (Ephesians 2:14) as well as literally "the One who is" (Revelation 1:8).

64  A reference to John 15:1. Fascinatingly, Scripture not only refers to Jesus as the Vine but practically every other part of the plant as well: the seed (Galatians 3:16), the root (Revelation 22:16), the branch (Zechariah 6:12), and the fruit (1 Corinthians 15:23).

# ENGAGE: Group Study 1

**STARTER**   If you could give the Bible a subtitle,
what would it be?

**TRIVIA**   What type of tree was known to many ancient
civilizations as "the tree of life"?[65]

**REFLECT**   Who is the most selfless person you have ever met?

**PONDER**   How is church different than a social club with
singing?

**JOURNAL**   In what ways are you most selfish?

**BOIL IT DOWN**   Cheerful service flows from the fully
trusting heart.

**BRING IT UP**   What makes it so hard to trust God?

**LIVE IT OUT**   Write your own gospel contrast:
"I . . ., yet Jesus . . ." Then share with a friend.

---

65   The date palm, due to its shade and fruit keeping weary travelers alive in the desert, was known as the tree
of life in many ancient civilizations. In Israel, it also signified immortality, appearing on the walls of the
Temple and the doors of the Holy of Holies (1 Kings 6:29-35), as well as in Ezekiel's vision of the new temple
(Ezekiel 40:16-37, 41:18-26). Even the scientific name for the date palm, *Phoenix dactylifera*, alludes to the
legendary bird that stood for death and resurrection. For deeper study, consider Leviticus 23:40, Psalm
92:12, John 12:13, and Revelation 7:9.

# 2

# MOSES THE ADVOCATE

*"They forgot the God who saved them . . .*
*So he said he would destroy them—*
*had not Moses, his chosen one,*
*stood in the breach . . ."*
—Psalm 106:21-23 (NIV)

I MAGINE BEING NEWLY ENGAGED AND searching for the ideal minister to perform your wedding. Even close your eyes for a few seconds if it helps.

What would make for a great wedding officiant? Perhaps you envision someone kind, honorable, and well-kept. Maybe "well-spoken" or "confident" top your list of ideal traits. Regardless, one thing is certain: God's pick would not have been yours.

Throughout the Old Testament, God uses marital language to describe his love covenant with Israel for a reason: He married her. Keep in mind, God had no need for a wedding planner; He had that done before the world even began.[1] He did, however, desire a master of ceremonies. So, after centuries of engagement through covenants of old, the time finally came for the King of the Universe to hire His officiant. And on that day, in the middle of the desert, out of all the people in the world, God revealed his first-round pick: **a stuttering murderer.**[2]

The officiant himself was shell-shocked, and who could blame him? Not only was he informed through a talking bush on fire—the guy couldn't even pass a background check.

Meet Moses, great-grandson of Joseph's brother Levi.

After Joseph and his brothers passed away in Egypt, their descendants multiplied rapidly, and a new pharaoh enslaved them out of fear. As the Israelites continued to grow in strength, the oppression worsened until this pharaoh decreed all newborn Hebrew boys to be thrown into the Nile.

Moses, having been rescued from this massacre and raised among Egyptian royalty, burned with anger as he witnessed brutality against His people, the Israelites. One day, after seeing an Egyptian beat one of his kinsmen, Moses "looked this way and that, and seeing no one, he struck down the Egyptian and hid him in the sand."[3] Then, instead of owning up to murder, Moses fled to the wilderness where he tended sheep for forty years. Slow of speech and full of guilt, somehow this shepherd was God's chosen officiant.

So why did God Almighty first-pick a man with this résumé on Mount Sinai? It wasn't because of his job experience or interview skills; God simply selects whomever He wills.[4] That said, there is a quality Moses possessed that the Lord graciously favors: humility.[5]

---

1   God's plan of redemption through Christ was not a knee-jerk reaction to the fall of mankind. Scripture is clear that the Father makes all things work out according to His plan, from the iniquity of the Amorites to the arrest of Jesus to the election of the saints. For more on the sovereign plan of God, see Genesis 15:6, Matthew 25:34, Acts 2:23, Romans 9:21-24, and Ephesians 1:10-11.

2   The use of "first-round" is comical in part; however, it is also an allusion to Moses rejecting God's job offer and Aaron becoming the spokesperson instead. Of course, this did not surprise the Lord per se, but it did anger him. See Exodus 4:13-14.

3   An excerpt of Exodus 2:12 (ESV). Unlike the fanciful scene in the famous 1998 film *The Prince of Egypt*, this verse makes it clear that Moses' crime was premeditated, secretive murder—not some public accident.

4   See Deuteronomy 7:7-8, Psalm 115:3, and Romans 9:15-24.

5   To be clear, there is nothing a man can do to earn the grace of God. By definition, grace is unmerited. Therefore, the words in the corresponding section are carefully chosen. Moses may have possessed the quality that God loves to bless, but that doesn't mean Moses developed it. No part of Moses' election should be attributed to his own doing.

His meekness may have only been kernel-size at the blazing bush, but boy, did it ever grow. In an oft-overlooked passage, the book of Numbers plainly states, "Moses was very humble, more than any person who was on the face of the earth."[6] No matter how you slice it, this is extremely significant. The Bible is full of promises for the humble, from grace to wisdom to salvation itself.[7] Jesus Himself even declared, "Whoever humbles himself like this child is the greatest in the kingdom of heaven."[8] Clearly then, if we wish to be great for God and see His "Kingdom come," it's time we explore the treasure trove of Moses' humble service.

Beginning with the all-important Exodus, it's not long before we run across the most powerful display of humble service in Moses' life. It may not get the airtime of the Ten Plagues or the crossing of the Red Sea—but it should.

Too often, the cinematic storylines overshadow the precious gems in between. Nevertheless, we will begin by unpacking the familiar highlights of Moses' journey and discovering the road he walked. In time, we'll arrive at his most admirable moment, where one man's humility saves a nation from the destruction it deserves.

> Too often, the cinematic storylines overshadow the precious gems in between.

Oh, and one more thing: look for Christ's fingerprints. They're everywhere.

## ON THE ROCKS

The Exodus from Egypt was not some casual favor in Israel's distant past. It was her wedding ceremony. The Red Sea parted, and Israel walked down the aisle, dressed in silver and gold and silk.[9] Then Moses, the

---

6   An excerpt of Numbers 12:3 (NASB).

7   These promises to the humble can be found in 1 Peter 5:6, Proverbs 11:2, and Psalm 18:17.

8   Matthew 18:4 (ESV).

9   A reference to Exodus 12:35-36, 14:22, and Ezekiel 16:10. Israel left Egypt looking like royalty.

officiant, led the bride in song.[10]

At Sinai, the procession climaxed, where she would meet her divine Groom. There, the Lord wrote and read the vows, proclaiming in love, "I'm yours."[11] The officiant echoed, an altar was built, and with one voice, Israel cried, "We do! We do!"[12] Consummated in blood, the pair was pronounced—God and wife.[13]

All began with such vigor and delight. The Lord Himself recounts it this way:

> "When I passed by again and saw you, behold, you were
> at the age for love . . . I made my vow to you and entered
> into a covenant with you, declares the Lord GOD, and
> you became mine. Then I bathed you . . . I clothed you . . .
> I adorned you with ornaments. . . . And your renown went
> forth among the nations because of your beauty, for it
> was perfect through the splendor that I had bestowed on
> you, declares the Lord GOD."
>
> —EZEKIEL 16:8-14 (ESV)

The passion was hot, the ceremony extravagant, but the honeymoon was over in a hurry. **Less than forty days in, Israel cheated on her Husband.**[14] Melting down her bridal rings, she fashioned a new lover—the golden calf—chanting before the idol with glee: "These are your gods, O Israel, who brought you up out of the land of Egypt!"[15]

Try to imagine God's grief, even from a human perspective. One day, mere weeks after your wedding, you come home from a lengthy business trip only to find your valuables weirdly sitting in a box by the front door.

---

10   A reference to Exodus 15:1-18. Interestingly, the first thing Moses does after he guides the Israelites through the Red Sea is lead them in song. To some degree, this parallels what will happen at the end of time (Revelation 15:2-3).

11   A reference to Exodus 20:2, the often-overlooked opening verse of the Ten Commandments. This concept is repeated throughout the Old Testament (Genesis 17:7-8, Exodus 6:7, Leviticus 26:12, Isaiah 41:10, Jeremiah 11:4, Ezekiel 36:28, and Hosea 2:23).

12   A reference to Exodus 24:3-7, where the people literally repeat the phrase, "We will do!"

13   A reference to Exodus 24:8. The blood is both a symbolic pointer to the virgin marriage bed, as well as a foreshadowing of the Cross.

14   This is explicitly pictured in Jeremiah 31:32.

15   Exodus 32:4 (ESV). The singing comes from Exodus 32:18. The "bridal rings" referenced were Egyptian earrings.

Upon entering the living room, you notice your engagement photos have been replaced with pictures of your next-door neighbor. Then you hear your spouse upstairs, singing about how loyal and loving that neighbor has been. At the foot of the stairs lay strange clothes mixed with the intimate garments of your spouse. You ascend the stairs, open the door, and find the two "dancing" about, laughing.[16]

What do you do?

This is precisely what the Lord Almighty experienced, but a hundredfold.[17] Less than two months prior at a gorgeous mountain venue, God and Israel were wed. A couple of fortnights later, their marriage was on the rocks. What began as mere impatience (waiting for Moses to return from climbing Mount Sinai) had become outright adultery.

Needless to say, God was infuriated. A reckoning was in order. Immediately, the Lord called to Moses with a message of wrath and grief:

> "Go down, for your people, whom you brought up out of
> the land of Egypt, have corrupted themselves . . . I have
> seen this people, and behold, it is a stiff-necked people.
> Now therefore let me alone, that my wrath may burn hot
> against them and I may consume them, in order that I
> may make a great nation out of you."
>
> —EXODUS 32:7-10 (ESV)

Hearing God's stark pronouncement had to have shaken Moses. First off, the Hebrew word translated "corrupted" had only been used by God to describe people one other time: right before the flood.[18] Moreover, the Lord switched from calling Israel "my people" to "your people," sharply dissociating Himself from His bride. This isn't to say He forsook her, but rather that Israel's adultery was so wretched that she no longer resembled the "woman" He married. Thus, grieved to the core, the Lord demanded

---

16  This is a combined reference to Exodus 32:6 (NASB) and Exodus 32:19. Some translations use "play" in 32:6, but the root Hebrew word has undertones of sexuality as seen in its use in Genesis 26:8. This also fits the common customs of the land and era, where people would worship graven images with orgiastic dancing.

17  This is not an exaggeration. God, being infinitely loving and utterly perfect, must have stronger emotions toward sin and betrayal than we can even imagine. Thus, "a hundredfold" is, if anything, a gross understatement. For graphic language about the scandalous adultery of Israel, see Ezekiel 16:15-38 and Jeremiah 31:32.

18  See Genesis 6:11-12, where Scripture records the shocking depth of humanity's depravity before the flood.

to be let alone.[19]

**Now put yourself in Moses' sandals.** For months, you repeatedly risk your life to rescue thousands of people from ruthless oppression.[20] Things get dicey, but God swoops in at just the time with miraculous deliverance. Three days later, the people you've led out of slavery start grumbling against you. A month later, they want to kill you, claiming their old bondage is better than your foolish leadership.[21]

Nevertheless, you continue to serve them, but they emphatically reject your guidance. Then one day, the Lord tells you if you simply sit still, He will wipe them out and make you the centerpiece of history. How would you respond, or would you at all?

Here's how Moses did:

> But Moses implored the LORD his God and said, "O LORD, why does your wrath burn hot against your people, whom you have brought out of the land of Egypt with great power and with a mighty hand? Why should the Egyptians say, 'With evil intent did he bring them out, to kill them in the mountains and to consume them from the face of the earth'? Turn from your burning anger and relent from this disaster against your people. Remember Abraham, Isaac, and Israel, your servants, to whom you swore by your own self, and said to them, 'I will multiply your offspring as the stars of heaven, and all this land that I have promised I will give to your offspring, and they shall inherit it forever.'"
>
> —EXODUS 32:11-13 (ESV)

This plea of Moses is one of the greatest examples of selflessness in history. With four short sentences, the humblest man on Earth pleaded

---

19  Often, humans use this phrase in distress simply to mean, "Caution: I'm processing intense pain," not that they actually desire seclusion. Similarly, the picture here is not of God as some inconsolable child; it's a lament on the brink of release.

20  The use of "thousands" is intentional, as there is reasonable evidence that the Exodus may have been between 6,000 and 20,000 Hebrews (instead of the traditional two million) due to a translation discrepancy. For more information on this position, check out "The Number of People in the Exodus from Egypt" by Colin J. Humphreys, as well as "How Many Came Out of the Exodus of Egypt" by Jeff Benner.

21  The rebellious desire to stone the leaders of Israel referenced is found in Numbers 14:10. Some believe the people were only attempting to stone Joshua and Caleb, but with the vast amount of grumbling against Moses and Aaron prior, it seems likely that the people's indignation was directed at all four leaders.

for heaven's mercy to come upon the very people who tried killing him and his friends.[22] That kind of service puts the world on notice. That kind of love always wins.

## THE NECESSITY OF ADVOCACY

Studying Moses' humble response will change your life if you let it.[23] Naturally, we get inspired by stories of great heroes who have sacrificed dearly for others. This passage is that and far, far more. Moses' prayer to God that day is the epitome of leading servanthood, the blueprint of humility, the blinker that turns us right toward Christ. While deeply profound, it's structurally quite simple: there's a position of reverence, a priority for reputation, and

> Studying Moses' humble response will change your life if you let it.

a promise on record recited. Moses did three things: revere, resolve, and represent.

### STEP ONE: REVERE

When faced with a crisis, what you do first says a lot about who you are.

Forty years before Sinai, Moses' gut reaction was murder. Now, it's intercession. This reversal alone displays the transformational power in walking with God over time. Moses went from a stuttering, sheepherding felon to leading the people of Almighty God. But how?

The best place to start is reverence. According to Proverbs, "The [reverent] fear of the LORD [that is, worshiping Him and regarding Him as truly awesome] is the beginning *and* the preeminent part of wisdom [its starting point and its essence]."[24]

---

22  "Tried" here simply means they discussed it as a viable option. While no record of a legitimate assassination attempt is found in Scripture, planning how to kill someone is still a version of "trying" to do so. Moses also believed he was headed for assassination long before this moment, as seen in Exodus 17:4.

23  The confidence behind this statement is derived from Psalm 19:7-11.

24  An excerpt of Proverbs 9:10 (AMP).

This is precisely what we find at the beginning of Moses' prayer. After hearing the Lord credit him for bringing Israel out of Egypt, Moses immediately redirects all praise back to Whom it belongs. On top of that, Moses emphasizes the "great power and mighty hand" of the Lord, communicating just how worthy the Lord is to be praised. The same will be true in eternity.[25]

In the West, many of us have lost this adoration, developing instead a view of God as a benevolent grandpa who takes us to ballgames and buys nice cars for us. This must stop. Jesus was not just some good moral teacher full of interesting stories and clever suggestions. He was the lowly Servant we've come to adore, the reigning Savior we require. **If we see Him wrongly, we will serve Him poorly.** As one scholar, T.D. Alexander put it, "Worship, to be true, must be based on a right perception of God. The book of Exodus emphasizes the importance of knowing God as he truly is, and not as we imagine him to be."

To *worship* is literally to "pay worth." Such was the starting point for Moses, the bedrock of his plea.

### STEP TWO: RESOLVE

After adopting a position of reverence, Moses wasted no time addressing his highest priority: God's reputation. Israel's disobedience was making the Lord look bad, but if He wiped them out completely, the surrounding nations would only mock Him worse. To stand by and see that unfold was not an option. Not on Moses' watch.

People defend fiercest what they love dearest. This is why the "survival instinct" is so strong—because people love themselves, a lot.[26] Unfortunately, such self-advancement carries far beyond the preservation of life; a few thumb flicks on social media make this painfully clear. We defend our ideas and honor tooth and nail, but do we do the same for

---

25  The twenty-four elders shall sing of the Lord's worthiness (Revelation 4:10-11), as well as the four living creatures (Revelation 5:8-10), millions of angels (Revelation 5:11-12), harp-holding saints (Revelation 15:2-4), and really every created being in existence (Revelation 5:13).

26  Even those who claim to hate themselves really only hate their perceived dysfunction compared to those around them. At the bottom of such loathing is still a preoccupation upon the self. Attention is a primary indicator of love. This also resolves the apparent contradiction between Ephesians 5:29 and those committing self-harm.

God?[27] When someone uses "Jesus" as an expletive, do we speak up? Of course, God doesn't *need* us to defend Him. It simply communicates our love for Him when we do.[28]

**Thinking of God being publicly ridiculed wrenched the heart of Moses—as it should ours.** His heart for God's glory gave him a zeal for selfless service. How much better our world would be if every self-proclaimed Christian cared about God's reputation like Moses did.

Instead, all too often, Jesus' jersey[29] gets worn by fair-weather floozies taking His name in vain.[30] Imagine if thousands took *your* name, claiming to be in *your* family, and then acted like fools. Soon, things start showing up in your news feed tied to your family's name—drunkenness, prostitution, and the like. Your neighborhood starts to avoid you. You get weird glances at work. Eventually, your family is mocked, even hated, by people you've never even met. *That is God's experience.*

> People defend fiercest what they love dearest.

Moses implored God to relent, not because he loved God's people so much, but because *he loved God* so much. What started as reverence bloomed into resolve. For Moses, nothing eclipsed the importance of God being rightly viewed by the world.[31] His mission was simple and his mind was determined: magnify God at all costs. Similarly, our souls ignite with

---

27  To defend God "tooth-and-nail" is not a call to vehemence or violence, but rather gentle correction when the Lord we (claim to) love is spat upon.

28  Surely, the main way to "defend" God is to live lovingly while claiming to represent Him. As representatives or ambassadors for Him (2 Corinthians 5:20), we are called to do far more than speak up. Still, our response to the mockery of our Lord reveals our level of love for Him.

29  Olympic athletes talk about the honor of representing one's country—the weight of putting on such a jersey. When people claim Christianity, they are publicly putting on the most scrutinized jersey the world has ever seen. No team has higher expectations than God's. If a hateful Olympian disgraces his country, how much more a loveless Christian disgraces his Christ! Olympians represent their country. Christians represent Love Himself.

30  This is a reference to the third commandment as seen in Exodus 20:7. To *take* someone's name doesn't mean to say it irreverently; it doesn't mean to *say* it at all. Taking someone's name is to publicly identify as a member of their immediate family. We know this to be true most readily from adoption and marriage. From day one (well, technically day six), God ordained marriage to represent the future union between Christ and His Bride, the church (Ephesians 5:32). This is why it's not misogynistic for a woman to take the name of her husband—it reflects how we identify with Christ! It is no coincidence that the Bible repeatedly uses both adoption and marriage to illustrate a person coming to faith in Jesus Christ, thereby joining "the household of God" (Ephesians 2:19, ESV). For more on spiritual adoption, see Romans 8:14-23 and Ephesians 1:3-6.

31  This must be the priority of the church in every age, the Great Commission (Matthew 28:19-20) at its finest.

purpose when our telescopes are zoomed in on God's supreme worth.

If this all sounds too mystical or somewhat up in the air, just keep reading. Moses' final sentence tells us precisely where to land.

### STEP THREE: REPRESENT

No one told Moses to intercede for Israel. He didn't get a group text asking for prayer; His words came straight from his heart.[32] That said, it's not as if Moses mustered up some heroic spirit of bravery. When confronted with this crisis, he simply reverted to his default setting—trust in the promises of God.

When God married Israel, His covenant with her was codified. Now, fifty days later, God's bride was running away. Still, while Moses was surely shaken by the thought of nations mocking his Savior, something even deeper fueled his cry. Some four hundred years earlier, through the mouth of Jacob, God had promised that the coming Messiah would come from the tribe of Judah.[33] Well, Moses was a Levite. If God wiped out His frolicking calf-worshipers and restarted the nation with Moses, He'd be breaking His own Word. Thus, even after the Lord told His servant to let Him alone, Moses found the courage to pray.

**This was Moses' secret sauce: dependence on God's faithfulness.** Time and again, God brought Moses to the brink of collapse. At first, like countless leading servants in Scripture, he spent time in the wilderness alone.[34] Then came the testing of trust as he stared down death at the Red Sea. And really, that was just the beginning. On the other side, Moses would face intense thirst, hunger, exhaustion, and even betrayal—yet he endured.

Initially, these may seem like unfortunate events to be pitied, but

---

32  In a sense, Scripture declares that all human words come straight from the heart (Luke 6:45). The point here, however, is that no one implored Moses to intercede. He did so as a natural outcropping of his love.

33  A reference to Genesis 49:8-12. Moses is generally accepted as the primary author of the Torah, either receiving accounts predating him by oral tradition or direct revelation from God. Hence, Moses would certainly have been familiar with the blessing of Genesis 49, especially considering his plea in Exodus 32:13 is a direct quotation of the Abrahamic covenant recorded in Genesis 22:17 that was recited to Isaac and Israel as well (Genesis 26:4, 28:13-15).

34  The great messengers of the gospel all share this wilderness experience. Joseph walked sixty-five miles from Hebron to Dothan alone, later being thrown into prison. Elijah fled into the wilderness in 1 Kings 19. John the Baptist resided in the wilderness as prophesied in Isaiah 40. Paul spent three years in the wilderness as recorded in Galatians 1:17-18. And most notably of all, Jesus Christ was led into the wilderness by the Holy Spirit in Matthew 4:1. If you find yourself in the wilderness, don't grumble. Hope is on the horizon.

not to God. Whether in sports or work or war, training requires testing. As Franklin D. Roosevelt said one time, "A smooth sea never made a skilled sailor."

The same is true for faith. Moses' default setting became relying on God's promises, and it literally saved a nation. The faith of one humble advocate ushered in mercy—one lowly shepherd who laid it all down for the glory of God and the rescue of rebels.

So it is with Christ.[35]

---

35 To be clear, Moses did not live a perfect life or die for the forgiveness of sins; however, as Exodus 32:32 shows, Moses was so determined to see God's people saved that he implicitly offered his seat in heaven for them (much like Paul's lament in Romans 9:1-3). Of course, even this would not have sufficed, as Psalm 49:7 (NIV) makes clear: "No one can redeem the life of another or give to God a ransom for them." Still, the gospel rings forth, as Christ was condemned for us.

# HIDDEN GEMS

## JESUS: OUR FAITHFUL FIANCÉ

Israel disassociated herself from God out of impatience for His servant, Moses, to return. ⟶ Jesus was sent to associate with us, demonstrating God's perfect patience in love. *(John 3:16, Philippians 2:7, 1 Timothy 3:16)*

Moses redirected praise to God, proclaiming Israel belongs to the Lord. ⟶ Jesus redirected praise to His Father, proclaiming, "Mine are yours!" *(John 5:19, 8:28, 17:9)*

Moses put God's fame first. ⟶ Jesus put His Father's fame first. *(John 8:50, 17:4-6)*

Moses sought mercy and grace for his opposers, pleading to see them live. ⟶ Jesus sought mercy and grace for His enemies, dying to see them live. *(Luke 23:24, Matthew 5:44, Romans 5:10, Acts 2:36-41)*

Moses ascended Mount Sinai, received the Law in fire, and 3,000 idolators were killed in the end.[36] ⟶ Jesus ascended to heaven, sent the Spirit in fire, and 3,000 believers were saved in the beginning. *(Acts 1:9, John 15:26, Acts 2:3-4, 2:41)*

Moses, of the priestly Levite tribe, interceded for Israel, God's unfaithful bride. ⟶ Jesus, our priestly Mediator, still intercedes for the saints, His soon-to-be bride. *(Hebrews 4:14, 1 Timothy 2:5, Romans 8:34)*

**BOTTOM LINE:**

Jesus awaits us with festal robes, a glass sea, and a great song, for we are His. *(Revelation 15:2-3, 19:8, 21:3)*

---

36   See Exodus 19:3, 19:18, 20:1-17, and 32:28. The Jewish celebration in remembrance of this event is known as Shavuot or the "Festival of Weeks," commemorating the seven weeks between the Passover and the giving of the Law. In Christianity, the corresponding holiday is called Pentecost, meaning "fiftieth," commemorating the seven weeks (forty-nine days) between the crucifixion and the giving of the Spirit (on the fiftieth day). Therefore, the Apostles were celebrating the giving of the Law at the precise time its effective fulfillment took place!

# WRAP UP: Cold Feet

While servanthood packs the pages of Exodus, Chapter 32 transcends them all. With disaster approaching, in the eye of the hurricane, Moses still chose to serve. There's a reason why—six times in Scripture—Moses is called "my servant" by the voice of God.[37] Stuttering murderer turned wedding officiant, Moses was surely special.[38] Deuteronomy 34:10 (NLT) leaves no doubt: "There has never been another prophet in Israel like Moses, whom the LORD knew face to face." Nevertheless, Moses is *not* the main character of Exodus. God is.

After rising from the grave, the gospel of Luke tells us that Jesus found two of his disciples, "and beginning with Moses and all the Prophets, he explained to them what was said in all the Scriptures concerning himself" (Luke 24:27, ESV).

Did you catch that? The top of Christ's resurrected to-do list was preaching the Old Testament and how it's all about *Him*! Embracing this is pivotal to "accurately handling the word of truth."[39] Well before wondering how a verse might apply to us, we should ask: *How does this point me to Christ?*

In short, this world is not about us. **Though the wedding feast of the Lamb awaits, self-centeredness can give us cold feet.**[40] When we follow the world—treating pain with indulgence—the senses only grow numb. Soon, our frostbitten toes scream for slippers instead of the peace they are called to carry.[41] This must change, especially within the church.

Thankfully, intercession thaws our frozen phalanges. The key is

---

37  The verses declaring Moses as such are Numbers 12:7-8, Joshua 1:2-7, 2 Kings 21:8, and Malachi 4:4. This is tied with the six such references to Job, second only to King David. It's also noteworthy that Moses is additionally called "the servant of the Lord" twenty times in Scripture.

38  Sometimes we can become indignant at Moses' story, thinking, "Of course he trusted God. I would too if pillars of fire ripped through the clouds!" Adopting this mentality, however, neglects the power of Scripture. For centuries, the Israelites longed for their Messiah, desperate to understand how the pieces would fit together. Now, God's commands may not come through thunderclouds, but why want that over His Word?

39  An excerpt from 2 Timothy 2:15 (NASB95).

40  A reference to Revelation 19:9 (NLT). It should be noted for clarity that not all are invited to the wedding feast—only those who know and love Christ.

41  A reference to Isaiah 52:7 and Nahum 1:15. Paul connects these passages to evangelism in Romans 10:14-15. Even the armor of God contains this concept of feet clothed in readiness to share the gospel (Ephesians 6:15).

humility. You can't be stiff-necked and still bow your head.[42] To truly stand tall, we must kneel.[43]

As we dive further into the practice of servanthood, God quilts our rags into capes. The nasty pasts from which we once ran get redeemed for the sake of His glory. Nothing can stop the counsel of His will; our shortcomings don't stand a chance. Bring your stutters or felonies or whatever else before Him.

Transformation awaits you.

---

42  See Exodus 34:8-9 (ESV). The bowing of the head in ancient cultures was a sign of submission, because it exposed the back of the neck as if to say, "My life is yours for the taking." Refusing to bow, therefore, was payable by death as it communicated a refusal to pledge one's life in allegiance.

43  Kneeling isn't just an act of submission. In Hebrew, the word בָּרַךְ (barak), translated "kneel" in verses like Psalm 95:6, is also translated "bless" throughout the Old Testament. For more study, see H1288 at BlueLetterBible.org.

# ENGAGE: Group Study 2

**STARTER**   How would you respond if someone asked you, "Why should I pray for others?"

**TRIVIA**   What is the only psalm attributed to Moses, and for what is it famous?[44]

**REFLECT**   Do you care about God's reputation? Can others tell?

**PONDER**   Where does humility come from, and what can be done to grow it?

**JOURNAL**   In what ways are you most selfish?

**BOIL IT DOWN** Compassionate intercession flows from a heart that delights in God.

**BRING IT UP**   What is easy to start subconsciously worshiping?

**LIVE IT OUT**   Make a notecard of names. Tape it to your phone. Pray for them at each use.

---

44   Psalm 90 is the only psalm attributed to Moses, known primarily for verse 12.

# 3

# DAVID THE REDEEMER

*"I will establish one shepherd over them,*
*and he shall feed them—My servant David.*
*He shall feed them and be their shepherd."*
—Ezekiel 34:23 (NKJV)

A NY TIME THE LORD REPEATS Himself, it's a signal to pay attention. As we continue our walk through the Old Testament, the call to servanthood only grows louder. After Moses intercedes at Sinai, he receives the rest of the Law, which includes thirty-three commands about serving.[1]

Basically, the Law says *live to give*—a simple yet shocking directive. In the ears of the selfish, it's like an alarm that gets louder and louder the longer it's ignored. God thunders with urgency—"Wake up, sleeper, rise from the dead!"—but selfish hearts simply grunt and turn over.[2] Sadly, some spend their entire life this way, forever slapping the snooze button,

---

1   This is counted from the English Standard Version using BlueLetterBible.org. The book of Deuteronomy alone has twenty-six such instances.
2   An excerpt of Ephesians 5:14 (NIV). Strangely, this is actually a repurposed citation of Isaiah 60:1-2 that Paul intentionally adapts to directly reference Christ.

irritated that God would dare wake them from their narcissistic naptime.[3]

In Moses' day, such grumbling became a staple among God's people.[4] Then, at the end of Deuteronomy, Moses dies, and his assistant Joshua receives the leading servant baton. A man of great faith and zeal for the Lord, he was passionate about service. If Joshua's life isn't enough proof, his dying words say it all:

> "Now therefore fear the LORD and **serve** him in sincerity and in faithfulness. Put away the gods that your fathers **served** beyond the River and in Egypt, and **serve** the LORD. And if it is evil in your eyes to **serve** the LORD, choose this day whom you will **serve** . . . But as for me and my house, we will **serve** the LORD."
>
> —JOSHUA 24:14-15 (ESV)

Time and again, as they conquered the land God promised, Joshua reminded the people not to forget the Lord. At first, Israel obeyed and everything seemed peachy.[5] But as soon as Joshua's generation passed away, so did all allegiance to the Lord.[6]

Thus, judges were sent to provide course correction, but Israel's idolatry only deepened.[7] Judges 10:6 (NLT) summarizes this dark period best: "They abandoned the LORD and no longer served him at all."

After centuries of stubbornness, such rebellion finally came to a head as Israel, discontent with God, demanded a king to rule them instead. Initially, they were given Saul, whose reign was rocky at best. Then one day, there came a boy from Bethlehem who would turn everything upside

---

3    This may sound harsh or judgmental, but it's a straightforward fusion of Romans 13:11 and 2 Timothy 3:2. Paul refers to those in spiritual darkness as being asleep and ravenously selfish. For more, see 1 Thessalonians 5:6-7.

4    Israel's grumbling was not a few isolated incidents. It characterized the journey at large (see Numbers 14:27).

5    Judges 2:7 (ESV) even says, "the people served the LORD all the days of Joshua, and all the days of the elders who outlived Joshua."

6    A reference to Judges 2:10. This should be a stern wake-up call to those mature in the faith, especially parents and the elderly. Are we training up young people to serve the Lord with joy? Are we passing down stories of all He has done in our lives? Our example should demonstrate that serving God is far more than ritualistic behavior modification. Our service should look like joyful hospitality that welcomes and blesses all those made in God's image.

7    The time period referenced is from the death of Joshua to the coronation of King Saul, also known as the period of the Judges. Scholars disagree as to the exact duration, but Acts 13:20 gives a rough figure of 450 years. Regardless, the period of the Judges lasted at least several hundred years.

down. All he needed was faith, five smooth stones, and a Philistine.

Enter David.

Have you ever wondered why the story of David and Goliath is so famous? Out of all the majestic moments in Scripture, somehow it nearly rises to the top. Even most non-Christians know the gist: boy meets giant, rock meets forehead, and the crowd goes wild. There are plenty of flashier miracles in Scripture, but few get the same press. What's the deal?

For starters, people love *Cinderella* stories. Everyone digs a good underdog, and David surely was one. When we first meet the lad, he's a shepherd boy tending the woolies—the lowest job in society.[8] David, however, would soon conquer Goliath and skyrocket from sheep-shearer to superstar. Eventually, he'd be crowned king, commit murderous adultery, and be called a man after God's own heart—a curious life indeed.[9]

> Have you ever wondered why the story of David and Goliath is so famous?

Unfortunately, the bulk of David's story is often overlooked in the face of these blockbuster events. Many of his significant relationships and memories end up being footnoted or forgotten. This is especially shocking considering the enormous emphasis that Scripture places on David. After all, his name appears in the Bible a whopping 1,094 times![10] (That's 128 more than Jesus.)[11] Plus, the Lord refers to Him as "my servant" twenty-three times.

---

8   Shepherding was so low on the totem pole that a shepherd's testimony was not considered valid in court at the time. So, in very God-like fashion, who did the Lord choose to first testify to the Messiah's birth in Luke 2? The shepherds! It is often those the world deems worthless that Our Redeemer loves to bless.

9   Surely, being "after God's own heart" doesn't mean the Lord condones David's egregious sins. It simply means on the whole, David sought the presence, justice, and mercy of God—not that he was somehow the most virtuous man on Earth.

10  This is from the English Standard Version. Translations differ on precise counts, as some scholars prefer to insert names instead of manuscript pronouns more often for clarity (among other reasons). As a fascinating aside, in the ESV, the names "David" and "Jesus" are both found in the exact same number of verses (925).

11  The difference depends on which translation is referenced, but most are quite similar. The English Standard Version sports 966 uses of the name "Jesus," though a few uses refer to men other than Jesus of Nazareth (see Luke 3:29 and Colossians 4:11). The only exception in this regard is the New International Version, which uses the name "Jesus" 1,301 times! For the best explanation for such a disparity, see the footnote above.

No one else in Scripture comes close.[12]

So what made David so special? When it comes to servanthood, what was *his* finest hour?

In man's eyes, slaying Goliath may be David's most impressive accolade, but if loving service is God's greatest commandment,[13] then David's slingshot bravery wasn't his magnum opus.[14,15] While undoubtedly remarkable, a different chapter in David's story likely pleased God most. It's not well known, and it's not flashy. There are no enemies vanquished or demons cast out. It's the simple story of a king's promise, a boy's nightmare, and the kindness that brought them together.

## THE KING'S REACH

First, a bit of history.

Just before David conquers Goliath, the Lord tells King Saul that his royal reign is over due to the magistrate's arrogant disregard for God's direction. So naturally, as the harp-playing shepherd boy David becomes the people's new hero, Saul grows insanely jealous. Soon, spears are thrown and armies are dispatched, all to end David's life.

Meanwhile, Saul's son Jonathan becomes David's best friend, so David promises unfailing kindness toward Jonathan's family.[16] Shortly thereafter, the Philistines attack, Saul takes his own life, and Jonathan dies in battle. David then ascends the throne, overcomes a civil war, and defeats all surrounding enemies. And in that moment, when peace is restored after years of bloodshed, King David remembers his promise.

---

12  The nation of Israel, also called "Jacob", has twenty-three references in this manner as well, but is not mentioned here in Chapter 3 because only individuals are being compared. Fascinatingly, if you include the seventeen times Moses is called "the servant of the LORD," then he also has exactly twenty-three references in this manner.

13  To support the use of "loving-service" over the usual "love," see Deuteronomy 10:12 and 11:13.

14  There's no biblical evidence to believe David ever feared Goliath or even saw his offer to fight as a risk. On the contrary, David's actions and words leading up to the event are profoundly relaxed. Therefore, while it certainly displays his intense faith and obedience to the Lord, it isn't the most vivid example of love.

15  Most scholars place David between fifteen to nineteen years old when he fought Goliath. Saying that was King David's greatest moment is kind of like telling the president of the United States that he's been going downhill since high school.

16  Interestingly, this "unfailing kindness" in 1 Samuel 20:15 is the very same Hebrew word "*kheh-sed*" used for God's unfailing love throughout the Old Testament.

Such is the stage of 2 Samuel 9, where the story really picks up. David, out of love for his late friend Jonathan, begins looking for Jonathan's descendants to bless them. He even sends for an old servant of Saul named Ziba to ask if anyone is left. Ziba reports back that there is only Mephibosheth (pronounced *Meh-fib-o-sheth*), a long-forgotten son of Jonathan, living in hiding far away. Immediately, David sends a squadron to bring him in.[17]

This, ironically, was Mephibosheth's worst nightmare.

See, when a new king rose to power, it was common practice to exterminate all family members of the previous ruler to expunge any potential for revolt. David had the opposite intentions, but few knew what he was planning. Understandably then, when David was coronated, Mephibosheth's nurse took up the five-year-old and fled, terrified that the young lad would be put to death. In her haste, however, the little boy fell and became paralyzed in both his feet.[18]

In 1000 BC, there were no wheelchairs; this debilitating injury meant Mephibosheth would crawl, be carried, or be hoisted onto an animal for the rest of his life.[19] Add that to being orphaned young, having no extended family, and knowing that soldiers may come cut off his head at any time. Welcome to Mephibosheth's world.[20]

But here's the even crazier thing. **So much of Mephibosheth's story, from the very beginning, overlaps with ours.** In fact, it goes all the way back to Eden. Judging the Lord to be a selfish tyrant, Adam and Eve took matters into their own mouths, separating themselves from the King.[21] They also hid from the One bent on blessing them, racked with fear of judgment and death. Ever since, mankind, having lost the ability to

---

17  Curiously, this is the precise counterexample to when Saul sent squadrons to bring David in. In those situations, Saul was out to kill. Here, David was out to bless. With this in mind, one gets a taste of Romans 5:10.

18  This glimpse of Mephibosheth's childhood is found in 2 Samuel 4:4, curiously inserted in what seems to be a completely unrelated narrative.

19  Also, though crutches are often depicted with Mephibosheth, they would not have been an option. At least one leg must be partially functional for crutches. He was completely lame in both feet.

20  Basically, to all those who feel like they're on the edge of breaking down with no one there to save them, Mephibosheth would likely sing, "Welcome to my life."

21  The comparison is drawn to Mephibosheth's nurse who, judging the "lord" of that land to be a selfish tyrant, took matters into her own hands and wound up tragically separated from the king.

walk freely,[22] crawls around in spiritual despair—full of selfish tyranny.[23] After all, what you believe about God's nature defines what you become.[24]

Thankfully, the Lord doesn't leave us to die in the hole we've dug ourselves. Full of grace, He does precisely what David did—He reaches out.

Imagine the scene when David's men come to carry Mephibosheth away.[25] It must have seemed to the boy, now a teenager, that the jig was up. Perhaps the soldiers tried communicating David's kind intentions, but how could Mephibosheth believe such a claim? After all, when your grandfather repeatedly tries murdering someone, that someone usually isn't too fond of your family.

Still, whether Mephibosheth went screaming or silently, the youngster was brought before the king.[26]

## THREE IN ONE

When Mephibosheth arrives at the foot of the throne, he immediately falls on his face in reverence.[27] Surely, death was his expectation. At once, Mephibosheth's name is called. His fear and trembling must have been immense: the nightmare was coming true. "Here is your servant!" he cries out, counting himself like a sheep to be slaughtered.[28]

And then, the unthinkable happens.

King David, having the authority to end Mephibosheth's life, blesses him instead. "Do not fear," says the king, "for I will show you kindness for the sake of your father Jonathan, and I will restore to you all the land

---

22  This is a reference to humanity's universal slavery to sin as expressed in John 8:34 and Romans 6:6, apart from Christ.

23  A reference to the inner war between flesh and spirit, as the flesh keeps man from doing the good he desires, as seen in Galatians 5:17. Crawling in the dirt of despair is an illustration of the dirty hopelessness that sin instills apart from God's direct intervention.

24  Believe He is nothing, and that's what you'll come to. Believe He is everything, and you'll live like you have it. Believe He's aloof, and all will turn vain. Believe He is life, and even death will be gain.

25  Interestingly, though he was clearly brought to David, 2 Samuel 9:6 simply says that Mephibosheth "came to David." It may be that this language was intentionally employed by the Holy Spirit to connect to other verses regarding salvation such as Psalm 42:2, Matthew 11:28, and John 6:44 in light of 1 Peter 3:18.

26  As will each of us one day, regardless of our submission or lack thereof. See Romans 14:12.

27  A reference to 2 Samuel 9:6 (NASB). This is also what all people will do before the King of Kings on the last day according to Romans 14:11 and Philippians 2:10.

28  An excerpt of 2 Samuel 9:6 (NASB). This sounds wonderfully close to the "Here am I, Lord" of Isaiah 6:8. Also, the sheep to be slaughtered is a subtle reference to Psalm 44:22 and Romans 8:36.

of Saul your father, and you shall eat at my table always."[29]

Take a moment to let that sink in. Just when the guillotine seemed primed for slicing, grace came abounding instead.[30] Picture Mephibosheth in that precious moment when compassionate, extravagant love extinguishes his fear of death. In a flash, his old life was dead and gone. The new had come.

The deeper we look into David's threefold promise, the better it gets. His declaration spelled out a sacred fresh start for Mephibosheth, overhauling what he knew life to be.

> Just when the guillotine seemed primed for slicing, grace came abounding instead.

In essence, it gave Mephibosheth a new set of ABCs: Acceptance, Blessing, and Communion.

### PROMISE ONE: ACCEPTANCE
### "Do not fear, for I will show you kindness for the sake of your father Jonathan . . . "

Groveling and paralyzed, Mephibosheth bowed before the throne as the king's first shocking words were spoken: "Do not fear!" This is the single most repeated command in all of Scripture and, by design, the beginning of David's promise.[31,32]

These three crystal-clear words perfectly align with what Mephibosheth, and every human heart, needs most: security.[33] Before

---

29  An excerpt of 2 Samuel 9:7 (ESV).

30  This is simply illustrative language for sure-fire execution, as the gallows was invented in 1760 (though hangings date back to the Persian Empire in 500 BC), and the guillotine in 1792. In David's day, around 1000 BC, execution would have almost certainly been by stoning or sword.

31  In one of Jonathan's covenants with David, he told David to "fear not." Thus, it was appropriate for David to pass along the same message to Mephibosheth as he delivered his own covenant with the son of his late friend.

32  Fascinatingly, while the command to "fear not" appears over one hundred times in the Bible, it first arises in Genesis 15:1 as a springboard to God's unconditional covenant ceremony with Abram. The connections between this archetypal covenant and that of David (with both Jonathan and Mephibosheth) are shocking. They do not, however, fall within the scope of this chapter, and are encouraged for personal study.

33  Hosts of psychologists agree that "confidence" is the most universally attractive trait, and for good reason. People are fond of what they value most, and there's nothing more basic than the desire to be secure. Seeing security portrayed in others, even if feigned, comes with a natural sense of gravitation.

any loving acceptance can come home to roost in our hearts, first our fear must go. So, like an angel heralding good news of great joy, David first speaks to the condition of his hearer's heart, to the terror that had surely gripped Mephibosheth since kindergarten.[34,35]

Of course, David does not stop there, just as a builder does not stop after the foundation is laid. Relational security is not the goalpost; it's the gateway that allows growth to begin.[36] Thus, just as perfect love casts out fear, so David, looking on Mephibosheth with the love of heaven itself, launches into a proclamation of his covenantal kindness.

This was no small promise. Be careful not to hear "kindness" and envision a plate of Grandma's chocolate chip cookies or some playground hand-up after falling off the monkey bars. The Hebrew word translated as "kindness" is none other than חֶסֶד (kheh-sed)—the exact same word consistently used for the unfailing, benevolent, zealous love of God! David wasn't promising favors, but *favor itself.*

This favor isn't something Mephibosheth won. **Grace hinges on kindness, not deservedness.** Mephibosheth's story makes this clear. Even though he was the grandson of crooked Saul and therefore fearful of death, Mephibosheth was shown *kheh-sed* through the promise to his father, Jonathan.

Fittingly, salvation comes the same way—by grace. We all are descendants of a crooked man in Adam,[37] living in fear of the King's judgment.[38] And yet we too can be shown *kheh-sed* by the King through

---

34  The angelic news beginning with "fear not" can be seen in many passages. For one, see Luke 2:10.

35  We do not know if Mephibosheth was an educated man. The reference to "kindergarten" is simply a playful allusion to the fact that his nurse took him and fled in fear when he was five years old. Mephibosheth being a teenager is not specifically stated in Scripture but inferred by many scholars due to the timing of David's reign.

36  It is the author's opinion that this is the first of four things for which we (to some degree) are all "SAPS": Security, Acceptance, Prosperity, and Significance. People seem to progress through these four desires somewhat chronologically as they journey through life, not by leaving one behind, but rather building on the previous. Thus, these desires broadly represent the most common longings of infants, adolescents, young adults, and adults, in corresponding order.

37  A reference to Romans 5:12. This is not to finger-wag at Adam, but merely to draw the connection to Mephibosheth's grandfather being the reason he feared judgment.

38  Scripture makes it clear that the human heart knows of its inevitable interview with God. For those who have received the knowledge of the truth and live to the contrary, a "fearful expectation of judgment" is palpable (Hebrews 10:27, ESV). And for those who do not claim to believe in judgment (or in God at all), the Bible asserts that still—likely buried under mounds of pain and pleasure and pride—there is an awareness of the soul's accountability to its Maker (Romans 1:18-21, 2:14-16). Either way, the resultant fear of death enslaves (Hebrews 2:15).

the promise to our father, Abraham.[39]

When our hearts get a hold of this grace (or as it gets a hold of us), things change. All the internal pressure to survive or succeed is at last released. Cares that used to consume us start melting away. Even the fear of judgment fizzles like carbonation set free. That said, our lives don't go flat; they transform! The selfishness that used

It's like trading soda for fruit juice. Both taste sweet, but only one is nourishing.

to dominate our cognition gets replaced with generosity. It's like trading soda for fruit juice. Both taste sweet, but only one is nourishing.

Because of his covenant with Jonathan, King David didn't let Mephibosheth rot in fear. David accepted him in love, and as if that promise wasn't enough, he tacked on two more.

### Promise Two: Blessing
**". . . and I will restore to you all the land of Saul your father . . ."**

The second phase of David's promise might be the most esoteric of the three, but that only makes the unfolding all the sweeter. It picks up right where the first left off, referencing Mephibosheth's family line again. This time, however, the focus is on his grandfather Saul,[40] the tyrant who relentlessly attempted to murder David. Normally, this would've been a death sentence, but David promises to *restore* all of "Saul's land" to the paralyzed boy on the floor.

To put this in context, Saul had been the king of all Israel (and a greedy one at that). "The land of Saul" would have been the modern-day

---

39  To be clear, Abraham is known as the "father" of all who share his faith in Jehovah (Romans 4:16-18, Galatians 3:29). He is not the father of everyone, as Jesus makes clear in John 8:39-44. This relationship to Abraham is critical to salvation, just as Mephibosheth's relation to Jonathan was the whole reason David showed the boy kindness. Mephibosheth was blessed because his father Jonathan was a friend of (the soon-to-be) King David. Similarly, those of faith today are blessed because their father Abraham (Galatians 3:7) was a friend of the King of the Universe (2 Chronicles 20:7, Isaiah 41:8, James 2:23). It all ties back to covenants.

40  The text says "Saul your father," but here the use of "father" is simply a Hebrew expression for "ancestor." Clearly from the rest of the passage, Mephibosheth's literal father was Jonathan (see 2 Samuel 4:4 and 9:9).

equivalent of a billionaire's estate.[41] Also, like David's first promise, it's an unconditional guarantee. There's no "Might you please accept my offer, young lad?" or "If you do what I say, cripple, I'll be kind." This is an example of God's unstoppable, irresistible, soul-hugging love on full display. One can almost taste the sovereignty echoing through those two most important words: "I will."[42]

This is precisely how the King of Glory calls His own.[43] Especially when it comes to salvation, God is in the business of gracious *I wills*, not expectant *You betters*.[44] Nothing Mephibosheth did earned him the restoration of his inheritance. Such grace was set in motion before he was even born. So it is for those of faith—not that we will all receive mansions, but that the land of our grandfather Adam will one day be restored to us: Eden![45]

> Especially when it comes to salvation, God is in the business of gracious I wills, not expectant You betters.

It's all foreshadowed right here in the story. Grandpa Saul, due to his defiance of God's direct order, lost dominion over Israel and all the land he was given, but King David, upon subduing all the surrounding nations, rose to bless the remnant of Saul's line and restore the land.

---

41  We aren't told specifically how much land belonged personally to King Saul, but according to 2 Samuel 9:10, it took at least thirty-six people to take care of it, so the comparison to a billionaire's estate is warranted.

42  For a deeper dive into the security, acceptance, and blessings that bloom from God's sovereign "I will" declarations, see Genesis 12:1-3, Isaiah 41:10, Isaiah 46:11, and Ezekiel 17:24.

43  Throughout the Bible, David is likened to Christ. Later in life, Mephibosheth even says of David, "My lord the king is like *the angel of God*"—an Old Testament title commonly attributed to Christ Himself. King David was by no means perfect, but many of his words and actions foreshadowed He who was to come. Jesus not only answers to the name "Son of David" in Matthew 20:31-32, but even His last words in all of Scripture bear the same mark, as He says in Revelation 22:16, "I am the root and the descendant of David, the bright morning star."

44  This is said with the assumed understanding that God surely holds each of us responsible for all decisions made and words spoken. For everything we do and say, we will give an account (Romans 14:12, 2 Corinthians 5:10). However, when we focus primarily on the dos and don'ts of Scripture, we lose sight of grace, thus striving powerlessly to fulfill the Law. Such pharisaical attitudes produce the very lovelessness God aims to extinguish. Paradoxically, it's only when we confess our helplessness to live up to the *you betters*, focusing instead on the sufficiency of Christ, that we become increasingly enabled to live and love appropriately. The secret to a life of loving obedience is learning to cherish His. See John 6:38, Philippians 2:8, and Hebrews 12:2-3.

45  For a fascinating study on the remnant of Israel being restored like Eden, check out Ezekiel 36:22-36. For a more general application of Eden being restored to all of God's people, compare this to Revelation 21:9-22:5.

In the same way, ol' Grandpa Adam, due to his defiance of God's direct order, lost dominion over Eden, and yet there will come a day when the King of Kings, upon subduing all other nations,[46] will rise to restore the inheritances of *His* people.[47]

Before moving on, it's critical to note that these "inheritances" are eternal, not earthly. While it's true that Mephibosheth was given immense earthly wealth by King David, this is not something that comes prepackaged with biblical salvation.[48] Sadly, Western culture has become so bloated with the love of money that many define blessing by bank statements alone. Even pockets of the church have succumbed to a so-called "prosperity gospel" that says, "Come to Jesus so He can bless you and make you rich."

> No mansion is big enough to fill a human heart.

But there's no pot of gold at the end of that rainbow, only greed. No mansion is big enough to fill a human heart. Only the great kindness of the King can do that. And David saved the best kindness for last.

### PROMISE THREE: COMMUNION
### " . . . and you shall eat at my table always."

At first glance, David's final promise to Mephibosheth may seem like small potatoes. The untrained eye might be tempted to write it off as merely a nice gesture, categorizing it among modern phrases like "my door is always open" or "*mi casa es su casa.*" Don't let that happen.

A permanent seat at the king's table must not be compared to inviting some friends over for dinner. Like in any home, to hold a lifelong seat at the dinner table means you are *family*. Five minutes

---

46  An allusion to the reaching of the nations with the gospel (Matthew 24:14), the fullness of the Gentiles coming in (Romans 11:25), and the literal striking down of all the nations when Christ comes in glory (Revelation 19:15).

47  The use of "inheritances" here refers to the notion of different Promised Land allotments (Joshua 13-24) and how they foreshadow "a better country" (Hebrews 11:16) that is promised to those who believe (John 14:2-3). Even deeper, because all followers of Jesus are called "priests" in the New Testament (1 Peter. 2:4-9, Revelation 1:6, 5:9-10), there is a glorious connection between believers and the Old Testament priests—the Levites—whose inheritance was not land but God Himself (Numbers 18:20, Deuteronomy 10:9).

48  The closest the Bible comes to such an earthly prosperity guarantee is Mark 10:29-30. With careful study of this passage, however, it becomes apparent that this prosperity describes access to the shared wealth of all believers who are following the command to be deeply hospitable. It's not about "ownership."

ago, Mephibosheth's choices seemed like the guillotine or the gallows. From now on, it would be chicken or steak. In a flash, the groveling paralytic became royalty.

There's one more important thing to notice here. Just like the two previous promises, David didn't offer—he declared. **This wasn't an invitation. It was adoption.**

All three of King David's promises vividly illustrate God's gift of salvation, but this is undoubtedly the capstone. Right away, clear connections can be made to events like the Last Supper and the wedding feast of the Lamb. Both involve us dining with the King of Kings as a family. With a bit of diligence, one can also find multiple quotes from the lips of Christ linked to this concept of eternally feasting with the Master in His Kingdom.[49] Even so, if that's where we stop, we've missed the crown jewel.

Rewind some eight hundred years[50] to the life of the original son of promise, Isaac, and we see the similarities. After watching both of his parents die, Isaac, perhaps at an all-time low, is sought out by God, who declares:

> "I will be with you and bless you, for to you and to your descendants I will give all these lands, and I will establish the oath which I swore to your father Abraham."
>
> —GENESIS 26:3 (NASB)

As if that wasn't enough, God reinforces it in the very same chapter:

> "Do not fear, for I am with you. I will bless you and multiply your descendants, for the sake of My servant Abraham."[51]
>
> —GENESIS 26:24 (NASB)

It's no accident that David's promise to Mephibosheth is nearly identical to God's covenant with Isaac. Both boys are sons of promise

---

49  Some examples of these passages are Luke 12:37, 14:15, and 22:30.

50  Timelines prior to the conquest are a bit dicey, but according to a few different sources such as the "Amazing Bible Timeline," tracing genealogies backward yields approximately 1896 BC to 1716 BC for the life of Isaac. For more study on this topic, see the article titled *Isaac* at AmazingBibleTimeline.com.

51  This is also the very first occurrence in Scripture of God directly calling someone "My servant."

and recipients of blessing. Both covenants were given for the sake of their fathers. Time and again, the New Testament speaks of believers as "children of promise," just like Isaac.[52] Salvation isn't merely about being rescued from the fire. It's about orphans experiencing the joy of being adopted into the family of the King.

Imagine if you were a paralyzed youngster hearing all these promises. How would you respond? Like a game show contestant who just won the showcase? Not Mephibosheth. His reaction speaks volumes:

> "Who is your servant, that you should show such kindness
> to a dead dog like me?"[53]
> —2 Samuel 9:8b (NLT)

Really, this type of incredulous humility should be our response to every good thing that comes our way, especially the promises of God Almighty. King David lavished grace upon the son of his friend; how much more does the infinite King of Kings do so upon us! Amazingly, for those who are of faith, the Gracious Governor of the Universe doesn't condemn. He says, "Tonight, we're having spaghetti and meatballs."

You're invited.

---

52  Two verses that speak directly to this concept are Romans 9:27-28 and Galatians 4:28.

53  This is yet another connection with David's past, as David called himself a "dead dog" when Saul was pursuing his life in 1 Samuel 24:14.

# HIDDEN GEMS

## JESUS: OUR GRACIOUS GOVERNOR

Mephibosheth kept his distance—lame and fearful—until King David brought him near. ➤ We keep our distance—lame and fearful—until King Jesus brings us near. *(Luke 14:21, Ephesians 2:14, Hebrews 10:27)*

King David sought out the crippled Mephibosheth without anyone convincing him to do so. ➤ King Jesus seeks out the crushed in spirit without anyone convincing Him to do so. *(John 6:44, John 15:16, Romans 9:16, 1 John 4:19)*

King David's love shocked Mephibosheth because the boy expected to be put to death. ➤ King Jesus' love shocks our consciences because we deserve to be put to death. *(Romans 1:32, Romans 6:23, 1 John 3:1)*

King David's profound kindness and care was rooted in his covenant of old. ➤ King Jesus' immeasurable kindness and care is rooted in His eternal covenant. *(Jeremiah 31:33, Luke 22:20, Ephesians 2:7, Hebrews 13:20)*

King David received Mephibosheth as a beloved friend at the royal table. ➤ King Jesus receives us as His beloved friends at His royal table. *(Isaiah 25:6, Luke 14:13, Luke 22:30)*

King David blessed Mephibosheth with servants who helped him in his toil. ➤ King Jesus blesses us with His servants who help us in our toil. *(2 Corinthians 4:5, Hebrews 1:14)*

**BOTTOM LINE:**

Jesus loves us in our lameness, offering an identity that overcomes. *(2 Corinthians 12:9, Hebrews 12:13)*

# WRAP UP:
# Happily Almost After

Mephibosheth's story is so much more than a random historical event that took place three thousand years ago. What happened speaks to the very heart of the human condition. As the story concludes with all the promises fulfilled and a great Disney finish in sight, the last line swoops in with a spiky reminder: "He was lame in both his feet."[54] Mephibosheth's life had radically transformed, but he still couldn't walk on his own. **The king didn't save him from his pain and paralysis; he gave him new life within it.** The disability remained, but one shared day at a time.

This grace is the way of Christ—the beauty and power of going low.[55] For grace to be amazing, we must first realize we aren't. The higher we see ourselves, the lower we treat God. Heavenly love is like rain. Crops depend on it for life, and so do we, yet often we balk at the thought of being dependent on anything or any One. As a result, many treat God like some passive summer breeze rather than the very breath in our lungs. Over time, "God" becomes nothing more than a spiritual box fan. So instead of raising the sails of their souls, people put their faces in front of the vent—and still expect to be moved.

Mephibosheth was paralyzed, utterly incapable of coming to the king, yet his lord sent servants to carry him in. Expecting to die, Mephibosheth found life—and life to the full. So it is with us and God. No one comes before the Throne of Grace unless the Father ushers them in. God first seeks us, not the other way around.[56]

And just like David, our King sends servants to bring us in—messengers

---

54 An excerpt of 2 Samuel 9:13 (ESV).

55 An allusion to both the heart of Christ as described by Him in Matthew 11:29, as well as the humility of His incarnation seen in verses like Psalms 8:5, Philippians 2:7, and Hebrews 2:7.

56 Such concepts of God being the ultimate Initiator can be seen throughout the Scriptures, perhaps most strikingly with regards to salvation in John 6:44 and Luke 19:10. The converse is also cemented in the canon, that "no one seeks for God" on their own (Romans 3:11, ESV). Similarly, Jesus made sure the Twelve knew that they became disciples not because they chose Him, but because He chose them (John 15:16).

of the Good News.[57] He replaces our fear of judgment with His loving promise of *kheh-sed*. Over time, as we experience such unfailing love, we learn to show Him and others the same. Ultimately, through a most glorious exchange, our hearts ditch selfishness for a life devoted to sharing and showing "the affection of Christ Jesus."[58]

In the end, we serve because He first served us.[59]

---

57  This could be said of the angels in Luke 2:10 as well as the preachers of Romans 10:14-15 and 2 Corinthians 4:5. Interestingly, the NASB even inserts the noun "messengers" into 2 Samuel 9:5 to describe those sent by David to retrieve Mephibosheth. This only furthers the point as the word for "angel" literally means messenger, and followers are implicitly called the same by Christ in John 13:16. That said, it is debatable whether angels assist in the lead up to salvation or sanctification alone, centering around Hebrews 1:14.

58  An excerpt of Philippians 1:9 (ESV).

59  1 John 4:19 uses the same phrasing to famously speak of love, but it is equally true that Jesus first served us (Mark 10:45), and out of the freedom we have received by the ransom he paid, we live to do the same (Galatians 5:13).

# ENGAGE: Group Study 3

**STARTER**   Mephibosheth's name translates in English to "The end of shame." How does this connect to his story?

**TRIVIA**   Five times in Scripture, people respond to God's pronounced favor with an incredulous "Who am I?" Three were by David, one by Solomon. Who was the other one to declare this great phrase?[60]

**REFLECT**   Does God's kindness amaze you like it did Mephibosheth? When was the last time His goodness took you by surprise?

**PONDER**   From a biblical standpoint, how might fear and paralyzed feet be connected? (*Consider Isaiah 52:7 and Romans 10:15.*)

**JOURNAL**   Who is someone you don't know very well that you could be compassionate or generous toward, and what might that look like?

**BOIL IT DOWN**   God's kindness is unstoppable, turning fear into feasting.

**BRING IT UP**   Why is trusting God's kindness so challenging?

**LIVE IT OUT**   Make a plan with a friend to bless someone in need this week.

---

60   The other "Who am I?" came from Moses. The associated verses are Exodus 3:11, 1 Samuel 18:18, 2 Samuel 7:18 (repeated in 1 Chronicles 17:16), 1 Chronicles 29:14, and 2 Chronicles 2:6.

# 4

# ISRAEL THE WANDERER

*"Who is as blind as my own people, my servant?*
*Who is as deaf as my messenger?*
*Who is as blind as my chosen people,*
*the servant of the LORD?"*
—Isaiah 42:19 (NLT)

H AVE YOU EVER WONDERED WHICH words appear most frequently in the Bible?

Well, thanks to either the advent of computers or someone with way too much time on their hands, wonder no longer. The words have been tallied, and the votes are in. In first place—the undisputed, undefeated champion of the world—is "Lord," coming in at 7,803 appearances.[1] The silver medal, also by a wide margin, goes to "God" at 4,375 appearances.

---

1   The count of 7,803 includes both the all-caps "LORD" which translates the divine name YHWH, as well as the title "Lord," the English rendering of the Hebrew "Adon/Adonai." According to BlueLetterBible.org, the lion's share is from YHWH, occurring some 6,521 times. All word counts are from the NASB95. Also, this ranking does not take into account pronouns (he, she, it), prepositions (of, to, in), conjunctions (and, but, so), or determiners (this, the, those). It is sheerly focused on meaningful words—nouns, adjectives, verbs, and the like.

(After all, the Bible is God's autobiography.)

But what comes in third? Believe it or not, sneaking onto the podium and weighing in at a whopping 2,571 occurrences—the man, the nation, the legendary contender: "Israel"!

Yes, throughout the biblical narrative, other than God Himself, the main character of the Bible is not Adam or Moses or David—it's *Israel*. Without a doubt, the name was so important that God Himself picked it.

Plus, Israel was more than just a BC concept: the name appears some seventy-five times in the New Testament. Time and again, the Apostles weave together the idea of serving in the body of Christ and belonging to Israel, God's chosen nation. Needless to say, studying Israel is critical to understanding God's plan of salvation and service.

**Prepare yourself, though. It's messy.**

Israel's history begins with Jacob, the scrawny momma's boy from Genesis 32.[2] After twice cheating his brother Esau, Jacob feared for his life. Eventually, he devised a plan to make amends, sending Esau 780 animals worth nearly $1 million today.[3] After delivering the massive herd, however, something radical happened. Scripture records that an unnamed "man" suddenly began wrestling with Jacob.[4] Curiously, this "man" dislocates Jacob's hip, blesses him, and, at the climax of the smackdown, changes Jacob's name to Israel.[5]

Thus, it's accurate to say that before Israel was a nation, Israel was a person—a name. Make no mistake, though: Israel is no ordinary name. As one Hebrew dictionary puts it, "The meaning of Israel is not singular

---

2   This is by no means a derogatory remark regarding Jacob. It's a reference to the favoritism his mom Rebecca showed him as seen in Genesis 25:28.

3   This was calculated by simple internet searches that yielded the following figures: two hundred ewes at $250 each, twenty rams at $450, 420 goats at $200, forty cows at $2,800, ten bulls at $4,500, thirty donkeys at $1,000, thirty camels at $15,000, and thirty baby camels at $5,000 for a total of $930,000.

4   There is considerable debate over the identity of the unnamed "man." Some believe he was simply an angel, as Hosea 12:4 seems to state. However, the verse continues with God saying Jacob "spoke with *us*," implying the Godhead was manifestly present. Moreover, Jacob was given the name "Israel" because he was said to have "striven with God" (Genesis 32:28). Jacob showed no signs of knowing that the "man" was more than simply human until after the fact, when he boldly declared, "I have seen God face to face, yet my life has been spared" (32:30). This mirrors the accounts of people not initially recognizing the resurrected Jesus.

5   Such a name change seems eerily similar to that of God toward Sarai (who became Sarah) and Jesus toward Simon (who became Peter). There are no accounts of an angel changing someone's name in Scripture. This furthers the case for the "man" being Christ pre-incarnate, though such a position raises questions of its own.

and distinct but consists of many nuances and facets and **bulges with theological significance**."

Indeed, many have debated its Hebrew roots through the centuries. Check out the frontrunners in the chart below and how they all connect to the grand narrative of Scripture.[6] Could a single name, just six letters, communicate the entire Christian gospel?[7]

| "ISRAEL" MEANING | SOURCE | NOTES | CONNECTIONS |
|---|---|---|---|
| God rules, or God persists | *Brown-Driver-Briggs Hebrew and English Lexicon* | The Hebrew verb "sarar" means to rule. God's sovereignty and His persistent pursuit of man are central in Scripture. | PSALM 103:19 1 TIMOTHY 1:16 HEBREWS 13:8 |
| He who contends with God | *New American Study Bible* footnotes | To "contend" means to be unyielding, doubly exposing man's refusal to surrender and doggedness to endure. | JOB 40:2 ISAIAH 45:9 ACTS 5:39 |
| He has become a receptacle in which God can be received and retained | *Abarim Publications' Biblical Name Vault* | The indwelling of God, whether in the Tabernacle, the Temple, the person of Christ, or a believer is richly woven throughout Scripture. | EXODUS 31:3 EZEKIEL. 36:27 JOHN 14:23 1 CORINTHIANS 3:16 |
| He will be prince with God | *Jones Dictionary of Old Testament Proper Names* | The Hebrew noun "sar" means chief or ruler. Believers will reign with Christ, as He is the "Prince of Peace." | ISAIAH 9:6 ACTS 5:31 2 TIMOTHY 2:12 |

Of course, receiving this new name was only the beginning. Israel would go on to father twelve sons (Joseph and his brothers) amid a devastating famine. Through a strange blend of hatred and heroism,

---

6   For an exhaustive dive into the various root words that inform the meanings presented, check out the page of Abarim Publications' online database entitled *Biblical Name Vault: Israel.*

7   Look what curiously happens when you string the meanings together: "God rules, (and yet) he who contends with God becomes a receptacle in which God can be received and retained, (until the day) he will be prince with God."

these boys would become the progenitors of the famous twelve Jewish tribes. Eventually, what began as one man would become a kingdom, all from a starving family in the desert. But how?

The story of Israel's ascent as a country is no Disney film. Honestly, it would be rated R, if not worse.[8] Recapping it alone is hard to stomach: four hundred years of backbreaking slavery, mass infant drownings, then forty years of death in the desert, thirty years of bloody wars, some three hundred fifty more on the brink of collapse, and finally the forty-year reign of a murderous, demon-oppressed king in Saul who ends up committing suicide.

> The story of Israel's ascent as a country is no Disney film.

This was the Israel that King David inherited, chaos and all. With David, however, came a new chapter in Hebrew history. Widely regarded as Israel's greatest king, David ushered in his nation's golden age.[9] His military victories brought rest to the region. His temple preparations amassed resources. Indeed, by the time the torch was passed to his son Solomon, Israel's meteoric rise was well underway.

But so was temptation.

## OUR KINGDOM COME

Solomon's reign was the pinnacle of Israel's prominence. Controlling the vast majority of modern-day Israel, Gaza, Jordan, Lebanon, and Syria, Solomon's kingdom functioned as the global center of trade.[10] Every year,

---

8   If this claim seems harsh, read the following passages in succession and imagine them realistically depicted in a movie: Exodus 1:22, 32:27-28; Numbers 14:35; Joshua 6:21; and Judges 19:29.

9   In Ecclesiastes 2:9, Solomon claims to have surpassed all others before him in greatness, but this is specifically regarding wealth. By countless sacred Jewish writings, David is emphatically declared Israel's greatest *overall* king. Therefore, it may be said of David that the shepherd became the GOAT (Greatest of All Time). This is doubly true of Christ, who, being the Chief Shepherd (1 Peter 5:4), became both the supreme "King of the Jews" (John 19:21) and humanity's scapegoat for sin (Leviticus 16:10).

10   According to 1 Kings 4:21, Solomon ruled not only over Israel but the surrounding kingdoms as well, receiving tribute from them all the days of his life. 1 Kings 4:34 states that people from all nations came to hear his wisdom, solidifying the "global center" description above. In riches and wisdom, he was supreme (1 Kings 10:23).

Solomon brought in some 50,000 pounds[11] of gold from far-off lands, which today would be worth $1.8 billion.[12] There was so much gold in Israel, silver was considered worthless. Solomon made a throne of gold, shields of gold—even his water bottle was gold.[13]

In no time, King Solomon became the single most powerful man in the world. The nation he ruled, Israel, had officially gone from a handicapped wrestler to a starving family to a record-breaking empire. Talk about rags to riches!

Under Solomon, the golden Temple was built, a structure so magnificent that it would become known as one of the seven ancient wonders of the world.[14] Twenty chariot cities were constructed to house Solomon's 40,000 horses. He even built an entire navy that carried ivory, monkeys, and peacocks.[15] Zoos, vineyards, aqueducts, palaces—Solomon had it all. Where, though, would it lead him? And where would he lead Israel?

It's often said that suffering brings out people's true colors. Well, so does abundance. At first, it seemed King Solomon wanted to make Israel great and God's name known, but it soon became about himself. The more Solomon had, the more he wanted, and the way to get more was by collecting *wives*. So, that's what he did.

> It's often said that suffering brings out people's true colors. Well, so does abundance.

---

11 See 1 Kings 10:14. A "talent" in ancient Hebrew culture was a unit of measurement for weighing precious metals. One talent weighed around 75 pounds, and Scripture curiously records Solomon importing exactly 666 talents of gold every year, equating to just under 50,000 pounds. Whether Solomon's wisdom and gold connects to Revelation 13:18 is up for debate and not within the scope of this book.

12 This is a rounded estimate using $35,075 per pound of gold, the market price in the spring of 2024.

13 A playful reference to 1 Kings 10:21a, where it records "drinking utensils" being of pure gold. The shields of gold were two hundred in number and each weighing just over fifteen pounds. This equates to a modern-day value of $426,000 per shield, not to mention the absurd impracticality of a shield made from one of earth's softest metals.

14 The seven ancient wonders of the world are not universally agreed upon, but some sources do list Solomon's Temple. For more information, see the article titled *The Seven Wonders of the World* by GlobalSecurity.org.

15 A reference to 1 Kings 10:22. It is unknown why Solomon would choose apes to lug back from distant lands. Two main theories exist. Either he maintained a personal zoo for entertainment, or he studied these animals. Either way, he certainly was fascinated by such creatures, as he included them in his teachings (1 Kings 4:33).

Beginning with the princess of Egypt, King Solomon married seven hundred female dignitaries from all the surrounding nations. When these wives arrived on the palace grounds, though, they brought along their gods, customarily worshipped in two main ways: public orgies and child sacrifice.

That didn't bother Solomon. He built altars to each one.[16]

Never once does God call Solomon "my servant," and for good reason. There were only three no-no's in the Law for kings of Israel: no amassing horses, no collecting wives, and no procuring great sums of gold.[17] Solomon struck out swinging on all three pitches. Instead of trusting the Lord to save, he amassed weapons. Instead of trusting the Lord to satisfy, he chased lust. And through it all, what mattered most? His bank account.

When hearts lose sight of servanthood, anything becomes fair game.

Do these vices sound familiar? Solomon had horses; we have nukes. Solomon had hundreds of wives; we have thousands of porn stars. Public orgies aren't gone; they just moved from street corners to smartphones. Meanwhile, the love of money is sold as good fun—just look at the ads for the Powerball lottery. And perhaps worst of all, life in the womb is not highly valued.[18]

When hearts lose sight of servanthood, anything becomes fair game. Solomon's life started strong: wealth, wisdom, and accomplishments

---

16  (Caution: the following description is exceedingly graphic.) Imagine the great holy Temple in all its glory, the gold gleaming in the sunlight. Then imagine seven hundred altars scattered around the area, each with its own grotesque half-human, half-animal brass statue. Underneath the hollow metal, priests stoke roaring fires, turning the surface red hot. Surrounding the statues, public orgies rage forth as one by one, fathers lay their newborns on the god's hands, melting their children alive. All the while, musicians beat drums loud enough to drown out the screams of the sacrificed. This actually happened.

17  A reference to Deuteronomy 17:16-17. Fascinatingly, what follows those prohibitions is a single exhortation explaining what a king should do instead: personally handwrite a copy of the Torah (the first five books of the Bible) and read from it every day of his life.

18  This can be seen by a variety of metrics, from the incidence of fatherless newborns to fetal alcohol syndrome to pregnancy termination. For instance, if you count abortions as deaths, they would by far be the leading cause of death in the world. Public data sets on this topic of course do not account for life in the womb. For example, according to the organization Our World in Data, heart disease was the leading cause of death worldwide at 18.5 million deaths a year in 2019. Meanwhile in 2019, there were 73 million abortions. This number nearly quadruples that of heart disease and well exceeds all the deaths *combined* for that year (55 million).

galore. And yet, the wisest man in the world became an utter fool. This didn't happen overnight. The devil plays the long game, inching ambition toward arrogance, gain toward greed. Solomon's idolatry wasn't a crime of passion. Most sin isn't. It was the gradual erosion of a soul bent inward.

The sobering story of Solomon's downfall serves as a grave warning against seeing oneself as king. From the moment Israel became a nation, the people struggled to decide who knew best. Eventually, the demand for an earthly sovereign won out. But humans need softened hearts, not stronger leaders.

Too often, Western culture snarls for justice and benefits with clenched fists, but white knuckles don't make helping hands. Harmony doesn't come through the hatred of evil. It emerges from the love of ultimate Good.[19]

> Harmony doesn't come through the hatred of evil. It emerges from the love of ultimate Good.

## OUR WILL BE DONE

King Solomon began Israel's avalanche of pride, but he sure didn't finish it. At his death, the kingdom split, never to unite again.[20] Two hundred fifty years of evil kings would follow, climaxing in a gory exile at the hands of the Assyrian Empire. Just like that, God's chosen nation became a remnant of slaves. For centuries, Israel refused to serve her Savior, swollen with selfish ambition. The dam had been cracking for generations. Then came the flood.

Of all God's proclamations of "my servant" in Scripture, only one is negative. With the Promised Land in ruins and exile on the way, the Father bellowed this grievous lament over Israel:

---

19  Ultimate Good is a wink to the "Good Shepherd" and "Good Teacher," Jesus Christ.

20  Of course, Israel became a unified nation again in 1948, but not as a unified *kingdom*. That said, in a sense, one could view the millennial reign of Christ as such, but that is not within the scope of this work.

Who is as blind as my own people, **my servant**? Who is as deaf as my messenger? Who is as blind as my chosen people, the servant of the LORD? You see and recognize what is right but refuse to act on it. You hear with your ears but you don't really listen . . . **Who will hear these lessons from the past** and see the ruin that awaits you in the future?

—Isaiah 42:19-23 (NLT)

So far, we have studied various servants of the Old Testament and how they all point to Christ. This chapter does the same but in reverse. Rather than examining one focal event, we will trace the primary pivots in Israel's story, discovering what caused the kingdom to crumble (and so many others since). Broken into three main eras—the Exodus, Conquest, and Kingdom—these seven hundred years of history boil down to bite-size sections, all aimed at answering the same question: What poisoned Israel's servanthood, and what would have cured it?

The goal here is to study what cheerful servanthood *doesn't* look like and build awareness of common spiritual landmines before the shrapnel flies. God included Israel's downfall in His Word for a reason. As the apostle Paul put it:

These things happened to them [Israel] as examples and were written down **as warnings for us**, on whom the culmination of the ages has come.

—1 Corinthians 10:11 (NIV)

The sirens are blaring. Who will heed them?

### PIVOT ONE: THE WILDERNESS

The first of the three Israelite pivots unfolded just after their deliverance. Given their dramatic exodus from Egypt, God's people thought they were headed for paradise. The Hero had rescued the damsel in distress. Shouldn't prosperity follow?

What the Hebrews found across the Red Sea shocked them: a barren wasteland. Within three days, they were exhausted, dehydrated, and at their wit's end. Finally, happening upon a pool of undrinkable bitter water, their morale broke: the bitterness before them took root within.[21] Grumbling quickly traveled from their guts to their lips.

"What shall we drink?" they seethed.

So Moses, their great advocate, cried out to the Lord, who "showed him a tree; and he threw it into the waters, and the waters became sweet."[22] What a miracle! At the sound of a single prayer came provision for an entire nation.

Sadly, Scripture records no praise or response of thankfulness from Israel. The people pouted, got what they wanted, and seemingly moved on. Many more moments like this would follow, as Israel became increasingly hard-hearted. God hadn't led them into a land of posh comforts like they expected. He wasn't interested in simply removing them from slavery; God wanted to remove the slavery *from them*—the slavery of self-centeredness.

Their murmurs evidenced a grave heart condition, just like in the medical field. To a cardiologist, a murmur is a recurring sound heard in the heart through a stethoscope that is usually a sign of disease or damage. In Israel's case, hundreds of thousands of people thundered forth their bitter murmurs. No stethoscope was necessary.

"Would that we had died in Egypt! At least there we had pots of meat and bread to the full," they jabbed. "Or would that we had died in this wilderness! Let us choose a leader and go back to Egypt."[23]

Realize just how sharp of a slap this was to the face of God. Egypt murdered Israelite infants, enslaved their children, and beat their adults for centuries. And *that* was better than life with the Lord? Stripped of their last few comforts, their priorities became plain. It wasn't communion with God they wanted; it was the good life.[24] They had come to be served, not to serve.

---

21  Such bitterness connects to multiple passages about rebellious hearts who say, "I will be safe, even though I persist in going my own way," when in reality there is poison and disaster afoot (Deuteronomy 29:18-19, NIV). Other passages in the same vein are Jeremiah 9:13-15, 23:14-15, and Hebrews 12:15.

22  An excerpt of Exodus 15:25 (NASB95).

23  These quotes are a combination of Exodus 16:3 and Numbers 14:2-4. Such a fusion of multiple grumbling instances is intended to highlight the addictive nature of the sin presented.

24  "They" in this instance is a generalization of the Hebrew people at the time. Surely, Moses and select others desired communion with God. But on the whole, Scripture does not record the people ever praying to their Heavenly Liberator for help when in the wilderness.

How many people still come to God with this attitude? Too often, salvation is presented as a permanent boarding pass to a life of bliss. As a result, souls look to exit oppression with toxic expectations of all the flowers and fidget spinners their hearts ever wanted. But God doesn't save us so our dreams will come true. He longs to show us that, without Him, all those dreams are really nightmares in disguise.

The problem is humanity's default desire: instant gratification. We're quickly addicted to ourselves, and stubbornly opposed to admitting it. Consider the progression: It took a few hours for God to get Israel out of Egypt. It took forty years to get Egypt out of Israel. And it took only one generation for the entire nation to turn its back on the one true God.

> We're quickly addicted to ourselves, and stubbornly opposed to admitting it.

When Moses ascended the mountain, what did the Israelites do? They built and worshipped a golden calf—the ultimate symbol of milk and meat. Then, "the people sat down to eat and to drink, and rose up to play."[25] Those forty wilderness years were one large grumble tumble, as they waltzed in the desert instead of bowing their knees.

Eventually, many even wished to die rather than submit to their Savior, and so, after countless moments of mercy, God gave them what they asked for. After all, life always ends one of two ways: we either say yes to God, or God says to us, "Have it your way."[26]

### PIVOT TWO: THE CONQUEST

The desert wasn't pretty, but what came after was arguably worse. When Israel first entered the Promised Land, Moses' understudy, Joshua, led the people to remain faithful. Scripture even goes so far as to say:

> "And the people served the LORD all the days of Joshua, and all the days of the elders who outlived Joshua, who

---

25   An excerpt of Exodus 32:6 (ESV).
26   There can only be one Burger King, and appointing ourselves is a whopper of a mistake.

had seen all the great work that the LORD had done
for Israel."

—JUDGES 2:7 (ESV)

Life was good. The people had their inheritance. And that's when the
second pivot came. For the first time since Egypt, the tribes had their
comforts back, this time without slavery. The land of plenty was theirs
at last.[27] How would they respond?

Not well.

In one of the most tragic turnarounds in history, Scripture records
that immediately after Joshua and the elders died, "there arose another
generation after them who **did not know the LORD or the work that
he had done for Israel.**"[28] For decades, God had delivered one miracle
after another: freedom from Egypt, bitter water becoming sweet, bread
and meat from heaven, rescue from fiery serpents, parting the Jordan
River, the conquering of Jericho, and more. So after all that, how could a
generation possibly rise up that knew nothing of those awesome events?
Simple: they weren't taught to care.[29]

It's impossible to overstate the importance of discipleship. Joshua's
generation didn't train up their youth well, and the result was utter
disaster. Scripture minces no words in relaying just how swiftly everything
spiraled as soon as Joshua's gang was gone:

> And the people of Israel did what was evil in the sight of
> the LORD and **served the Baals**. And they abandoned the
> LORD . . . they went after other gods . . . they abandoned
> the LORD and **served the Baals and the Ashtaroth** . . .
> Then the LORD raised up judges, who saved them out
> of the hand of those who plundered them. Yet they did

---

27  While Israel hadn't completed the conquest properly, they had still done so to the point where Joshua
    could "dismiss" them to take possession of their respective inheritances as seen in Judges 2:6.

28  An excerpt of Judges 2:10 (ESV).

29  Given the people's proclamation in Joshua 24:16-18, they clearly knew "of" the works God had done for
    Israel, just not in a personal way. They had been told the stories, but that's all they saw them as—stories.
    While this new generation of Israelites may have abandoned the Lord for multiple reasons, it's fair to infer
    that their lack of intimacy with God was due in part to the lack of discipleship shown them. Proverbs 22:6
    (BSB) makes this clear: "Train up a child in the way he should go, and when he is old he will not depart
    from it."

not listen to their judges, for they whored after other gods and bowed down to them . . . whenever the judge died, they turned back and were more corrupt than their fathers, going after other gods, **serving them** and bowing down to them.

—JUDGES 2:11-19 (ESV)

In a few short years, Israel went from widespread devotion to wretched desertion. Soon, she would downright forget the Lord.[30]

**All it took for Israel to collapse was a generation that didn't prioritize discipleship.** Sure, Joshua and his peers were mighty men of faith. They even built memorials to commemorate certain works of the Lord.[31] However, when it came time to pass down that faith, they choked—big time. The youth were given the wealth and rituals, but they needed discipleship—personal training in the way they should go. Without that guidance, the God of their fathers became no more than a rule master of meaningless tradition, and cheerful servanthood dissolved.

The West has experienced similar descents into idolatry. Focusing so intently on behavior, attire, and attendance, many nations have experienced rapid declines in church involvement. Let's face it: when delight in the Lord gets replaced by dutiful obedience, the human heart looks for love somewhere else. Souls long for a glorious hero to adore, not some do-and-don't list. Such burdensome rigidity sends young people straight through the stained glass, metaphorically speaking. The church shatters, and the kids move on.

> Souls long for a glorious hero to adore, not some do-and-don't list.

People wonder why the "don't know, don't care" mentality toward faith is skyrocketing in the West.[32] Look no further than Joshua & Co.,

---

30  The "forgetting" of the Lord is explicitly mentioned in Judges 3:7, among other places.

31  These memorials can be found in Joshua 4:20, 7:26, 8:28-29, 8:30-32, 10:27, 22:34, and 24:26-27.

32  For a thoughtful article describing the ongoing collapse of organized religion in America (written by an agnostic), see "Three Decades Ago, America Lost Its Religion. Why?" by Derek Thompson of *The Atlantic*.

who taught the Law and shared the stories but failed to foster connection with God. Faith became an ideology, worship a routine, and the next generation said no thanks. The same is true today. It's tempting to point the finger at a lost generation and wag our heads with disgust, but a widespread exodus from the church doesn't happen overnight. It's more like organ failure due to a long-neglected disease.

All the while, the warning resounds: apathy toward discipleship breeds indifference toward God.

## PIVOT THREE: THE KINGDOM

Israel's final pivot wouldn't come for another three hundred years.[33] For two centuries after Joshua's death, the Lord sent judges to course-correct Israel, only to see the nation delve deeper and deeper into sin. Then one day, the people had enough. Fed up with being overtaken by other nations (in judgment), Israel decided what she needed was an earthly king. *After all, God surely hasn't protected us,* they thought.[34] Thus, the very Savior who rescued them from Egypt, the Provider who sustained them in the wilderness, the Banner that afforded them the Promised Land—the King of the Universe—was rejected.[35]

Immediately, their plan backfired. Expecting a political paragon in King Saul, Israel received a murderous madman. In David, though a man after God's heart, they plummeted into civil war. Then in Solomon, along with the Temple, came oppression and child sacrifice.[36] Slowly, Israel's final, fateful pivot was unfolding.

Following the death of Solomon, the kingdom split. His son, Rehoboam, took the southern region (henceforth called Judah), while Solomon's old right-hand man Jeroboam nabbed the northern territory, which kept the name Israel. At first glance, it may seem like this gave the North a

---

33 This is a rough number denoting the time from Joshua's death (~1245 BC) to that of Solomon (931 BC).

34 This mentality fermented over time and eventually birthed unabashed rebellion as seen in Jeremiah 44:16-18.

35 "Banner" as a name for God is a reference to Exodus 17:15. The phrasing of "rejected" is the precise language God uses for this event in 1 Samuel 8:7, because putting people in the place of God is a disastrous idea.

36 While 1 Kings 9:22 clearly states that King Solomon did not make slaves of the Israelites and the enslavement of conquered peoples was nothing new to his time, the use of "oppression" here is largely in reference to 1 Kings 12:4, when the people plead with Rehoboam to lighten the heavy yoke and hard service instituted by Solomon.

chance at a fresh start, but in reality, it was the reverse. In a sense, the coffin was being nailed shut.[37]

Israel had spent centuries grumbling and abandoning God, distancing themselves from their Redeemer. Sincere worship was rare at best. When the kingdom split in two, those in the northern half were physically separated from the Lord's presence, since the Temple was in Jerusalem—in Judah.

King Jeroboam, though, was no dummy. If his constituents were to continue worshipping Yahweh, they would have to travel down to rival Judah to celebrate the annual feasts. This had to be stopped, or his sway would slip with the people. To do so, Jeroboam first excluded all the true priests from leading worship. In their place, he appointed his own. (Ironically, the true priests all moved to Judah.[38])

That, however, wasn't enough. Looking to squash any chance of losing power, Jeroboam threw his knockout punch to the spleen of Israel's servanthood: He brought back the golden calf. In fact, he built two.

What made this strategy so effective? Jeroboam set one of mankind's oldest traps: the dangled carrot of convenience. Just listen to the christening words Jeroboam spews as he debuts his two hairless heifers:

> "It is too much trouble for you to worship in Jerusalem. Look, Israel, these are the gods who brought you out of Egypt!"
>
> —1 KINGS 12:28B (ESV)

This repurposing of the infamous Sinai sedition worked like a charm. Every king who succeeded Jeroboam dug Israel a deeper ditch. For two hundred years, one after another, Israel's rulers endorsed these heavenly heifers until 732 BC, when Israel got eviscerated by Assyria.[39]

In all that time, not a single king removed the golden calves (or goat

---

37  Still, it should be noted that throughout history, God saves a remnant of Israel who faithfully follow Him. For more study on this concept, see Genesis 45:7, Judges 5:13, 2 Kings 19:30-31, Ezra 9:8-15, Isaiah 10:20-22, 11:11, Jeremiah 23:3, Micah 2:12, Zechariah 8:6-12, and Romans 11:5.

38  This is explicitly mentioned in 2 Chronicles 11:14-16, where Scripture notes that along it wasn't just the Levites who abandoned ship and headed for Judah, but every single person who still sought the Lord left with them.

39  Scripture goes to the length of explicitly stating that almost every Israelite king walked in the sins of Jeroboam, with the exception of Shallum (who reigned only one month) and Hoshea (who did unique evil; see 2 Kings 17:2). Otherwise, each king was individually indicted, as seen in the following list of verses: 1 Kings 15:30, 15:34, 16:13, 16:19, 16:26, 16:31, 22:52; 2 Kings 3:3, 10:29, 13:2, 13:11, 14:23, 15:3, 15:18, 15:24, and 15:28.

demon altars[40]) that Jeroboam built. The idolatry was so rampant that even the Southern Kingdom of Judah was infected.[41] Eventually, they too would be gruesomely exiled, though God would spare a remnant.

It was an epidemic then, and it's still going strong. The church today is by no means exempt, especially in the West, where the ease of life seems to have largely neutered cheerful servanthood among those who claim to follow Christ. After all, when bank accounts boom, dependence on God often shrivels up.[42]

Jeroboam's golden calves may seem like some antiquated foolishness, but they're alive and well. In the 21st century, some kneel to the calf of wealth; others to fame and ease. The question is not whether these heifers exist; it's whether they'll be worshipped.

The sordid story of Israel's downfall shows the world what happens when humans decide self knows best. It reminds us how quickly a nation can fall when it takes its eyes off the one true God. When it comes to America, as Ronald Reagan once declared, "If we ever forget that we're one nation under God, then we will be a nation gone under."

Yet no matter how far humans fall, the Lord's arm is never too short to save. In fact, as the next chapter reveals, saving might just be His favorite thing to do.

---

40  A reference to 2 Chronicles 11:15, especially in the Legacy Standard Bible (LSB). Different versions translate this "satyr" concept in a variety of ways, but all point to a goat-like demon. Such worship was not a new thing, either, as evidenced by Leviticus 17:7 written some four hundred years earlier. A throng of commentators make the connection from these goat idols to satanic worship and even devil depictions through the ages, such as that of Baphomet. Detailing such, however, is not within the scope of this work.

41  This tragedy is confirmed in 2 Kings 17:19 and displays how, if you are surrounded by the wrong crowd long enough, you will almost certainly join in (1 Corinthians 15:33). Put simply, corruption is corrosive.

42  Technically, our dependence on God never actually decreases, only our perception of such dependence. Here, the use of "dependence" refers to the active awareness and subsequent lifestyle of a heart looking to God for provision.

# HIDDEN GEMS

## JESUS: OUR FORSAKEN FORERUNNER

| | |
|---|---|
| Moses cut down a tree and threw it into bitterness to offer Israel drinkable water. | Jesus, the Tree of Life, was cut down and thrown into bitterness to offer us living water. *(Psalm 1:3, Matthew 26:38, Revelation 22:17)* |
| Israel wandered the wilderness for forty years, soon dying for their ungrateful disobedience. | Jesus wandered the wilderness for forty days, soon dying for His gracious obedience. *(Matthew 4:1-2, John 5:19, Philippians 2:8)* |
| Israel deserted God once they entered the Promised Land. | Jesus was deserted by God and man so that we could enter the Promised Land. *(Matthew 27:46, Mark 14:50, John 14:3)* |
| Israel rejected God their King, demanding a man in the place of God. | Jesus was rejected by Israel, who mocked their crucified King: God in the place of man. *(Acts 4:11, Matthew 27:42, 2 Corinthians 5:21)* |
| Israel sought to please themselves, did so, and wound up crushed. | Jesus sought to please His Father, did so, and wound up crushed. *(Isaiah 53:10, Mark 1:11, John 5:30, John 8:29)* |
| Israel stiffened their neck like their fathers, abandoning all the commandments of the LORD. | Jesus bowed His neck to His Father, fulfilling all the commandments of the LORD. *(2 Kings 17:14-16, Matthew 5:17, Matthew 26:39)* |

**BOTTOM LINE:**

Jesus' servanthood isn't what our flesh wants, but it's what our souls need. *(Galatians 5:17, 1 Peter 2:16)*

# WRAP UP:
# Head, Shoulders, Knees, and Toes

God's love for Israel boggles the mind. It transcends the plot of every box office hit in history. Imagine the tagline on a movie poster: "King of Creation gets blamed, forgotten, and traded for cows by the people He chose to bless." No, it's not the most uplifting tale, but certainly one that we should learn from.

The wealth of wisdom that can be gleaned from Israel's collapse is inexhaustible.[43] Like Solomon, you can be the wisest, wealthiest leader in the world, but without cheerful servanthood, disaster approaches. Like Jeroboam, you can build your own religion, but eventually your sandcastle will collapse.

The lessons are many, but they all boil down to one central idea: God must be the one we serve, not the waiter who takes our orders. Otherwise, in the desert come the grumbles. In the battle, the heart forgets. And if we rise to wealth and power, we naturally spoil ourselves.

The reverse is also true. **To grow in faith, we must do what Israel largely didn't: stick to the basics.** After all, before we can hope to run, we must master how to walk.[44] For a simple pneumonic, consider the age-old exercise jingle, "Head, Shoulders, Knees, and Toes."

First and foremost, our *heads* must be on straight, celebrating God's kindness instead of our excellence. Pride comes before the fall, and forgetting one's salvation is like a running back taking the field without a helmet—not good.

Next is the *shoulders*, where we learn to entrust our burdens to the Lord. Only then can we help bear the burdens of others and fulfill the

---

43 Scripture is crystal clear: Israel's wandering took place as an example of what *not to do*. Paul details this in 1 Corinthians 10:6-11.

44 This is an allusion to the tragic choices of how Israel's kings "walked in all the ways of Jeroboam" (1 Kings 16:26) along with God's call for us to contrastingly "walk by the Spirit" (Galatians 5:24-25). Heeding such warnings puts the bumpers in our bowling lanes. It turns our gutter ball lives into strikes we don't deserve.

law of Christ.[45] The third key is that growing in faith requires bent *knees*. Remember, to a king, bowed service is not optional. Loyal love means full allegiance, not just casual shout-outs.[46]

And lastly, perhaps above all else, Israel's story reminds us that sin can subtly sink your life. One minute, you're standing on the edge of the pool, dipping your *toes* in delight; the next, you're at the bottom of the deep end.

Israel kept on playing with poison, and eventually, it cost her everything. Though God promised never to forget Israel, she forgot her King.[47]

Will we?

---

45  This is a reference to Galatians 6:2, where the apostle Paul sums up the fullness of Christ's commands in four simple words: "Bear one another's burdens." Such is the foundation of the late Dr. Tim Keller's fantastic assertion that all real love is substitutionary sacrifice.

46  For more on this, see the vivid instances of bowed knees before the Lord in Isaiah 45:23, Philippians 2:10, Ephesians 3:14, and Revelation 4:10-11.

47  This promise is found multiple places, most notably in Isaiah 44:21.

# ENGAGE: Group Study 4

**STARTER**   If Solomon was the wisest man to ever live (1 Kings 3:12), why did he make such awful decisions later in life? Discuss.

**TRIVIA**   As mentioned in the chapter, the three most common words in Scripture are *Lord, God*, and *Israel*. Can you guess the rest of the top ten?[48]

**REFLECT**   Solomon literally had the entire known world at his beck and call (1 Kings 10:24). Would it be good for you to have that power? Why or why not?

**PONDER**   Luke 2:52 says Jesus "kept increasing in wisdom" while growing up. How does someone increase in godly wisdom? *(Consider Job 28:12-28, Psalm 90:12, and Proverbs 2:1-10.)*

**JOURNAL**   In what ways are you most prone to wander from God, and who can you confess this to that will hold you accountable?

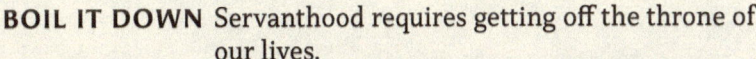

**BOIL IT DOWN** Servanthood requires getting off the throne of our lives.

**BRING IT UP**   What actions would accompany becoming wiser?

**LIVE IT OUT**   Copy a chapter (or book!) of the Bible by hand like Solomon should have.[49]

---

48   Rounding out the top ten are: 4. King (2,529), 5. Son (2,358), 6. Man (2,214), 7. People (1,956), 8. Land (1,816), 9. House (1,747), 10. Men (1,652). These are according to the NASB95 as counted by BlueLetterBible.org.

49   A great resource for embarking on this handwriting journey is *The 17:18 Series*, a collection of journals based on the command of God in Deuteronomy 17:18 for all kings to write their own personal copies of Scripture.

# 5

# THE ⊕NE T⊕ COME

*" . . . listen to the words of my servants the*
*prophets whom I send to you urgently . . . "*
—*JEREMIAH 26:5 (ESV)*

S INCE TIME BEGAN, HUMANITY HAS longed to know the future.
From the position of the stars to reading the lines on a palm, our
methods betray our desperation. Figuring out what lies ahead is not just
for the eccentric spiritualist, either. The quest for predictive power reaches
far beyond the fortune cookie into a curious realm where superstitions
and Wall Street algorithms coexist: a land of hunches and war tactics,
sports betting and sneak peeks. The anxious fixate on the future; the
foolish shrug it off. Ultimately, the future is where *what if* meets *what's*
*next*—which just so happens to be the very climax of the Old Testament.

For hundreds of years, God patiently endured the faithlessness of
His bride, Israel. Relentlessly, He reached out to her, but the more He
called, the further she ran away.[1] The same selfishness that plagued the

---

1    The concept of God's people spurning Him the more they are called to return is laid out in Hosea 11:2.

patriarchs kept snowballing.[2] Everyone did what was right in his own eyes, and eventually, it all came crashing down.[3]

Thankfully, that's not how the story ends.

**The climax of the Old Testament isn't the destruction of God's people; it's the promise of their redemption.** The final seventeen books of the Old Testament were all penned by prophets—men sent by God to declare what was (and partly still is!) to come.[4]

Not only that, the Old Testament is filled with these futuristic declarations.[5] Israel was handed the forecast; she had prophets every stumbling step of the way.[6] Over and over, God detailed the future, yet over and over, the people laughed it off. It wasn't the truth Israel lacked; it was the ears to take it in. The following three passages make this painfully clear:

"Since the day that your fathers came out of the land of Egypt until this day, I have sent you all **My servants the prophets**, daily rising early and sending them. Yet they did not listen to Me or incline their ear, but stiffened their neck; they did more evil than their fathers."

—JEREMIAH 7:25-26 (NASB95)

"Also I have sent to you all **My servants the prophets**, sending them again and again, saying: 'Turn now every man from his evil way and amend your deeds, and do not go after other gods to worship them . . . but you have not inclined your ear or listened to Me."

—JEREMIAH 35:15 (NASB95)

---

2    This is true on the whole, though there were certainly short periods of repentance and right living. The most notable examples of such pious seasons can be seen through the lives of Joseph, Joshua, Josiah, and Nehemiah.

3    This notion of Israel doing whatever they wanted comes directly from Judges 17:6 and 21:25, resonating with Deuteronomy 12:8 and Isaiah 53:6.

4    Some of the prophecies in these books have yet to be fulfilled in their entirety, especially ones relating to the glorious second coming and final judgment of God. Of course, these books are not ordered chronologically, but in general they speak to what the future holds for Israel and Judah post-exile.

5    One Bible scholar, Barton Payne, counts 1,817 distinct predictions in Scripture, astronomically more than any other sacred writing.

6    The problem was that Israel treated God like the weatherman. The prophecies were simply nice suggestions she could never fully trust.

"Yet I sent you all **My servants the prophets**, again and again, saying, 'Oh, do not do this abominable thing which I hate.' But they did not listen or incline their ears to turn from their wickedness . . ."

—JEREMIAH 44:4-5 (NASB95)

Eight times God calls the prophets "My servants."[7] Through them came warnings, promises, and even invitations from on high, yet rarely were they believed or heeded. Often, their messages packed an unwelcome punch, exposing the idolatry at hand. Sprinkled throughout their writings, however, were detailed prophecies of eventual redemption centered on a single, mysterious figure—the Messiah.

In Hebrew, the term "Messiah" means *anointed one.* For an ancient Jew, anointed meant one of two things: either a priest was being ordained for ministry, or a king was coming to power.[8] With the coming Messiah, both were in play.

Stopping there, though, would only scratch the surface. These were prophecies of an ultimate Anointed One, not just a hierarchal human. For example, one passage declares He will reign forever; another calls Him "Mighty God."[9] And these are but two of the 574 Old Testament verses referring to this glorious king-priest on the way![10]

Piecing these together reveals the Messiah to be not just an earthly deliverer but, incredibly, the Creator Himself.[11] That said, these prophecies aren't all sunshine and rainbows.[12] Yes, the Messiah is often painted in triumph and glorious strength, but Scripture also foretells his torturous death. This surely puzzled the Jews. How could the Mighty God come in power to redeem His people yet be mocked, stripped, beaten, and killed?[13]

---

7   These passages are 2 Kings 9:7, 17:13; Jeremiah 7:25, 26:5, 29:19, 35:15, 44:4; and Zechariah 1:6 in the NASB95.

8   For a verse displaying the anointing of a priest, see Exodus 30:29. For the anointing of a king, see 1 Samuel 10:1.

9   The verses alluded to are Daniel 7:13-14 and Isaiah 9:6-7, respectively. For more, see Psalm 2.

10   While different scholars have different counts, the 574 alluded to comes from the works of J. Barton Payne.

11   Remember, "The Creator" is an accurate title for Jesus, not only because He is God, but the Bible clearly states in Colossians 1:16 that all things were created by Him and through Him and for Him.

12   That said, the rainbow was a sign of God's promise to never destroy "all flesh" again—hinting at remnant salvation (Genesis 9:15)—and the Messiah is called the "Sun of righteousness" (Malachi 4:2) as well as the "sunrise" (Luke 1:78-79) that shines on us (Ephesians 5:14). So, considering all the promises of God find their "Yes" in Christ (2 Corinthians 1:20), perhaps in a way all the prophecies really are sunshine and rainbows.

13   These are allusions to Psalm 22, Isaiah 53, and Micah 4:14.

More than that, why would God Almighty choose to suffer so much for people who repeatedly reject Him?

This answer is the foundation of Christianity and all healthy relationships. It's the centerpiece of this book and even the gospel itself: cheerful, compassionate servanthood is the key to life and the call of Christ.

Not convinced? The Messiah said it Himself—He "came not to be served but to serve, and to give his life as a ransom for many" (Mark 10:45, ESV). In a sense, His purpose on earth was the same as ours—service in love.[14] Israel expected a conqueror, but they got someone far greater.

Sadly, they didn't see it that way. Should they have known better? Did any of these prophets speak of the Messiah coming so humbly?

Yes, but only one.[15]

Out of all the Old Testament seers, when it comes to messianic prophecy, there's clearly one frontrunner. Even the New Testament writers clearly favored one above the others, quoting his book fifty-five times! (The next highest is seven.)[16] In fact, his writings are so interconnected to other parts of Scripture that some scholars literally refer to the book as a "miniature Bible."[17]

Truly, there's nothing else like it: the book of Isaiah.[18]

---

14   To be clear, verses like Luke 19:10 also seem to declare a singular purpose regarding Christ's first coming, which would seem to seek and save the lost. While one could argue that by making disciples, we too are called to that mission, humans obviously cannot save each other. Thus, the point being made is not that our purpose is identical in breadth or application; Christ's purpose was surely higher, deeper, and wider than ours. Rather, it is simply to say that as imitators of Christ (Ephesians 5:1-2), we naturally share in His purpose.

15   This statement specifically refers to the aspect of being called a servant. Several of the Old Testament prophets speak to the suffering or humility of Christ in other ways, just not as comprehensively or flagrantly as Isaiah.

16   This count comes from Peter Krol, author of *Knowable Word: Helping Ordinary People Learn to Study the Bible*. The book of Psalms is quoted sixty-eight times, but this is not mentioned because, though it contains multiple prophecies, the book isn't categorized as primarily prophetic. Consequently, second place, with a mere seven quotes, goes to the book of Zechariah.

17   While certain "coincidences" in Isaiah are obviously more than accidents, how deep these connections go is a point of debate. For example, there are sixty-six chapters in Isaiah and sixty-six books in the Bible. Some see correlations between each chapter in Isaiah and its corresponding Bible book (in number order), while others believe this to be wishful thinking. It is, however, obvious that Isaiah is divided into two main parts: Chapters 1-39 (largely judgment) and 40-66 (largely redemption)—just like the Old Testament's thirty-nine books are divided from the New Testament.

18   Even the Hebrew name "Isaiah" has bizarre connections to Christ. As Abarim Publications puts it, "The name Joshua is the Hebrew form of the Greek name Jesus, and most probably the name by which Jesus was known by his contemporaries. Jesus consistently quoted the book of Isaiah, possibly because this book appears to be entirely about Him, but perhaps also because the name Isaiah is almost identical to the name Joshua with the two segments reversed." Moreover, the name Isaiah means "Yah is salvation," profoundly close to the meaning of Jesus, "Yah will save."

# REDEMPTION SONGS

Living in the eighth century BC, Isaiah witnessed the collapse of the Northern Kingdom and the eroding faith of Judah in the south. Thus, for his thirty-nine chapters (much like the thirty-nine books of the Old Testament), his message is fairly simple: judgment is real, and repentance is necessary.[19]

Suddenly, however, Chapter 40 switches gears, and salvation swoops on in. The Messiah, previously only hinted at, arrives in full force. Nearly all the rest of Isaiah's chapters revolve around this Anointed One, including what may well be the greatest chapter in the entire Old Testament: Isaiah 53.[20] Soon, we'll be examining this brilliant treasure, but first we must at least briefly explore the block of passages to which it belongs—a treasure trove of prophecies called "The Four Servant Songs of Isaiah."

## SONG ONE

As an introduction to the first song, in Chapter 41, God pronounces a plan of redemption over His broken yet beloved servant Israel, twice calling her "my servant."[21] Then, after a brief advisory on the futility of idols, He launches into song number one. Listen to how it begins:

> Behold, **my servant**, whom I uphold,
>> my chosen, in whom my soul delights;
> **I have put my Spirit upon him**;
>> he will bring forth justice to the nations.
> He will not cry aloud or lift up his voice,
>> or make it heard in the street . . .
> He will not grow faint or be discouraged
>> till he has established justice in the earth;
>> and the coastlands wait for his law.
>
> —Isaiah 42:1-4 (ESV)

---

19 Technically, they weren't "his" chapters, as chapter divisions didn't arrive for nearly 2000 years until 1227 AD with the work of Stephen Langton.

20 This claim of Isaiah 53 being the "greatest" has been made by multiple acclaimed commentators. For one example, check out the Precept Austin website at preceptaustin.org. and search for "Isaiah 53 commentary."

21 This takes place in Isaiah 41:8-9, where the nation of Israel is clearly in view, as God speaks of calling them from the farthest corners of the earth. In other places, the name "Israel" is representative of other entities.

God addresses the anthem once again to "my servant," but this time He's not referring to Israel. Someone far greater is in view.

Israel had grown faint and discouraged plenty of times; they were exiled for heaven's sake.[22] No, this was the Messiah, the Christ to come—just ask Matthew. After Jesus withdrew from a gang of murderous Pharisees, Matthew records that Jesus quietly healed many so prophecy would be fulfilled, and then the apostle quotes this very song![23]

Years later, his fellow disciple Peter connects the dots when he preaches:

> "You yourselves know what happened throughout all Judea, beginning from Galilee after the baptism that John proclaimed: how **God anointed Jesus of Nazareth with the Holy Spirit** and with power. He went about doing good and healing all who were oppressed by the devil, for God was with Him."
>
> —ACTS 10:37-38 (ESV)

And that's just song one.

## SONG TWO

A few glorious chapters later, God gives us the sequel. This time, however, the Messiah starts with the microphone. Speaking to the coastlands, He picks up right where song one left off:

> Listen to me, O coastlands,
>     and give attention, you peoples from afar.
> The LORD called me from the womb,
>     from the body of my mother he named my name.
> He made **my mouth like a sharp sword**;
>     in the shadow of his hand he hid me . . .
> And he said to me, "You are **my servant**,
>     **Israel**, in whom I will be glorified."
>
> —ISAIAH 49:1-3 (ESV)

---

22  Quite literally, everything works out for "heaven's sake" as the Bible specifically states that God "works all things according to the counsel of His will" in Ephesians 1:11. The entire world exists to glorify Him.

23  See Matthew 12:14-21. Interestingly, the New Testament quotation is not identical to the Old Testament reading.

Immediately, the song oozes with messianic overtones, especially in referring to His mouth being like a sharp sword. (Thrice in the book of Revelation this very illustration is used to describe the mouth of Jesus in glory.[24])

Then, just when it seems clearly about the Christ, the speaker is curiously called "Israel." Surely this isn't referring to the nation, for the speaker is an individual "me"; nor is it Israel the patriarch, long dead and gone. Rather, it is One who will perfectly embody what Israel was not, who will live up to the name "Israel" as the true Prince of God. It's God's own Son,[25] whom the song later describes as "one deeply despised, abhorred by the nation, the servant of rulers."[26]

Of this Servant, the Father's heart sings:

> "It is too light a thing that you should be **my servant**
> to raise up the tribes of Jacob
> and to bring back the preserved of Israel;
> I will make you as a light for the nations,
> that my salvation may reach to the end of the earth."
> —ISAIAH 49:6 (ESV)

The Restorer of Jacob, the Light of the world, the greatest promise in history—Israel the nation, meet Israel the Messiah.

### SONG THREE

Still, God's redemption recital is only half over. In the very next chapter, Isaiah 50, the third song rings forth. Again, the Messiah is handed the mic, but this time He speaks to His pain:

> I offered my back to those who beat me,
> my cheeks to those who pulled out my beard;
> I did not hide my face

---

24 The three passages referenced are Revelation 1:16, 2:12-16, and 19:15. These powerfully connect to others like Psalm 149:6, Hosea 6:5, Ephesians 6:17, and Hebrews 4:12 regarding the Word as a sword.

25 This is a reference to the connections between "Son of Man" in Revelation 1:16 with Daniel 7:13, as well as the reappropriation to Christ in Hosea 11:1 and Matthew 2:15.

26 An excerpt of Isaiah 49:7 (ESV), which connects to other foreshadowings of the Messiah as the Suffering Servant in Psalm 2:2 and 22:16-18, for example.

> from **mocking and spitting**.
> Because the Sovereign LORD helps me,
>> I will not be disgraced.
> Therefore have I set my face like flint,
>> and I know I will not be put to shame...
> Who among you fears the LORD
>> and obeys the word of **his servant**?
>
> —ISAIAH 50:6-10 (ESV)

Imagine how the Jews must have felt reading this passage: their Messiah, the great holy Deliverer to come, would be tortured, mocked, and spat on. Why? How? And by whom?

Talk about a plot twist. Sure, the Roman soldiers swung the whips and drove the nails, but only at the demands of the Sanhedrin and the mob. Israel was promised a Savior, while the Savior was promised torture. Indeed, the Messiah would be beaten bloody, rejected by those He'd come to save.

Christ knew this prophecy full well—He proclaimed it seven hundred years in advance.[27] How much more then can we appreciate that glorious moment when the Savior boldly "set his face to go to Jerusalem."[28] He knew what would come and still He went cheerfully, for the joy set before Him.

## THE FINAL SONG

This brings us to the pinnacle of all messianic prophecy, the fourth and final servant song. So vividly does it depict Christ that many Jewish rabbis skip over it in synagogue.[29] Nicknamed "the forbidden chapter," Isaiah 53

---

27  Seven hundred is a rounded estimate. It may well be closer to eight hundred depending on when Isaiah wrote Chapter 50. Regardless, it's also worth noting that the Messiah predicted these events while writing in the *past tense*, as if to say, "Consider it done."

28  An excerpt of Luke 9:51 (ESV).

29  The rabbis claim the reason they skip this passage in the weekly Old Testament readings is because it does not fit the theme of comfort and consolation allotted for that particular Sabbath day. Thus, they read halfway through 52 and then skip to Chapter 54. This is a tragic irony, as they simultaneously call their awaited Messiah the great consoler and comforter. In so doing, they rightly recognize that eternal consolation comes only through the Messiah, as Simeon demonstrates in Luke 2:25-35 and Paul in 2 Corinthians 1:5. The problem is, in trying to explain away Jesus of Nazareth, they dismiss perhaps the most vivid, shocking, power-packed prophecy about their Messiah in their Scriptures—Isaiah 53!

stands as God's overture for the ages on the beauty and power of cheerful servanthood.[30] Comprised of three main parts, this grand anthem walks through the Messiah's humble life, unjust death, and eternal reward. Bluntly, it's the gospel in a nutshell, and it's time to dig in.

## THE FINAL SONG, PART I
### He Shall Walk Humbly (Isaiah 52:13-53:3)

Right off the bat, the song unabashedly revolves around exalting the Christ to come. Unlike modern Western culture, however, it's not because the Messiah will arrive exceedingly rich or handsome or talented. He's exalted because He chose humiliation; He's lifted up because He bent so low. Check it out:

Behold, **My servant** will prosper,
He will be high and lifted up and greatly exalted.
Just as many were astonished at you, My people,
So His appearance was **marred more than any man**
And His form more than the sons of men.
Thus He will sprinkle many nations,
Kings will shut their mouths on account of Him;
For what had not been told them they will see,
And what they had not heard they will understand.[31]
—ISAIAH 52:13-15 (NASB95)

The connections to Jesus in this short section alone are staggering. First, take the phrase "high and lifted up." This is only used four other times in the Bible, and they're all in Isaiah with each instance centering on God alone being enthroned in glory.[32]

---

30  Technically, the fourth servant song includes the last three verses of Isaiah 52 as well, but for the sake of brevity, these astonishing verses are usually spoken of as if part of the following chapter, Isaiah 53.

31  As an aside, it's shocking that the NASB95 translators chose not to capitalize "servant" in verse 13, as if they don't attribute the verse to the Messiah. This sure seems like an egregious (albeit rare) error on their behalf.

32  See Isaiah 2:13-14, 6:1, 33:10 and 57:15. In the Isaiah 2 passage, the Lord declares a day of reckoning for everyone who acts "high and lifted up," communicating that He alone is truly exalted. The other three verses are much more direct, majestically thundering the glory of the Most High. It's also worth noting how in Isaiah 57:15, God reigns in "a high and holy place" and yet simultaneously dwells with the lowly—another pointer to Immanuel, "God with us."

To use such language regarding this "Servant" would only be appropriate if He, too, were enthroned in the heavens, sharing in the Father's glory. Yet in the first servant song, the Father makes plain that His glory is not up for grabs, saying, "I am the LORD; that is my name; I will not give My glory to another."[33]

Therefore, it seems that this Servant *is God Himself* while somehow being *distinct from God*. Is this not precisely how Jesus described Himself? Consider these three sayings:

+ "I and the Father are one."[34]

+ "I came forth from the Father and have come into the world."[35]

+ "And now, Father, glorify me in your own presence with the glory that I had with you before the world existed."[36]

Still, the well runs deeper. Multiple times, Jesus uses this very same language of being "lifted up" when prophesying His own death and resurrection. For example, just before the wildly popular John 3:16, Jesus declares, "And as Moses **lifted up** the serpent in the wilderness, so must the Son of Man be **lifted up**, that whoever believes in him may have eternal life."[37] Then later, just after the triumphal entry, He proclaims, "And I, when I am **lifted up** from the earth, will draw all people to myself."[38]

Sadly, the people railed against this, snapping, "We have heard from the Law that the Christ remains forever. How can you say that the Son of Man must be lifted up?"[39]

If only they had read their scrolls of Isaiah.

Truly, the connections to Christ in this section abound.[40] Not only does the language match up, but the events predicted took place. His face

---

33  An excerpt of Isaiah 42:8 (ESV).
34  John 10:30 (ESV).
35  An excerpt of John 16:28 (NKJV).
36  John 17:5 (ESV).
37  John 3:14-15 (ESV).
38  John 12:32 (ESV).
39  John 12:34 (ESV).
40  More connections exist in this passage than this work has room for. For instance, "He will sprinkle many nations" can be connected to Moses ratifying the (marriage) covenant between Israel and God in Exodus 24:8. This profound connection is fleshed out fully in Hebrews 9:19-26. It is how we are "sprinkled clean" in Hebrews 10:22, and perhaps even the salvific water-sprinkling of Ezekiel 36:25-29.

did get "marred" beyond recognition—beaten with a staff and caked in blood from the thorns on his brow. He really did get lifted up—on a cross to die and from the grave to rise. And now He is ascended, so highly exalted at the right hand of the Father that every mouth—kings and serfs alike—will one day confess that Jesus Christ is Lord.[41] It all centers upon the cheerful servanthood of Jesus. He walked in humility, and for that, He was exalted.[42]

> It all centers upon the cheerful servanthood of Jesus.

One short stanza of the opening section remains. Truth gems are also plentiful here:

> Who has believed our message?
> And to whom has the arm of the LORD been revealed?
> For He grew up before Him like a tender shoot,
> And like a root out of parched ground;
> He has **no stately form or majesty**
> That we should look upon Him,
> Nor appearance that we should be attracted to Him.
> He was despised and forsaken of men,
> A man of sorrows and acquainted with grief;
> And like one from whom men hide their face
> He was despised, and **we did not esteem Him.**
> —ISAIAH 53:1-3 (NASB95)

Predicting the Messiah's torture didn't make Isaiah real popular. After all, it's far easier to neglect harsh truth than grapple with it.[43] What the prophet wrote here would drive the dagger even deeper. Not only would their heavenly Deliverer be beaten beyond recognition; He would come to this earth *tender and lowly.*

---

41  A reference to Philippians 2:9-10, Acts 5:31, and Romans 3:19 (ESV).

42  This promise was declared by Christ Himself multiple times: "Those who exalt themselves will be humbled, but he who humbles himself will be exalted." (See Matthew 23:12, Luke 14:11, and Luke 18:14)

43  Both the apostle John and apostle Paul leverage Isaiah 53:1 to emphasize Israel's rejection of her own Savior in John 12:38 and Romans 10:16, respectively.

This was an outrage. In ancient Jewish society, noble birth and public pomp was everything. To say their triumphant Rescuer would arrive like a root out of parched ground—meaning with no majesty at all—sounded like a mockery of His literal worth. Moreover, Isaiah's prophecy brought forth a hideous thought: the Savior as an *actual servant*.

Then, to top it off, Isaiah throws his most grievous grenade of all. It wouldn't just be tyrannical Gentiles who would scorn the Messiah. The Jews would despise their own King to come.[44]

You can begin to see why some rabbis have "forbidden" the reading of Isaiah 53. Every line feels like a wink from Jesus, but He wasn't what Israel wanted. The Jews anticipated a godly Goliath, not some pious softy.[45] They wanted a warlord, not the nativity.

> They wanted a warlord, not the nativity.

Virtually every expectation required a reversal. A tender shoot with no money or majesty, sorrowful, despised, and forsaken—*this* was God's Royal Redeemer? The humility stank to high heaven. How could such grandeur come from next to nothing?[46] As Nathanael, one of the twelve disciples, would say, "Can anything good be from Nazareth?"[47]

Yes. It can.

## THE FINAL SONG, PART II
### He Shall Suffer Willingly (Isaiah 53:4-10a)

Even after such a grand opening, Part II of Isaiah's final Servant Song

---

44  This can be seen through Isaiah's use of the word "we" in Isaiah 53:3, as he wrote to the Jews. Even if taken to mean "we humans" in general, this still would include the Jews as rejectors of the Messiah. Also, while surely Jesus was also the great Prophet and ultimate High Priest, the phrase "king to come" was chosen to emphasize the mockery He endured at the Cross like in Matthew 27:42.

45  Surely, Jesus wasn't actually a "softy" in the sense of a flimsy pushover. This sentence refers instead to the Jews' *perception* of a tenderhearted Jesus. Ironically, the only people he was really "harsh" to was them!

46  This is precisely the question mankind should ask about creation—the question all evolutionists hem-and-haw over, because it's unanswerable apart from the self-existent I Am.

47  An excerpt of John 1:46 (NASB). Fascinatingly, the Hebrew word "Nazareth" literally means "City of Shoots" or "Sproutville." Even the name itself testified to the Messiah, allowing Matthew to claim the prophets said "he would be called a Nazarene" in Matthew 2:23, while no such prophecy exists. Over and over, the Old Testament refers to the Messiah as a "branch" or "shoot," connecting the dots between His radical humility and Nazareth as seen in the following: Isaiah 4:2, 9:6, 11:1; Jeremiah 23:5; and Zechariah 3:8, 6:12.

doesn't disappoint. The connections to Christ burst forth like backyard fireworks. That said, the mood is hardly celebratory. What follows from Isaiah's quill depicts some of the heaviest truths in the world. If Part I felt weighty, brace yourself:

> Surely he has borne our griefs
>> and carried our sorrows;
> yet we esteemed him stricken,
>> smitten by God, and afflicted.
> But he was pierced for **our transgressions**;
>> he was crushed for **our iniquities**;
> upon him was the chastisement that brought us peace,
>> and with his wounds we are healed.
> All we like sheep have gone astray;
>> **we have turned**—every one—to his own way;
> and the LORD has laid on him
>> the iniquity of us all.
>
> —ISAIAH 53:4-6 (ESV)

If this section doesn't shock the system, not much else will. It's hard enough to picture God's Royal Rescuer beaten and belittled. To see oneself *as the cause* of said torture sickens the soul. But it's true. The Cross wasn't some tragic case of God-slaughter where innocent people accidentally killed the wrong guy, nor was it merely the fault of ancient mobsters. Isaiah makes it plain: our transgressions, our iniquities, our fault. *We are the villains too.*

Thankfully, Isaiah doesn't leave us condemned. Sandwiched between all the doom and gloom, the prophet reveals a blessed gamma ray of hope.[48] Not only will the Messiah take our burdens upon Himself, not only will He endure our just punishments, but we will obtain peace and healing through His crushing demise. Still, rejoicing at this point seems backward: Who cheers at the gruesome death of a loved one, regardless

---

48 On the electromagnetic spectrum, gamma rays have the shortest wavelength and thus the most densely packed power. They are only emitted by nuclear explosions, lightning, black holes, and stars. Therefore, the imagery holds nicely for this short burst of hope in Isaiah 53 of peace and healing through Jesus, the "great light" (Isaiah 9:2).

of how great an inheritance is left?[49]

*Unless, of course, the loved one doesn't stay dead.*

> Insulting a king is payable by death, and we've all done it.

Lastly, just in case the point wasn't made clear enough, Isaiah closes the stanza with a review; namely, all mankind is indicted of a single crime—turning away from God to go our own way.

It's the same poison of old, that hideous mantra of Judges when "everyone did what was right in his own eyes."[50] This is serious.

Insulting a king is payable by death, and we've all done it. *Someone* must pay the price; no good king lets all criminals off scot-free.

Just when it seems like mankind is going down in flames, however, the plot turns on its head.[51] Rather than punishing the deserving wretches we are, God—the Righteous Judge—lays on His perfect Servant the guilt of the world.

Part II of Isaiah's anthem finishes by revealing how the sacrifice would all take place. Remember, the Jews wanted a royal conqueror. Does this sound like one?

> He was oppressed, and he was afflicted,
>> yet he opened not his mouth;
> like **a lamb that is led to the slaughter**,
>> and like a sheep that before its shearers is silent,
>> so he opened not his mouth.
> By oppression and judgment he was taken away;
>> and as for his generation, who considered
> that **he was cut off** out of the land of the living,
>> stricken for the transgression of my people?

---

49  Such cheering is only made possible through the Resurrection. Without it, no inheritance would do (see 1 Corinthians 15:12-19).

50  Judges 17:6 (NASB). Also, Judges 21:25 and Deuteronomy 12:8 speak the same truth.

51  The wordplay within this sentence is intentional. Apart from Christ's atonement, mankind's rebellion will take him down in flames to the Lake of Fire. Only through Jesus—the "head" of every man (1 Corinthians 11:3), the "head" of the church (Ephesians 5:23), even the "head" over all things (Ephesians 1:22)—does the plot turn hopeful.

> And they made his grave with the wicked
>> and with a rich man in his death,
> although he had done no violence,
>> and there was no deceit in his mouth.    .
> **Yet it was the will of the LORD to crush him**;
>> he has put him to grief . . .

—ISAIAH 53:7-10A (ESV)

If they weren't before, the gloves are off now. Such a submissive depiction of the Messiah was undoubtedly a bare-knuckle punch to Israel's eye socket; this is *not* what they envisioned.[52] Oppression and affliction were the very things the Messiah was supposed to eradicate, not willingly accept! A lamb led to the slaughter sounds more like docile victimization than triumph. After all, what victory can come from being cut off and crushed?

Amazingly, the answer is *infinite*.[53] In the glorious words of Paul:

> For if by the trespass of the one (Adam), death reigned
> . . . much more *surely* will those who receive the abundance
> of grace and the free gift of righteousness reign in eternal
> life through the One, Jesus Christ.[54]

—ROMANS 5:17 (AMP)

One seed can produce millions more, but only if it first dies. In Genesis, God promised to bless the nations through Abraham's seed. At last, that Seed was on His way.[55]

Indeed, Jesus would be egregiously afflicted, yet He never once

---

52  The analogy in fact holds extremely well, for God says of Israel just a few chapters before: "Who is as blind as my own people, my servant?" (Isaiah 42:19, NLT) In fact, relentlessly in the Old Testament God speaks of Israel having eyes that do not see (Deuteronomy 29:4, Psalm 69:23, Isaiah 6:9, Jeremiah 5:21, Ezekiel 12:2), a concept reiterated by the apostle Paul in Romans 11:8-10. Likewise, Jesus states that He came to make the blind see and to make blind those who can see (John 9:39).

53  Not only does the Bible relentless speak of "eternal life," but Revelation 14:6 even calls the Good News "an eternal gospel."

54  In this verse, brackets were removed from the word "eternal" so the reader wouldn't think the author of this book inserted the word. The Amplified version adds words like "eternal" in brackets to help readers connect the dots.

55  The promises regarding Abraham's seed can be found in Genesis 12:7, 17:7, and especially 22:18. Christ being called the Seed in fulfillment of these promises comes from Galatians 3:16-19.

demanded justice.[56] His captors spat, but He forgave. Christ fulfilled every line of Isaiah's song, down to the wicked alongside Him at the cross and the rich man's tomb where He was laid.

Still, to the Jews, Christ was a disappointment. Ironically, Jesus' life didn't satisfy them, yet His death satisfied the wrath of God *for them*—if only they'd believe.

**Here's the point: the King of the Universe first and foremost wants to free us from ourselves, not our oppressors.** Selfish hearts need transformation, not independence. Christ didn't come to overthrow Rome like the Jews wanted, and for that He was tortured and nailed to a tree. In doing so, He illustrated how the highest love isn't to merely remove others from suffering, but rather to suffer on their behalf.[57] That's why all His signs and wonders mattered little to the mob: If Jesus wouldn't take away their pain, He was dead to them—literally. They made sure of it.

Selfish hearts need transformation, not independence.

It's easy to slap blame on those ancient mobsters, but how many of us treat God the same way? When our prayers go unanswered, or the money runs out, or loved ones die, we tend to flail our fists at the heavens as if the King owes us rebels more than He's already given.

What more, though, could He give?[58] The human heart howls for fairness, often forgetting the debt God paid for our bankruptcy. It's one thing to see Christ as a Savior who did the world a heroic favor, but accepting responsibility for the horror He went through is humbling.[59] If anyone had the right to scream "That's not fair!" it would've been the Messiah. But He

---

56  An allusion to Matthew 26:63, 27:12, and 27:14. In addition to Old Testament prophecy, this fulfilled both His teaching (Luke 6:30) and the later exhortations of Paul (1 Corinthians 10:24). To be clear, the justice that Jesus refused to demand was justice for crimes committed against Him personally. Christ definitely advocated for the just treatment of others (Matthew 23:23), thereby fulfilling the Law, the Psalms, and the Prophets (Deuteronomy 10:18, Psalm 82:3, Isaiah 1:17).

57  An allusion to John 15:13, where Jesus famously proclaims that the greatest love a man can have is to lay down his life for his friends. And yet, coupled with Romans 5:10, we see that Jesus went even a step further, laying down His life for His enemies!

58  An allusion to Romans 8:32, where God has already promised to give believers "all things." Meanwhile, mankind acts like Veruca Salt in the 1971 classic *Willy Wonka & the Chocolate Factory*, saying, "I want the whole world . . . give it to me NOW!"

59  There are two things in this world that, if you seek, you are 100 percent guaranteed to find: God and excuses.

didn't. For the joy set before Him, He served to the bitter end.[60]

### THE FINAL SONG, PART III
### He Shall Share Gladly (Isaiah 53:10b-12)

The anthem's first act was all about Christ's life. The second spoke to His death. Now, in the last couple verses, Isaiah finishes with a flourish. The Messiah's demise wasn't the end; it was the beginning. David was right: "Weeping may last for the night, but a shout of joy comes in the morning."[61]

Thus, get ready. The first half of this section can shock souls back to life.[62] In the words of the Messiah, "Come and see."[63]

> When his soul makes an offering for guilt,
>> he shall see his offspring; he shall prolong his days;
>> the will of the LORD shall prosper in his hand.
> Out of the anguish of his soul he shall see and be
>> satisfied;
> by his knowledge shall the righteous one, **my servant,**
>> make many to be accounted righteous,
>> and he shall bear their iniquities.
>
> —ISAIAH 53:10B-11 (ESV)

At last, the Good News arrived. Yes, Israel's Messiah would offer Himself for the guilt of man, but that's not where the story ends.

Right after prophesying about death and the grave, Isaiah flips the script once more. Suddenly, the Messiah seems alive and well again—meeting His descendants,[64] enjoying a long life, and prospering!

How could this be? Welcome to the most pivotal, controversial event

---

60 This is an allusion to Hebrews 12:2 (ESV), which says that believers should always be "looking to Jesus, the founder and perfecter of our faith, who for the joy that was set before him endured the cross, despising the shame, and is seated at the right hand of the throne of God."

61 Psalm 30:5 (NASB).

62 This is meant both figuratively and spiritually. The Ethiopian eunuch, though spiritually dead, was "made alive" (Ephesians 2:6) by the preaching of Philip beginning with this very chapter (Acts 8:32-39).

63 An excerpt of John 1:39 (KJV).

64 The Hebrew word in Isaiah 53:10 translated "offspring" is literally the word for "seed." This makes much more sense, as Christ did not have any biological children, but those who belong to Him are "Abraham's seed" (Genesis 3:29). It could also be connected to the Parable of the Sower, where "The seed is the word of God" (Luke 8:11), meaning the Messiah would witness "children of God" being born again through Him.

in human history: the Resurrection of Jesus Christ. What you believe about this one event affects every nook and cranny of your life, even how you live and think and dream. If the Messiah never rose, we are free to honor Him like a fallen war hero, spouting an occasional song or tip of the hat. (Many who claim to follow Christ sadly treat Him this way.) Perhaps we'd even try living more nobly in remembrance of His sacrifice, but in the end, honor would be optional.

If the ultimate Anointed One resurrected, however, then all bets are off. If the King beat death, then He reigns; and if He reigns, we must bow the knee.[65]

Out of all the "my servant" moments in Scripture, this is the centerpiece—the pot of gold to which all others point. What we've got here is the point-blank gospel, the great exchange.[66] As the apostle Paul said, "There is no righteous person, not even one . . . all have turned away."[67] So the "Righteous One" paid our debt.

The only One who deserved everything became nothing to take the wrath we earned. He bore our iniquities. He carried our sorrows. Jesus Christ, in the greatest love ever shown, "suffered once for sins, the righteous for the unrighteous, that he might bring us to God, being put to death in the flesh but made alive in the spirit."[68]

In Christ, we don't become "good enough," we become *righteous*. "He made Him who knew no sin to be sin on our behalf, so that we might become the righteousness of God in

> The only One who deserved everything became nothing to take the wrath we earned.

---

65  Literally, everyone will one day bow to King Jesus, either by choice or force (Philippians 2:10). Still, the word "must" in this context, if not careful, will be perceived as putrid as its moldy homonym (must-iness). Submitting to Jesus isn't about compulsion; it's the cheerful giving of the self (2 Corinthians 9:7).

66  "The great exchange" phrasing is generally first attributed to Martin Luther and now the title of a book by Jerry Bridges which Alistair Begg declares one of the top-ten books of all time. Sadly, though, with the extreme lack of evangelism in the Western church, the words of *Cool Hand Luke* simultaneously ring true: "What we've got here is a failure to communicate."

67  A reference to Romans 3:11-12, which is a citation of David's Psalm 53:1-3. In the chapter material, Paul's name was cited, as David doesn't use the word "righteous."

68  An excerpt of 1 Peter 3:18 (ESV). If a single verse in the Bible best represents the gospel message, this is probably it. (John 3:16 doesn't mention atonement for sin or the Resurrection.)

Him."[69] Without the Messiah, our best efforts are to God but filthy rags, putrid attempts to wipe away the blood on our hands.[70] In the dungeon of selfishness, Jesus Christ is the only Way out.

The goal of life, however, isn't just to escape; it's to be cherished, to be adopted by the Eternal Family—and He's the only Way in.[71] So whether Christ has been your Lord for decades or you're just getting to know Him, hear this: *Peace is found in repentance, not performance.* As Paul and Timothy put it (to the church!): "We beg you on behalf of Christ, be reconciled to God."[72]

The end is near. Only one more verse remains. Just when it seems like the Good News couldn't get any better, Isaiah finishes with a bang:

> Therefore I will divide him a portion with the many,
>     and **he shall divide the spoil** with the strong,
> because he poured out his soul to death
>     and was numbered with the transgressors;
> yet he bore the sin of many,
>     and **makes intercession** for the transgressors.
>
> —ISAIAH 53:12 (ESV)

What a conclusion. Not only will the perfect Messiah die for warped criminals, but He intends to share the reward with them too![73,74] How topsy-turvy the gospel is! Christ poured out His soul to death and now reigns as the King of Life.[75] Those who die to themselves end up inheriting

---

69   2 Corinthians 5:21 (NASB).

70   "Filthy rags" is an allusion to Isaiah 64:6 (NIV), where the actual Hebrew word translated "filthy" refers to menstruation, a graphic connection to our guilt as the "blood on our hands."

71   See John 1:12, Ephesians 2:19, and 1 John 3:1. The use of "Eternal Family" offers a double meaning, depicting adoption by the triune Godhead as well as the "household" of God.

72   An excerpt of 2 Corinthians 5:20 (NASB95).

73   "Warped" is an allusion to Psalm 78:57, as well as C.S. Lewis' writings in his *Space Trilogy* series about humans being "the bent ones," meaning bent inward with selfishness.

74   Isaiah promises such to "the strong," but he surely doesn't mean the muscular. The Hebrew word here, עָצוּם (*'aṣûm*), can either mean those mighty in number or valor, both of which ring true of believers in Scripture. God promised Abraham that his descendants would outnumber the sand kernels, which is fulfilled in the "great multitude that no one could number" before the throne (Revelation 7:9), as Paul calls all those of faith "children of Abraham" (Galatians 3:7). Believers are also called "more than conquerors" (Romans 8:37) by Paul and given "the victory through our Lord Jesus Christ" (1 Corinthians 15:57) as they "fight the good fight of the faith" (1 Timothy 6:12), faithfully enduring to the end (Matthew 24:13). Indeed, followers of God shall be mighty in both number and valor.

75   The title "King of Life" is not found in Scripture but can be reasonably fashioned from a fusing of John 1:4, 14:6, and Revelation 17:14.

eternal life. God chooses the foolish to shame those who think they are wise. Christians will be known by their love and yet will be hated by the world.[76] At every turn, a twist seems to appear. Perhaps that's because we're the twisted ones.

Out of all the lines in Isaiah's masterpiece, like any good writer, he saves something special for last. After being numbered with the transgressors, bearing their sin, being beaten beyond recognition, dying alongside the wicked, and then sharing His reward with them, the Messiah still kept serving.

If you've ever wondered what Jesus is doing now that He's ascended, here's your answer: He's praying for us![77]

Take that in. Christ prayed for people while on Earth; He even prayed for the forgiveness of those killing Him. But He didn't stop there. The apostle Paul says that even in glory, at the right hand of the Father, Jesus is interceding on our behalf. Think about that—for nearly two thousand years, the King of Kings has been in heaven, praying for His people. Scripture goes so far as to say, "He always lives to make intercession for them."[78]

It's His mission, as it should be ours—serving to the end of time.

---

76   The notion that those who die to themselves inherit eternal life is a reference to Luke 9:23-24. God choosing the foolish to shame the wise comes from 1 Corinthians 1:27. As for Christians being known by their love yet hated by the world, the corresponding passages are John 13:34-35 and 15:18-19.

77   We also know from John 14:3 that Jesus has been "preparing a place" for us, though it's possible He has finished that project already. His intercession, on the other hand, is clearly stated in Hebrews as continuing for all time (Hebrews 7:25).

78   An excerpt of Hebrews 7:25 (NASB95).

 # HIDDEN GEMS

## JESUS: OUR MAGNIFICENT MESSIAH

God promised that one like Moses—the humblest man on earth—would come to save. → Jesus embodied prophecy and walked humbly, coming as a servant to save the lost. *(Deuteronomy 18:15-19, Zechariah 9:9, Philippians 2:7)*

God promised one like a lamb—the sacrifice at Passover—would come to bear our sins. → Jesus came as the Lamb of God, being lifted up for the sins of the world. *(John 1:29, John 3:14, John 12:32)*

God promised the Messiah would willingly endure the mockery and malice of mankind. → Jesus served and suffered willingly, bearing our hatred with grace. *(Psalm 22:6-8, Matthew 26:67, Matthew 27:38-44)*

God promised the Messiah would take the wrath and punishment we deserve. → Jesus accepted the cup of wrath, being crushed and killed so we could be free. *(Matthew 26:39-44, Colossians 2:13-14, 1 Peter 2:24)*

God promised the Messiah would experience thirst and bitter agony at our hands. → Jesus shared gladly in the anguish of thirst so many may never thirst again. *(Psalm 69:21, John 19:28-30, Revelation 21:6)*

God promised the Messiah would share His reward with those who seek Him. → Jesus will share His glory and inheritance with the thirsty for all eternity. *(Romans 8:17, 2 Corinthians 3:18, Revelation 22:17)*

**BOTTOM LINE:**

All the promises of God are Yes and Amen in Jesus Christ our Lord.[79] *(Luke 18:31, Romans 15:8, 2 Corinthians 1:20)*

---

79  This is a paraphrase of 2 Corinthians 1:20 (ESV). As an aside, in Revelation 3:14, Jesus is given the name "the Amen."

# WRAP UP: Lean on He

All good stories present a conflict needing resolution. Some play out in theaters; others come alive in books or battlefields. No matter the medium, each one at its core echoes the grand theme of history and humanity's deepest need: the need for redemption.[80] From Genesis to Malachi, this was the ultimate mystery: Who would God send to redeem His world?

The last five chapters have all been spent revealing just how perfectly Jesus fulfilled the Old Testament narrative. Each aspect matters, but in the end, everything hinges on the Resurrection. The Righteous One, God's supreme Servant, either rose from the grave, or He was a sham. You can't call yourself one with God, predict your own resurrection, and just be a good dude. With Jesus of Nazareth, it's all or nothing. As the late pastor Tim Keller put it, "Crown Him or kill Him. Nothing in between."

What you believe about Jesus determines what you become. Consider Him a good moral leader, and you'll try to be one. Revere Him as King, and you'll soon reign at His side. He created all things, rules over all things, and in Him all things hold together. Lean on Him and live sturdy. Lean anywhere else and collapse.[81]

**It's crucial, no matter how big our bank accounts are, that we recognize our desperate reliance on the Messiah.** He isn't just some boost to our morning routine—He's the King, and He's called us to follow. Like Him, we must learn to disregard what's not fair and to carry what's heavy for others. Like Him, we must give of ourselves gladly and anticipate what is ahead. Like Him, we should cheerfully serve.

While those all sound good, following through isn't so easy. Temptations and trials lie close at hand. The world is surely a mess, but we aren't the victim—we're the cause. The solution, however, is not more education or less poverty or better leaders; it's a transformed heart through Christ Jesus.

---

80  In the words of reggae artist Bob Marley from "Redemption Song": "How long shall they kill our prophets while we stand aside and look? Some say it's just a part of it, we've got to fulfill the Book."

81  The language of "lean on" doesn't just refer to goodish support. It's to put your full weight upon Him, just as He described in Matthew 7:24-27.

# ENGAGE: Group Study 5

**STARTER**    How does studying biblical prophecy benefit someone's faith?

**TRIVIA**    In many versions of the Bible, the word "propitiation" is used to describe what Jesus became for us. Do you know what it means?[82]

**REFLECT**    At this very moment, Jesus Christ is at the right hand of the Father, praying for you! What might He be praying for you to change?

**PONDER**    If someone heroically dies for someone else, should it change the way the saved one lives?

**JOURNAL**    Are you absolutely certain that Jesus will share His inheritance with you forever? Where does that assurance (or doubt) come from?

**BOIL IT DOWN**    The Messiah served unto death, that we might find life in His name!

**BRING IT UP**    Is it healthy to feel like you owe God? Why or why not?

**LIVE IT OUT**    Write a letter to Jesus, thanking Him for what He went through for you.

---

82  In the KJV, "propitiation" is used three times (Romans 3:25, 1 John 2:2, 4:10). In the NKJV, ESV, and NASB, it is used four times—the extra passage being Hebrews 2:17. According to *Merriam-Webster*, propitiation means "the act of gaining or regaining the favor or goodwill of someone or something."

# PART II

## LOVE DESPITE ADULTERY IN THE LIFE OF HOSEA

*An Old Testament Highlight*

# 6

# BROKEN PROMISE LAND

*The LORD says, "O Israel, when I first found you,*
*it was like finding fresh grapes in the desert . . .*
*But then they deserted me for Baal-peor,*
*giving themselves to that shameful idol."*
—HOSEA 9:10 (NLT)

T O MANY BIBLE READERS, Hosea is no more than the name of a book
thumbed past.

The first of the so-called "minor prophets," Hosea often lives in the
shadow of his big brothers—Isaiah, Jeremiah, and Ezekiel.[1] Even when
the book of Hosea is read, it's not the easiest to follow. Hosea packed his
papyrus full of emotion, quickly shifting gears without notice. As one
expositor put it, "It is his heart that speaks; he is not careful to concentrate

---

1   The final twelve books of the Old Testament, prophets Hosea through Malachi, are called "minor" for their
    brevity in comparison to the "major" prophets. Traditionally, the book of Daniel is included in the major
    prophets, but being only a third the size of the three main amigos, Daniel does not receive big brother status
    in this work. Really, his writings deserve a category all their own. Even Sir Isaac Newton (whom Einstein
    called "the smartest man to ever live") would agree, calling one passage from Daniel "the foundation stone
    of the Christian religion."

his thoughts or to mark his transition; the sentences fall from him like the sobs of a broken heart."

On top of that, Hosea steeps his dialogue in historical know-how, frequently citing esoteric names like Ephraim and Jezreel. Thus, with such a jumbled style and strange cast, Hosea may appear peripheral or even unrelated to the person of Jesus.

*But it's just the opposite.*

**For some scholars, Hosea harbors the greatest messianic foreshadowing in all of Scripture.** Others have dubbed Hosea the second greatest love story ever told, "second only to the story which it illustrates"—God's unfailing love for His bride.[2] Regardless of rank, the book of Hosea stands as an absolute masterpiece of the gospel in action, more than seven hundred years before the Cross! For many, these writings remain a buried treasure, an unopened gift—until now.

To properly unwrap this prophetic present, we must begin by reading the related card:

> The word of the LORD that came to Hosea, the son of Beeri, in the days of Uzziah, Jotham, Ahaz, and Hezekiah, kings of Judah, and in the days of Jeroboam [II] the son of Joash, king of Israel.
>
> —HOSEA 1:1 (ESV)

This time stamp places the prophet Hosea as Isaiah's contemporary in an especially gory chapter of Israel's history.[3] By the end of Hosea's life, he would see six different kings reign, and four of them assassinated.[4] Precious little is recorded about these leaders, yet one refrain is repeated five separate times: Each king "did not depart from the sins of Jeroboam

---

2   Prominent commentators John Brown and J. Vernon McGee both hold this view. Similarly, reformed theologian Dr. James Boice calls Hosea "the second greatest story in the Bible."

3   King Menahem, for example, sacked a nearby city and "ripped open all the women in it who were pregnant" (2 Kings 15:16, ESV).

4   The stories of these kings can be found in 2 Kings 14-15. The names of those assassinated are as follows: Zechariah, Shallum, Pekhiah, and Pekah.

the son of Nebat, which he made Israel to sin."⁵ In short, the whole nation was collapsing into chaos, mimicking the sins of one man. But why?

Remember, after the death of Solomon in 932 BC, the Kingdom of Israel split. The North retained the name "Israel," but the South became known as "Judah." Jeroboam, a past servant of Solomon, immediately gripped the Northern throne. Fearful of his people sacrificing to God in Jerusalem (now a Southern city) and losing his governance, Jeroboam set up two golden calves in the North for mandatory worship.

As we discussed earlier, this may seem primitive, even innocuous—but such idolatry destroyed a nation. Jeroboam's public pronouncement delivered the ruinous venom: "Behold your gods, O Israel, who brought you up out of the land of Egypt."⁶ These calves were a fatal misdirection, just like at Sinai. Jeroboam's message was subtle yet clear: *Embrace your history but reject your Founder. Keep your insurance; just replace your Provider. Forget about God.*

Two hundred years later, we meet Hosea, and the venom is running its course. Israel is rotting from within. The commandments they were founded on? Discarded. The God that had blessed them? Despised. With their Savior expunged from memory, Israel got busy abandoning God.

**This is the backdrop of Hosea: a beloved people discarding their Beloved.** Jeroboam did not conjure a new tactic; he resurrected an ancient one—get the people to worship their wants. It worked in the Garden, and it worked at Mount Sinai. It would work in the Promised Land too. From Moses to Hosea, for roughly seven hundred years, Israel spread her legs to many different lovers.⁷ Some were objects and images. Others were kings offering military aid. Though vastly different in form, the same

> With their Savior expunged from memory, Israel got busy abandoning God.

---

5    The verses with this phrase are 2 Kings 14:24, 15:9, 15:18, 15:24, and 15:28.

6    An excerpt of 1 Kings 12:28 (ESV).

7    This may seem unnecessarily graphic or grotesque, but it's precisely the language of God Himself in Ezekiel 16:25 about the adulterous idolatry in Israel. For more on this, see Leviticus 17:7, Judges 2:17, Psalm 106:39, 2 Chronicles 11:15, and Hosea 4:12. Notice the connection to Jeroboam's goat demon altars to those in Leviticus!

sickness drove Israel to chase each one: the belief that God was not enough.

In the Garden, they thought God was holding back. At Mount Sinai, He was taking too long. For Jeroboam, He was a threat. Whatever the case, God was not to be trusted.

This is the backdrop for Hosea's Israel. It's also the story of his wife, Gomer.

## "I NOW PRONOUNCE YOU. . . PROPHET AND PRODIGAL"

Imagine being a young, eligible adult on the lookout for marriage material (if you aren't already). For years, you have loved the Lord and been cheerfully serving Him as you patiently wait for your match. Nevertheless, you're lonely, wondering if the family you've always wanted is in your future at all. Night after night, prayers leak out your lips for contentment and clarity. Years go by without an answer.

Then one day, while watching the news, your whole life changes. During a special report on the multibillion-dollar pornography industry, God's voice suddenly booms forth from heaven: "Go forth and marry a promiscuous woman who will have children that aren't yours. This will illustrate how My people have acted like whores, forsaking Me."[8]

How would you respond? Would you obey?

Somehow, some way, Hosea did.

For him, the above interchange wasn't a thought exercise; it was reality. The very first words Hosea heard from God were these:

> "Go, take to yourself a wife inclined to infidelity, and children of infidelity; for the land [Israel] commits flagrant infidelity, abandoning the LORD."
> —HOSEA 1:2 (NASB)

Talk about a shocking command! Perhaps even more astonishing, however, was the prophet's immediate response:

---

8    This is a blended paraphrase from Hosea 1:2 NLT and ESV.

"So Hosea went and married Gomer daughter of Diblaim,
and she conceived and bore him a son."
—Hosea 1:3 (BSB)

The prophet obeyed—no questions asked.

What an opening scene! Who was this Gomer, and how did Hosea find her? Was he even fond of her at all? Unfortunately, we don't know. The Bible gives little to no detail about Hosea's wife, Gomer, other than her mother being named Diblaim. Thankfully, the meanings behind Hebrew names often give clues to the individual's story. **In fact, unpacking the names in the book of Hosea is the master key to the treasure within.**

It's worth noting that names are far more important than we realize—both to us and to God. Throughout Scripture, God gives people names, changes people's names, and even takes a few for Himself. Three times, He sends angels to declare what a child's name should be.[9] Even in heaven, the name game will continue as each saved soul will be given a new moniker. To top it all off, God not only calls each of His children by name but the 200 billion trillion stars in the universe too.[10]

So, when God takes the time to include certain names in His Word, we should pay close attention. For example, the names of our newlyweds, Hosea and Gomer, tell a story by themselves. "Hosea" means "salvation," stemming from the same Hebrew root יָשַׁע (yasha) as the names Joshua and Yeshua (Jesus).[11] Meanwhile, "Gomer" translates to "complete" from the Hebrew verb גמר (gamar). Thus, we have a prophet named "Salvation" sent by God to make "Complete" his wife, even though she begins woefully unfaithful.

What story does that sound like? Well, listen to a few quotes from Paul to the church:

9   This is a reference to Genesis 16:11, Luke 1:13, and Matthew 1:21. Isaac was also named by God before birth, but it was not through an angel (Genesis 17:19).
10  The promise of new names to those in God's eternal kingdom can be found in Revelation 2:17. Regarding the naming of stars, Psalm 147:4 and Isaiah 40:26 reveal this intimate relationship between God and His creation.
11  For more on the translation history from the Hebrew "Yeshua" to the English "Jesus," see Dr. Mark Steven Francois' video on YouTube titled, *From Yeshua to Jesus: How We Got the Spelling and Pronunciation of the Name Jesus in English.*

+ "I promised you to one **husband**, to Christ . . ."[12]

+ "In Him you have been made **complete**, and He is the Head . . ."[13]

+ "For the husband is the head of the wife as Christ is the head of the church, his body, of which he is the **Savior**."[14]

+ "And I am sure of this, that he who began a good work in you will bring it to **completion** at the day of Jesus Christ."[15]

+ "If we are **faithless**, He remains faithful, for He cannot deny Himself."[16]

Yes, merely three verses into the book of Hosea, we are already given a glimpse of the gospel. Jesus Christ, "the Prophet who was to come"[17] and betrothed husband of the church, was sent by God to redeem a people prone to infidelity.[18] No wonder His name, Yeshua, is so close to Hosea.

Still, there is one more name in Hosea's opening we must not forget—Gomer's mother, Diblaim. No doubt it's easy to overlook such a briefly mentioned moniker, but doing so would severely limit one's grasp of Gomer's background. Make no mistake: God included Diblaim's name for good reason—a reason that reveals more than you'd think.

## EASY AS CAKE?

In Hebrew, the word "Diblaim" comes from a doubling of the root word דבלה (debela), meaning "fig cake." In other words, Diblaim literally means "two fig cakes." This may not seem like much, but alas, a pearl is hidden within the oyster.

In ancient Israel, fig cakes had a few specific uses. Some were used to

---

12  An excerpt of 2 Corinthians 11:2 (NIV).
13  Colossians 2:10 (NASB95).
14  Ephesians 5:23 (NIV).
15  Philippians 1:6 (ESV).
16  2 Timothy 2:13 (NASB95). This is a powerful verse assuring the repentant believer of salvation. Such confidence during dark times is so important that the apostle John wrote his entire first epistle to provide such assurance (1 John 5:13).
17  An excerpt of John 6:14 (HCSB).
18  Such a bent toward infidelity can be seen through the heart being deceitful above all else (Jeremiah 17:9), the abandonment of Christ by the disciples upon His arrest (Mark 14:50), as well as the line in Hebrews that commands us to lay aside "the sin which so easily entangles" (Hebrews 12:1).

honor royalty, others to revive the strength of the sick. Tracking down these fig cakes throughout Scripture will help unearth three crucial facets of Hosea's bride: her ancestry, affections, and allegiance. We shall gain great insight into Gomer's world while being reminded of the Savior we need.

It's time to cut the cakes.

### FACET ONE: GOMER'S ANCESTRY

To project where something is headed, one must study from where it has come. Well, in 750 BC, Israel bathed in prosperity. It had been seven hundred years since they left Egypt, yet Egypt hadn't left their hearts. The power and pleasure Israel witnessed in Pharoah had grown like a weed within them. In Israel's mind, she had paid her dues; now it was her turn to let loose. Whatever would make the Hebrews resource-rich, that's what they would worship. Of course, like all idolatry, this was a slow poisoning. Turning their backs on God didn't happen overnight.

In the ancient Near East, fig cakes were delicacies made for special occasions, celebrations of surplus—even for offerings in worship. Frankly, the Lord deserved every cake Israel had. After all, upon receiving the Promised Land, God's people vowed:

> The power and pleasure Israel witnessed in Pharoah had grown like a weed within them.

> "Far be it from us that we should forsake the LORD to serve other gods! It was the LORD our God himself who brought us and our parents up out of Egypt, from that land of slavery, and performed those great signs before our eyes. He protected us on our entire journey . . . We too will serve the LORD, because he is our God."
>
> —JOSHUA 24:16-18 (NIV)

What a difference, however, one generation can make. Entering the land of milk and honey, Israel was glad to serve Jehovah. Deliverance was fresh, so dependence was palpable, and the cakes came flooding in.[19] Joshua, though, feared this wouldn't last—and he was right.

Just before he died, Joshua recounted *all* the LORD had done, pleading with the people to always remember their Savior. But they didn't. Time passed, and with it, the memory of their Redeemer. Soon, praises due Yahweh were poured out to idolatrous statues instead. Whenever Israel experienced success, they thanked a block of wood. Such spiritual sleeping around, however, would bring far more doom than delight.

By Hosea's day, God had been practically erased from society. The same bride who emphatically declared her vows to the Lord was now spewing just the opposite.

"I will not serve!" snapped Israel.[20] "It is hopeless, for I have loved foreigners, and after them, I will go."[21]

**Brazenly, Israel's two fig cakes were on full display: comfort and conformity.** Her kings worked hard to rewrite history, erasing her vows of old. Now, pleasure was their god. Instead of celebrating Yahweh and conforming to His Kingship, she bent the knee to her neighbors—whoever would feed her fix. This was the ancestry of Gomer, or at least what was left of it.

Before moving forward, one critical takeaway needs to be addressed: Israel's issue was *not* her desire for comfort but rather her definition of it. To her, as well as for millions today, comfort comes through eliminating suffering. In essence, the agenda becomes minimizing pain to maximize pleasure.

For some, this means fighting to fit in, conforming to their surroundings. Others attempt to enforce this agenda on the world under the banner of "tolerance" or "co-existence," but there's one fatal flaw: suffering isn't the enemy. Any good parent knows this—cushy lives make spoiled brats.

Even in general, smooth seas don't make skilled sailors; they make

---

19  Technically, there is no evidence that Israel before the time of the kings made cakes of figs at all. Here, "cakes" is used symbolically to represent the general concept of Israel's faithful sacrifices at the time (which very well could have included fig cakes).

20  An excerpt of Jeremiah 2:20 (ESV). Though Jeremiah was a prophet to Judah after the time of Hosea, this prophecy was still addressed to "all the clans of the house of Israel" (Jeremiah 2:4) and in general, typifies the obstinance Israel showed toward the Lord before Assyria wiped them out.

21  An excerpt of Jeremiah 2:25 (ESV). See previous footnote for more context.

drowning victims when the storms do hit. Hence, wishing away suffering is wishing for a world of wimps. It may sound good—peace, pleasure, and the pursuit of happiness—but it's all a guise when God isn't the goal.

**The Bible paints a radically different picture of comfort and the path to find it.** For starters, Scripture cements Yahweh as "the Father of mercies and God of all comfort."[22] Thus, we see a correlation between compassionate mercy and durable comfort, neither of which can be found apart from the Lord.

Of all places, this link probably shines forth best in the book of Isaiah. After thirty-nine chapters filled with judgment, the book's grand turning point[23] arrives through the voice of the Father: "Comfort, yes, comfort My people!"[24]

Fascinatingly, the word translated "comfort" here is the Hebrew נָחַם (nâcham), which can mean both "to pity, console, or have compassion upon" and "to be sorry, suffer grief, and repent." It's the gospel packed in a single word.

Hebrew in hand, the Lord's message rings clear: heavenly comfort comes through genuine repentance. Nevertheless, Israel gave herself away like hotcakes, seeking the good life while running from the Source of it.

> The path to comfort is not self-care but submission, where the fullness of freedom is found.

We must not follow suit.

The path to comfort is not self-care but submission, where the fullness of freedom is found. Alas, one day God Himself would come down to prove it—leading the Way, proclaiming the Truth, and laying His Life down for us.

---

22 An excerpt of 2 Corinthians 1:3 (NASB).

23 Remember, the first thirty-nine chapters of Isaiah largely proclaim judgment, correlating to the thirty-nine books of the Old Testament. Then, just like its counterpart Matthew, Isaiah Chapter 40 turns on a dime with messages of salvation.

24 An excerpt of Isaiah 40:1 (NKJV). Note how this spectacular verse has multiple renderings. Not only can the word "comfort" also mean "repent," but even the phrasing allows for both a consoling tone (like a parent comforting a child) and a directive for us to comfort fellow believers.

## FACET TWO: GOMER'S AFFECTIONS

Since the beginning of time, offering food has communicated a certain sense of fellowship, a love that transcends barriers. Holidays gather hearts around tables for the same reason that romantic dates often include dinner: *sharing food shows affection.*

Likewise, in the desert, God gave Israel bread from heaven.[25] With grace, quail dropped from the clouds.[26] These gifts weren't meant, though, to be a one-way windfall. The book of Numbers is exceedingly clear: Israel was to offer food and drink back to her Glorious Groom.[27]

God didn't want spoiled brats or somber servitude; He wanted fellowship. Slowly, however, Israel's oblations became tired rituals instead of cheerful gifts, and she ultimately left her first Love. Woman was created to be a helper, yet God's wife became a harlot.[28]

Inevitably, the affections of the heart determine where our resources wind up. Time, money, food—they're all sold to the bidder we love the most. In other words, what we delight in, we give to.

This is where Diblaim's fig cakes provide our next clue. The Bible records three distinct ways fig cakes were *affectionately* purposed: **to heal, to revive, and to enjoy**. Together, these three actions demonstrate God's blueprint for affectionate relationships and how Israel was blowing it big time. Regarding healing, consider the story of King Hezekiah.[29] At only thirty-nine

> Inevitably, the affections of the heart determine where our resources wind up.

---

25  Far more than an Old Testament story, the bread from heaven powerfully foreshadows Christ as interpreted by Jesus Himself in John 6:51.

26  There are two very different instances where quail came from heaven. The event alluded to here is the generous gift of God in Exodus 16:12-15, not the plagued judgment quail of Numbers 11:31-35.

27  For a few examples of these food offerings, see Numbers 6:15, 15:24, and 28:9. For biblical support for calling God Israel's "Glorious Groom," see Isaiah 54:5, 62:4-5, Jeremiah 2:2, Ezekiel 16:8, and Hosea 2:16.

28  The words "helper" and "harlot" are allusions to Genesis 2:18 and Hosea 2:5, respectively. It should be noted that "helper" is by no means a condescending term. The Hebrew word עֵזֶר (*ezer*) translated "helper" in Genesis 2:18 regarding Eve is the exact same word used to describe God Almighty in many passages such as Exodus 18:4, Psalm 33:20, 70:5, 146:5, and Hosea 13:9.

29  Interestingly, 2 Kings 18:5 goes so far as to declare that King Hezekiah "trusted in the LORD, the God of Israel, so that there was none like him among all the kings of Judah after him, nor among those who were before him" (ESV). Somehow, this even surpassed the trust of Josiah, of whom Scripture declares, "Never before had there been a king like Josiah, who turned to the LORD with all his heart and soul and strength, obeying all the laws of Moses. And there has never been a king like him since" (2 Kings 23:25, NLT).

years of age, Hezekiah grew deathly ill. Upon being told he would surely die, Hezekiah cried out to the Lord with all his heart. Immediately coming to his aid was the prophet Isaiah, declaring, "Bring **a cake of figs**. And let them take and lay it on the boil, that he may recover."[30]

Hezekiah obeyed, and sure enough, he was healed. Similarly, Israel had God by her side—the infinite Healer—yet instead of crying out to Him, she settled for painkillers . . . stopgap pleasures to alleviate life's woes. As the Lord put it:

> "They do not cry out to me with sincere hearts.
> Instead, they sit on their couches and wail.
> They cut themselves, begging foreign gods for grain
> and new wine, and they turn away from me."
> —HOSEA 7:14 (NLT)

Desperate for relief, Israel sought the very addictions causing her pain. Badly broken, no quick fix would ever work. Car repairs don't come by playing with toy trucks or buying Super Glue; one must go to the Dealership. The same is true of souls—whether it's a pesky leak or a blown engine, we must take it to the Healer, not the harem.

Another use for fig cakes revolved around the revival of spirit and strength. Consider the story of David fleeing from his rebellious son Absalom into the wilderness. One day, after hearing their families had been taken captive and their city burned to the ground, David's army set off in pursuit of their enemies. Along the way, they found a sickly Egyptian man who had not eaten or drank in three days. Instead of passing him by, "They gave him a piece of a **cake of figs** and two clusters of raisins. And when he had eaten, his spirit revived."[31]

While this may seem trivial—surely, a hungry man feels better after eating—implications abound. For instance, the less man spends on dead idols, the more he has to uplift the weak. Put another way, to worship idols is to refuse the world the help it needs; to worship the Lord is to graciously give the self away.

---

30  2 Kings 20:7 (ESV).

31  1 Samuel 30:12 (ESV). To be fair, their hospitality was with the intention of gaining military information, not simple kindness.

Tragically for Israel, life became all about gain, not God. Thousands of years later, martyred missionary Jim Elliot would say, "He is no fool who gives what he cannot keep to gain what he cannot lose."[32] Hosea's Israel was doing the opposite: taking what she could not keep to lose what she could not regain.[33]

Finally, and perhaps most notably, fig cakes communicated heartfelt joy to the ancients. When the elders of Israel first anointed David as king, hundreds of thousands came to support him. Radiant unity permeated the land as these travelers came "with a loyal heart . . . of one mind to make David king."[34]

Here, during one of the most resplendent coronations the world has ever seen, alongside 340,000 armed soldiers, droves of people brought "abundant provisions of flour, **cakes of figs**, clusters of raisins, and wine and oil, oxen and sheep, for there was joy in Israel."[35]

What a celebration! Sadly, some three hundred years later, that loyalty was gone, that joy extinguished. Israel's delight was no longer in the Lord, and the desires of her heart grew ravenous. Her gluttony only bred more hunger; her focus was on her food.

Seek the Savior and find healing, revival, and joy; seek the self and go hungry.

When the heart is set on heaven, blessings come flooding in.[36] Seek the Savior and find healing, revival, and joy; seek the self and go hungry. Israel's figs, once baked with love, had turned into a cycle of numbing pain and ignoring infections. Selfishness had taken over, instead of cheerful sacrifice. In the words of the Messiah:

---

32  This quote is in reference to cheerful sacrifices made for the sake of Christ, which will be rewarded unimaginably in eternity.

33  This comes from the notion of Mark 8:36. "What she could not regain" refers to the opportunity to trust in Christ, something one forfeits forever when this life has passed.

34  1 Chronicles 12:38 (NKJV).

35  1 Chronicles 12:40 (ESV). The rounded 340,000 troops quoted comes from adding up the troops listed in 1 Chronicles 12:23-37.

36  A combined reference to Colossians 3:1 and Malachi 3:10. Here, "blessings" don't necessarily refer to external, earthly treasures. The blessings God guarantees to hearts set on heaven are the things that last, things that matter, like the fruit of the Spirit.

"For whoever wishes to save his life will lose it, but whoever loses his life for My sake and the gospel's will save it."

—MARK 8:35 (NASB)

If it's lasting satisfaction you desire, look no further. You won't find it anywhere else.

### FACET THREE: GOMER'S ALLEGIANCE

The last piece of Gomer's puzzle revolves around the use of fig cakes to honor royalty. Much like David's coronation, Israel initially celebrated Jehovah, her King. Time and time again, they promised to serve the Lord,[37] offering sacrifices and baked goods galore. In the years of the Judges, however, God's chosen people failed to rid the land of idolatry, and it came back to bite them—hard.

With each new generation, the gods of their neighbors became thorns in their sides. [38] Eventually, Israel would utterly reject God as her king, demanding a human one instead. And as Israel's allegiance turned to the wrong royalty, out the fig cakes went.

By the time Gomer was born, little good was left. Listen to the description from God Himself:

> There is **no faithfulness** or steadfast love,
>     and **no knowledge** of God in the land;
> there is swearing, lying, murder, stealing,
>     and committing adultery;
>     they break all bounds, and bloodshed
>     follows bloodshed . . .
> When their drink is gone, they give themselves
>     to whoring;
>     their rulers dearly love shame.
>
> —HOSEA 4:1B-2, 4:18 (ESV)

It cannot be overstated how dark the land had become. This is crucial

---

37  Disturbingly, there were many of these moments, seen in passages like Exodus 19:8, 24:3, and 24:7, as well as Joshua 1:16-17 and 24:21-24.

38  The prophecy in view is found in Judges 2:1-4, which tragically came to pass throughout the Old Testament.

to understand; otherwise, God's jarring command to Hosea makes little sense. After all, what good would it do for Hosea to marry a wife of harlotries and raise the children from her affairs? How would that help Israel? Undoubtedly, Hosea asked himself these questions, but he didn't let his lack of answers deter him from faithfully following God.

When it came to trusting his King, Hosea was all in.

See, cheerful servanthood requires complete devotion from the heart. (And where our heart goes, our fig cakes follow.) The best example is found in 1 Samuel 25 when King David's army is starving in the wilderness. He sends messengers to a rich man named Nabal asking for food, but they're pompously spurned. Nabal's wife, Abagail, however, rushes out to meet David personally and show him honor, that she might find favor with the king.

Along with her, she brings a massive feast packed on donkeys, including—you guessed it—*two hundred cakes of figs*! But it gets even better. Upon seeing David, she falls at his feet and utters one of the humblest entreaties ever recorded, seven times referring to herself as "your servant." King David, moved by her reverence, responds with mercy. Not only that, when Nabal dies of a stroke shortly after their meeting, David asks for Abigail's hand in marriage.

And how does Abigail respond? With her face bowed to the ground, she declares: "I am **your servant** and am **ready to serve** you and **wash the feet** of my lord's servants."[39]

*Serve, serve, serve.*

When it comes to marriage, Abigail had it down from the start: cheerfully serve your spouse ahead of yourself.[40] Unfortunately, with Israel, this was radically not the case. At the time of Hosea, the vows to God she said on Sinai were long gone. Of the fig cakes the Lord deserved, even the crumbs were being cast at the feet of lifeless idols. Just imagine God's heart when He heard His once-loving bride spew the following rebuff:

"We will not listen to your messages from the LORD! We will do whatever we want. We will burn incense and pour

---

39 An excerpt of 1 Samuel 25:41 (NIV). Imagine if Jesus repeated these very words to God the Father just before "taking the form of a servant" (Philippians 2:7, ESV) and washing the disciples' feet!

40 This is the primary motto of Developing Great Relationships, a biblically based ministry that produces servant-based relationships. For more information, visit DevelopingGreatRelationships.org.

out liquid offerings to the Queen of Heaven just as much as we like—just as we, and our ancestors, and our kings and officials have always done . . . **for in those days we had plenty to eat** . . . pouring out liquid offerings to the Queen of Heaven, and **making cakes** marked with her image . . ."[41]

—JEREMIAH 44:16-19 (NLT)

Let that sink in. Not only did the Israelites punt God from the throne of their lives, but they elected a fake queen in His place. Worshipping this "Queen of Heaven"—a Moon goddess[42]—demonstrates the idiocy of idolatry on multiple levels. For example, in an agrarian society, light from the Sun grew their food, yet Israel substituted the dark, lifeless moon for God, who literally is light.[43]

How inconceivable: The Sun of Righteousness swapped for a cold ball of rock.[44] Then again, doesn't modern man do the same—seeking pleasure in self-image while asserting life began with an exploding dot? It's ridiculous, and it's all related. Think about it: *We-centered beliefs create me-centered chaos.*

> Think about it: *We-centered beliefs create me-centered chaos.*

In short, God wasn't meeting Israel's expectations, so she left Him. Sadly, Gomer would do the same to Hosea.

---

41  Note that this passage, which is in the book of Jeremiah, was written to the Southern Kingdom of Judah after the exile of Hosea's Israel. Still, because the Southern Kingdom was infected with the idolatry of the Northern Israel (see 2 Kings 17:19), it is appropriate to implement this passage as a general description of Hosea's day.

42  Not all scholars agree on the identity of said queen, but as one encyclopedia puts it, "It is generally believed that the 'queen of heaven' is the moon." Ironically, as the bride of the King of Heaven (Daniel 4:37), Israel in a sense could've claimed the "Queen of Heaven" title herself!

43  Not only is Jesus the Light of the Word (John 8:12), but John even declares that God is light (1 John 1:5). Of course, this is not to say the Creator is a photon or wave of electromagnetic radiation. Rather, He is the perfect opposite of the dark, the way by which those who have been spiritually enlightened see the world (Ephesians 1:18). As C.S. Lewis said, "I believe in Christianity as I believe that the sun has risen: not only because I see it, but because *by it I see everything else.*"

44  Just like the moon, we don't produce any light or warmth in ourselves. All we have to offer is a reflection of who we serve. For Israel, her allegiance was earthly. Instead of relishing her Creator, she had fallen in love with the world, serving up meals to lifeless figurines. For the epitome of this attitude, see Malachi 3:14. Just one chapter later we find the term "Sun of Righteousness" (Malachi 4:2) describing the Messiah.

 # HIDDEN GEMS

## JESUS: OUR BENEVOLENCE BRINGER

Hosea's Israel was trying to find comfort and belonging in this world. ⟶ Jesus offers internal comfort and belonging in Him. *(Matthew 11:30, 2 Corinthians 1:5)*

Hosea's Israel should have been using her resources to heal and uplift the lowly. ⟶ Jesus used His resources to the fullest, healing and uplifting the lowly. *(Luke 7:21-23, James 5:14-15)*

Hosea's Israel relentlessly tried reviving and cherishing herself. ⟶ Jesus emptied Himself to forever revive and cherish us. *(John 6:53, Ephesians 5:29)*

Hosea's Israel chased satisfaction to the grave, constantly begging idols for their wants. ⟶ Jesus satisfied God's wrath to the grave, constantly giving beggars their needs. *(Luke 18:35-43, Philippians 4:19)*

Hosea's Israel brought forth devastation and division upon all she was given. ⟶ Jesus will bring forth the eternal restoration and unification of all things. *(Ephesians 1:10, Revelation 22:3-4)*

Hosea's Israel honored the queen of heaven, seeking blessing from the cold, dark moon. ⟶ Jesus honored the King of Heaven, now offering blessing as the bright morning star. *(2 Peter 1:19, Revelation 22:16)*

**BOTTOM LINE:**

Jesus devoted Himself to an unfaithful bride and is bringing her to completion. *(John 3:29, Ephesians 5:23-27)*

# WRAP UP: Go Me-Rrrr!

Back in Exodus, when God first called His bride, she was to be a hope-bringer on His behalf. Then selfishness took over, and Israel fell off the wagon. God gave her His name, yet she went about sullying it. Instead of honor, she brought Him shame while the world pointed and laughed, jeering, "Those who offer human sacrifice kiss calves!"[45] What a description of God's people. Talk about tragic.

The story of Old Testament Israel is not easy to digest. With all the broken vows and bloodshed, there are more twists and turns than a small intestine. Time and again, the Jews went from worship to wandering, relentlessly questioning whether God had their best interest at heart. Year after year, they waffled. Eventually, even Israel's precious anthem to love the Lord alone got swapped for a Vulcan-esque "Fit in and prosper!"[46] Nothing was ever enough.

Here was the problem: Israel thought suffering was the enemy, and it was her job to minimize it. **If things went well, her response was, "Go me!" When hardship hit, it was "Rrrr! Why me?"** From both sides, she grew full of herself, grading God's love by how much pleasure He was providing.

In the end, man is left with a choice: conform to the world or to the image of the King. The world says, "Insulate yourself from suffering. Eat your cake and have more too!" God says, "Share in the sufferings of my Son and others. Serve your cake and be satisfied forever."[47] Which we choose makes all the difference, for we give our fruits to what we worship, and what we worship defines us.

It all boils down to this: Live to eat, and you'll never have enough. Kneel to serve, and you'll feast forever.

---

45  An excerpt of Hosea 13:2 (ESV).

46  This "anthem" is known as the Hebrew Shema. Found in Deuteronomy 6:4-9, this passage is recited as the centerpiece of morning and evening Jewish prayer services to date. The worldly replacement phrase, "Fit in and prosper" is a reference to the famous Vulcan salute "Live long and prosper" on the old hit series, *Star Trek*.

47  This creative quotation of God is not verbatim in Scripture, but rather a blend of Romans 8:17, Galatians 6:2, and 1 Peter 4:13.

# ENGAGE: Group Study 6

**STARTER**  Would you rather live in Joshua's Israel with constant war yet faithfulness to God or Hosea's Israel with relative peace yet rampant idolatry? Why?

**TRIVIA**  There are only three Old Testament passages that Jesus quoted on more than one occasion: the Ten Commandments, the Golden Rule, and a verse in Hosea. Can you guess it?[48] (Hint: check Hosea 6.)

**REFLECT**  Just as Hosea pledged his steadfast love to promiscuous Gomer, God pledges His amazing grace to the church. In response, how should you treat those who are unfaithful to you?

**PONDER**  Hosea was given a hard command to marry and love Gomer. If you asked him about the purpose of marriage, what do you think he would say?

**JOURNAL**  When times got tough, Israel looked to the world for comfort. What do you tend to run to instead of God, and where does that end up taking you?

**BOIL IT DOWN**  Discrediting God triggers explosive selfishness.

**BRING IT UP**  How can Christians use their pasts to help themselves love God?

**LIVE IT OUT**  Get crafty by creating a memorial of all God has done for you!

---

48   The verse in Hosea that Jesus quotes on more than one occasion is Hosea 6:6, as seen in Matthew 9:13 and 12:7.

# 7

# SOME KIND OF FAMILY

*"What a sick heart you have,*
*says the Sovereign LORD . . .*
*for your mother loathed her husband*
*and her children, and so do you."*
—EZEKIEL 16:30A, 45A (NLT)

N O PROPHET HAD IT EASY. After all, messages of doom don't sit well with most audiences. Even glimpses of hope can taste like a cop-out to those in extreme suffering. Ears seek affirmation, but seers of the Old Testament rarely gave it. Thus, the prophets were rejected, mocked, and despised—just like the One to come.[1]

Sadly, social ostracism was only the beginning for these truth-speakers, Hosea included. Often, they were called to physically live out their messages and endure graphic hardships in the sight of the

---

1   The language here is an intentional parallel to the suffering of Christ, who endured heinous rejection and despisal (Isaiah 53:3), as well as mockery (Psalm 22:7), being in a sense the ultimate Prophet (Luke 4:24). It should be noted, however, that Jesus Christ was not simply a prophet as believed by Muslims, but God in the flesh.

populace. The prophet Ezekiel, for example, was tasked with lying on his side, bound in rope, for over a year. Imagine doing that for a couple of hours, let alone twelve months. Isaiah, in obedience to God, walked around naked and barefoot for *three* years as a portent of destruction descending on Egypt and Cush.[2]

These acts may seem strange. They were. God's people refused to accept His words through His prophets, so He put these men (and a few women) on display as a final flagrant warning.[3] In the words of The Bible Project, "Sometimes people need strange to shock them into hearing a message they'd rather not hear." While the assignments mentioned were undoubtedly grueling, Hosea's calling was the most gut-wrenching of all: marry an unfaithful woman and raise the children she births, even when they're not yours.

Enter Gomer, stage left.

When the narrative begins, only two things are known about Hosea's bride. First, the text calls Gomer "a wife of whoredom."[4] While harsh at first blush, God's wording is rightfully severe. Israel had sold herself to all sorts of lovers in pursuit of fleeting comforts, as would Gomer.

Still, Israel did not begin that way.

It is important to note that while some scholars believe Gomer was a prostitute prior to marrying Hosea, it is best to see her as initially chaste. Listen to the affectionate language God uses in describing Israel when the relationship was young:

> "When Israel was young, I loved [her], and out of Egypt I called [her] . . . I led [her] with cords of kindness, with the bands of love."[5]
>
> —HOSEA 11:1, 4A (ESV)

---

2   A reference to Isaiah 20:2-4. With incredible detail, this passage is one of many in the Bible that accurately predict the rise and fall of historical empires hundreds of years beforehand. Such power to foretell the future is arguably the greatest evidence humanity has for Scripture being divine, as pointed out by God Himself in passages like Isaiah 41:21-23, 43:9, 44:7, 45:21, and 46:10.

3   The label "prophetess" was attributed to five women in the Old Testament: Miriam, Deborah, Huldah, Noadiah, and unnamed prophetess in Isaiah 8:3.

4   An excerpt of Hosea 1:2 (ESV).

5   Though the original pronouns in this passage are masculine and are even at one point attributed to Christ (Matthew 2:15), the change to feminine pronouns here is warranted, as God switches back and forth throughout Scripture between referring to Israel as His beloved son and His beloved bride.

A cold, wanton woman does not match well with the affectionate Israel freshly rescued from Egyptian slavery. When first tasting such deliverance, delight was on her lips:

> "The LORD is my strength and song; he has become my salvation. He is my God, and I will praise him . . . Who is like you—majestic in holiness, awesome in glory, working wonders?"
>
> —Exodus 15:1-2, 11 (NIV)

Nevertheless, this didn't last. God married Israel, knowing full well she would relentlessly forget Him for other lovers. Now it was Hosea's turn, and he didn't bat an eye. Despite being guaranteed his snuggly bride would one day share sheets with other men, Hosea picked Gomer.[6]

**The other thing we are told about Hosea's bride is easy to overlook: her name, Gomer of Diblaim.** As discussed in the previous chapter, the name of Gomer's mother, Diblaim, offers key insights into Israel's infidelity. Briefly, we examined how the Hebrew name גֹּמֶר (transliterated "Gomer") most nearly means "complete," referring to the fulfillment of something in progress—good or bad. So, while Gomer's name foreshadows God bringing His bride to completion in Christ, there's a morbid connotation as well—the fulfillment of *sin*.

In Genesis, for example, the Lord vows to give Abram's descendants the Promised Land once all sin had reached its full measure:

> "And they shall come back here in the fourth generation,
> for the iniquity of the Amorites is not yet *complete*."
>
> —Genesis 15:16 (ESV)

So what was coming to completion in Israel this time? The very thing Hosea signed up to endure: adultery.

---

6    Likewise, centuries later, the Perfect Prophet picked us, imperfect as we are. Of course, Scripture adamantly asserts that God chose His children before the foundation of the world (Ephesians 1:4). Jesus "picking" us, however, is simply a reference to passages like Luke 6:13 and John 15:16 where Christ chooses His disciples, knowing full well they would desert Him (Mark 14:50).

## THE HARD WAY

For centuries, the Lord had pursued His bride. Faithfully, He had seen her through war, famine, calamity—the works. And yet, at every turn, Israel seemed to resist His divine affections. Repeatedly, the blessings God had for His people were derailed by selfishness. What took them forty years in the wilderness could've been walked in eleven days. In the Promised Land, her greed for more turned wealth into war. As Israel swelled with pride, the prosperity God desired to give His chosen people would've only made things worse.

So the spigot was shut off.

In a very real sense, Israel tried playing hard to get with God. She wanted Him to prove His usefulness, to spoil her rotten, to see just how far He'd go to chase her down. Meanwhile, she continued to play the field.

> As Israel swelled with pride, the prosperity God desired to give His chosen people would've only made things worse.

There are really only two reasons why people do this: either they want the benefits without commitment, or they're unsure the suitor is worth loving back. Tragically, both describe Hosea's Israel. She wanted all God's blessings but none of the boundaries, all His love but none of the submission—just in case He wasn't enough. And the worst part was this: she had already married Him!

This faithlessness typified ancient Israel (after the kingdom was divided), but that's not all. Such was Gomer's headspace toward Hosea, as well as most of us living in the West today: *I'll serve you—as long as you serve me. Then my love is yours! Unless, of course, I decide you're not worthy anymore.*

Ever so slowly, Israel's "till death do us part" had become "till I feel neglected or hurt or something better comes along."[7] In Israel's mind,

---

7   This is not to say that an abused spouse should remain in a setting of abuse. This does, however, poke at what is and isn't biblical grounds for divorce. Though the topic is way too complex for the scope of this work, a good place to begin personal study is the *Desiring God* article, "A Statement on Divorce & Remarriage in the Life of Bethlehem Baptist Church," as well as John Piper's personal work, "Divorce & Remarriage: A Position Paper."

God's love was directly correlated to her prosperity—the greater her surplus, the more favored she felt. This is one of the easiest lies to buy because it's built on a half-truth; namely, that you can tell how much God loves you by what He has given you.[8]

No playground is big enough, no Porsche is fast enough to keep the human heart satisfied.

No playground is big enough, no Porsche is fast enough to keep the human heart satisfied.[9] We always want more. So what is the Lord to do? Give us what we demand, or patiently let us scream? It's the question parents ask about their children and the question God asks about humanity: How does one bless a spoiled brat?

As God Himself put it in the book of Hosea:

> "The Israelites are stubborn, like a stubborn heifer. How then can the LORD pasture them like lambs in a meadow?"
>
> —Hosea 4:16 (NIV)

As much as the Lord longed to bless Israel, no wealth would heal her heart. Instead, she became like what she worshipped, as cold and lifeless as the golden calves she venerated.[10] Israel had spent the last 150 years worshipping golden cows, so a stubborn cow she became, continually kicking against the goads, mooing for more.

What patience the Lord of the Universe must have, always being evaluated for what He has to offer. How often He gets treated like a presidential candidate subject to our criticisms instead of being revered

---

8   Through an eternal lens, this would ring true. While on Earth, however, our calculations tend to operate on what we physically and emotionally experience. Hence, when suffering comes, if our sliding rule for God's love is based on what we experience, then He is deemed unloving. Through the Cross, however, the whole truth is revealed to include just one more little three-letter word: "You can tell how much God loves you by what He has given *for* you." For confirmation, see 1 John 3:16.

9   Surely "the promised Holy Spirit" (Ephesians 1:13-14) can satisfy the soul. Only God can (Psalm 63:5, 107:9). Still, though full faith in His promise can provide unwavering strength (Romans 4:20-21), only the fulfillment of such—the presence of God Himself—is able to turn thirst into satisfaction.

10  This concept of increasingly becoming like what we worship rings true no matter the object of our praise. If we worship lifeless idols, we become like them (Psalm 115:4-8, 135:15-18). If people become our "idols," our identity gets subtly wrapped up in them. And for those who do worship the one true God, they "are being transformed into his image with ever-increasing glory" (2 Corinthians 3:18, NIV). For the same happening to Israel, see Hosea 9:10.

as the King on the throne, where all things are subjected to Him. This was Israel's downfall and the poison of Gomer's marriage. Without realizing it, she had adopted a "What's in it for me?" mentality from her idol-worshipping neighbors. To her, infidelity made sense: If the grass seems greener, why not jump the fence and "make friends"?

Lo and behold, she would.

## FAMILY MATTERS

Scripture doesn't go into much detail about the marriage of Hosea and Gomer, but think of the anxiety Hosea must have battled after God revealed that his wife would inevitably cheat on him. That alone could've set things tumbling. Perhaps the prophet tried going above and beyond in serving Gomer, hoping his love could convince her to be faithful.[11] Maybe he set up rules and boundaries to try to keep her lasciviousness at bay. And what if Hosea told Gomer that she would betray him? As much as we might wish to know all the juicy details, what God does offer in His Word is tailor-made for the human heart.

Curiously, the storyline centers not on Hosea and Gomer's marriage but on the names of the three children they reared. At each birth, God personally declared to Hosea what the newborn was to be called and why. Thus, as the narrative of adultery unfolds, so does the grief of the Almighty.

Time to meet the kids.

### THE FIRSTBORN: JEZREEL

Hosea's first child happens in a hurry. Literally, in the very same sentence that we learn of Hosea's marriage to Gomer, Scripture also announces, "she conceived and bore him a son."[12] Now whether it was a honeymoon baby or years after the altar, we aren't told. All we know, at least initially, is that the first child was Hosea's, and it was a boy.

Still, before we dive into the newborn's God-given name, it's pivotal

---

11   A positive example of this mentality—living and praying in the hopes that God's declaration might be reversed—can be seen in David's week-long mourning over his dying son (2 Samuel 12:22-23).

12   An excerpt of Hosea 1:3 (ESV).

to recognize the significance of biblical firstborns:

+ **Abel** brought the firstborn of his flock as an offering.

+ **Jacob** pretended to be Esau, the firstborn, to steal his blessing.

+ **Joseph**, after Reuben defiled his father's marriage bed, was given the firstborn rights.[13]

+ **Israel** receives the title "my firstborn son" by the Lord.[14]

+ God even declares to Moses, "All the firstborn are Mine . . . both man and beast. They shall be Mine: I am the LORD."[15]

Consequently, Hosea's baby boy was a big deal. With all the excitement, it's likely the newlyweds even had a special name already picked out. Consider, then, what it must've been like for Hosea to hear this from heaven:

> And the LORD said to [Hosea], "Call his name Jezreel, for in just a little while I will punish the house of Jehu for **the blood of Jezreel**, and I will put an end to the kingdom of the house of Israel. And on that day I will break the bow of Israel in the Valley of Jezreel."
>
> —HOSEA 1:4-5 (ESV)

No doubt, this would've stung. While it's not unheard of to name children after places (think Dallas or Virginia), for Hosea and Gomer to name their firstborn son after the Valley of Jezreel would be like naming a child "Auschwitz." Out of all the cities in Israel, this is not the one you'd want to call your child.

Jezreel was known for one thing: gruesome slaughter. The first main event in this gory valley came four hundred years before Hosea when God led Gideon's army of three hundred against

> Jezreel was known for one thing: gruesome slaughter.

---

13  A reference to 1 Chronicles 5:1-2. Curiously, this detail about Joseph gaining the birthright is not recorded in the Genesis account at all. Only by this parenthetical sidenote in 1 Chronicles do we discover that the honor was given to Joseph.

14  A reference to Exodus 4:22-23 as well as the similar declaration of Ephraim in Jeremiah 31:9.

15  An excerpt of Numbers 3:13 (NASB95). See also Numbers 8:16-17 and Nehemiah 10:36.

135,000 bloodthirsty Midianites.[16] Famously struck with confusion, the Midianites wound up stabbing each other to death while their leaders' heads became war trophies. More disturbingly, the Israelites would immediately respond by attempting to enthrone Gideon over God and melting down their gold earrings to "play the harlot" in idolatry.[17] Thus, at best, the memory of Gideon in Jezreel would've brought forth notions of Israel's adultery amidst God's deliverance.

But that's not all.

The next time Scripture focuses on Jezreel isn't until three hundred years later when this valley sported the royal palace of the cruelest couple in history: King Ahab and Queen Jezebel.[18]

Here's the backstory. In those days, a man named Naboth owned a vineyard that King Ahab coveted. After an unsuccessful attempt to buy it from Naboth, Ahab pouts to his wife, who, in turn, devises a sinister plan to get Naboth killed. Hiring two false witnesses to testify that "Naboth cursed God and the king," her plan worked; Naboth was taken outside the city and stoned to death. So despicable was this betrayal in the sight of God that the Almighty declared wild animals would eat Ahab's entire family—and God doesn't lie.[19]

Indeed, the final act in Jezreel's blood-stained story fulfills that prophecy. A dozen years after Ahab's reign, a man named Jehu (of whom God spoke to Hosea) rises to power in Israel. Anointed to bring judgment upon the atrocities of Jezebel, Jehu proceeds to slaughter all the descendants of Ahab, piling seventy of their heads at the city gate.

Sadly, Jehu instantly develops a *go-me* mentality, caring more that others watch him wipe out evil than the evil rising up within him.[20] In one fell swoop, after killing every Baal worshipper in Israel, he winds up

---

16    The four hundred years is an estimate, a rounded number representing the span between approximately 1180-780 BC. The verse that confirms Gideon's battle happening in the valley of Jezreel is Judges 6:33.

17    This event takes place in Judges 8:22-27. Does this sound familiar? See Exodus 32:2-4!

18    The cruelest couple in history is not an exaggeration. It stems from 1 Kings 16:30-33, 18:4, 21:25-26, and Revelation 2:20.

19    The concept of God never lying is a reference to Numbers 23:19, Titus 1:2, and Hebrews 6:18. That said, He can "relent" like in Jonah 3:10, but this nuanced discussion does not fall within the scope of this work.

20    This evil within Jehu can be clearly seen in his arrogant remark recorded in 2 Kings 10:16. Talk about a desperately needed lesson for all the virtue-signalers of modern society in the West! Too often, the ones most ferociously fighting for "rights" turn into the most violent, venomous citizens of all.

worshipping idols himself.[21] Hence, God's punishment against Jehu for the blood of Jezreel can be summed up in this fashion: though he partly obeyed, he blew it in the end.

Now, with all the Jezreel pieces in place, the bigger picture comes into view. Hosea's firstborn represented an ominous reality—Israel's kingdom would soon be no more. Though the Lord worked miracle after miracle, Israel chose idols over her Husband. One after another, her kings served themselves. And throughout the Old Testament, God made it very clear: Should His people cheat on Him, He would scatter them among the nations.[22] Thus, by the time Assyria came to power, this painfully came to pass.[23]

Here, though, is where things begin to turn around. While the prophecy itself is grim, packed inside the name Jezreel is golden gospel hope. In English, Jezreel can translate to "God will scatter," but the name can also mean "God will sow."

So what in the Old Testament does God promise to sow? Well, in Isaiah, the LORD promises to sow "righteousness and praise."[24] In Psalm 97, He says, "Light is **sown** like seed for the righteous, and gladness for the upright in heart."[25] Then, through the prophet Jeremiah, the LORD declares He shall "**sow** the house of Israel and the house of Judah" into a new covenant.[26] And finally, nestled in the book of Hosea, God vows to Israel the glorious line: "I **will sow** her for Myself in the land."[27]

Then, in the New Testament, it gets even richer. Jesus Christ, whom God calls "the Righteous One, My Servant"[28] in Isaiah, became righteousness to us "that we might become the righteousness of God

---

21  References to 2 Kings 10:28-31. God never told Jehu to do this. It was purely maniacal, especially in light of the previous footnote.

22  See Deuteronomy 4:27 and 28:64, Nehemiah 1:8, Psalm 44:11, Jeremiah 9:16, and Ezekiel 12:15, 20:23, and 22:15.

23  Sadly, this would occur only twenty-five years after Hosea's death, namely the Assyrian exile of Israel. The final line of God's prophecy through Jezreel states that He will break the bow of Israel in the valley of Jezreel. This valley is also known as Megiddo, the site in the book of Revelation where the apocalyptic battle of Armageddon will take place (Revelation 16:16). Thus, many scholars believe that this prophecy has a double fulfillment—when Israel fell to Assyria in 722 BC, as well as in the end times.

24  An excerpt of Isaiah 61:11. Note that this is the last verse of a chapter Jesus quotes to launch His ministry in Luke 4:18.

25  Psalm 97:11 (NASB95).

26  An excerpt of Jeremiah 31:27 (NASB95). For "new covenant" language, read through verse 34, noting the similar Hosea-like language of God as Israel's "husband" in verse 32.

27  An excerpt of Hosea 2:23 (NASB95).

28  An excerpt of Isaiah 53:11 (NASB95).

in Him."[29] He brought forth praise from the mouths of infants, light to hearts in darkness, the oil of gladness to those who mourn. He is the seed promised to Abraham, the Word of God sown for us.[30]

Only through Jesus is the new covenant possible; only through Him will the Father's kingdom come. Above all, He is the leading Servant, the King who bids us come and die,[31] so that we might be sown for others. That way, instead of melting down earrings, we'll forever exalt Jesus as God's loving servant!

And just in case that wasn't enough, don't forget, Jesus was a firstborn too—of Mary, yes,[32] but also far more:

+ "The Son is the image of the invisible God, **the firstborn** over all creation."[33]

+ "For God knew his people in advance, and he chose them to become like his Son, so that his Son would be **the firstborn** among many brothers and sisters."[34]

+ "He is also head of the body, the church; and He is the beginning, **the firstborn** from the dead, so that He Himself will come to have first place in everything."[35]

+ ". . . Jesus Christ, the faithful witness, **the firstborn** of the dead, and the ruler of the kings of the earth."[36]

Alas, Jezreel may have been a prophecy of disaster, but make no

---

29  "Became righteousness to us" is a paraphrase of 1 Corinthians 1:30. The quote cited is an excerpt of 2 Corinthians 5:21 (NASB95). Other supporting verses in this same vein are Romans 5:17, Philippians 1:11, and 2 Peter 1:1.

30  A reference to Matthew 21:16, 2 Corinthians 4:6, Isaiah 61:3 (plus Hebrews 1:9), Galatians 3:16, and Luke 8:11, respectively.

31  The first half of the sentence is a reference to Dietrich Bonhoeffer's quote, "When Christ calls a man, he bids him come and die," in his world-famous book, *The Cost of Discipleship*. The end of the sentence is a reference to Matthew 13:37-38.

32  A reference to Luke 2:7. Surely, with Mary being a virgin, Jesus being her firstborn was obvious. For Luke to go out of his way to declare Jesus her "firstborn" is likely a nod either to Mary having other children after Jesus or the theological significance of Jesus being the firstborn as seen in the cited verses.

33  Colossians 1:15 (NIV).

34  Romans 8:29 (NLT). This is the verse directly after the popular (and often misused) Romans 8:28, which offers crucial context to the concept of God working all things "together for the good of those who love Him." This "good" is conforming believers into the image of God's Son, which necessitates suffering (Romans 8:17) and by no means guarantees earthly affluence or ease.

35  Colossians 1:18 (NASB95). Jesus being the head of the body can also be seen in Ephesians 1:22-23 and 5:23.

36  An excerpt of Revelation 1:5 (BSB). To see how this fulfills the Old Testament foreshadowing in David, check out Psalm 89:27.

mistake: the King of Heaven knows what He's doing. There are already so many connections to the One who came, and we still have two children to go.

## THE SECOND-BORN: LO-RUHAMAH

Unfortunately, things would get far worse in Israel before they would get better. Immediately after Hosea's firstborn becomes the personification of punishment, the Lord unloads an even grimmer name upon child number two:

> And she conceived again and bore a daughter. Then God said to him: "Call her name Lo-Ruhamah, for I will **no longer have mercy** on the house of Israel, but I will utterly take them away."
>
> —HOSEA 1:6 (NKJV)

This part of the story wrenches the heart. One would think that the obedient Hosea, after marrying a woman destined to cheat on him and naming their firstborn after a place of slaughter, would be rewarded in some manner. Instead, things just continue downhill. Regarding the firstborn, Scripture states that Gomer "bore him [Hosea] a son"; here, the text just says Gomer "bore a daughter."

In other words, this baby girl wasn't Hosea's.

Imagine the depth of grief that must've come over the prophet. Who knows just how doggedly he served Gomer, assuring her of his love. Still, Gomer decided her husband wasn't enough. Perhaps she viewed him as rigid and unfun, a stick-in-the-mud who's hyper-focused on obeying God. Maybe she grew jealous of Hosea's attention, feeling unseen as he ministered to the nation. Whatever the case, whether greed or envy or lust or pride, she gave in to serving herself.

As a result, what should've been a great celebration in the birth of a daughter may well have been one of the most painful days in Hosea's life.[37] Each time he called out to his baby boy Jezreel, reminders shot forth of the

---

37 While it's not guaranteed that Hosea knew Lo-Ruhamah wasn't his right away, surely things were woefully off-kilter in his marriage.

gory downfall Israel faced. Now, he was to raise a daughter who wasn't his. Not only that, but God told him the baby girl's name was to be Lo-Ruhamah, Hebrew for "No mercy" or "She that never knew a father's love."[38]

*Yikes.*

Try to fathom how Hosea must've felt when holding that little girl. Surely, he wept, sensing the depth of God's anguish over Israel. Gomer's adultery wasn't an outlier; it was par for the course.

The same could be said of Israel. For decades, God's chosen nation punted her heavenly Husband for short-lived sensuality. This caused more and more children to grow up doubly Fatherless—spiritual orphans in fractured families. Over time, marriage got swapped for lust, and children out of wedlock became the norm.

Meanwhile, incessant wars kept costing kids their dads. And with all the fake priests and twisted history, just like in Judges, along came generations "who did not know the LORD or the work that he had done for Israel."[39] Thus, as the decades passed, so did the knowledge of a father's love. What a vicious cycle it was—one that Western civilization knows all too well.

Out of all the epidemics the modern world faces, fatherlessness may well be the most devastating. Particularly over the past half-century, the number of children born without daddies has absolutely skyrocketed in the West—especially in America. For example, in 1963, 6.3 percent of American births were by unmarried mothers. By 2020, that number grew to 40.5 percent—**a whopping 543 percent increase**.[40]

> Out of all the epidemics the modern world faces, fatherlessness may well be the most devastating.

Meanwhile, the divorce rate doubled and the marriage rate

---

38  The translation "No mercy" can be seen in the ESV rendering of Hosea 1:6. "She that never knew a father's love" comes from the *International Standard Bible Encyclopedia*, page 1426.

39  An excerpt of Judges 2:10 (ESV).

40  The citations for all statistics referenced in this section can be found in the Endnotes at the back of the book. Also, an unmarried mom does not guarantee a fatherless home, but it dramatically increases the chances of such.

plummeted.[41] Subsequently, the rate of American kids living only with their mom more than tripled. These days, a fourth of all children in the United States, **some 18.4 million**, live without a full-time father. That's 18 million Lo-Ruhamahs who don't know a consistent father's love.

The effects of such broken families are staggering:

+ Fatherless kids are **twenty times** more likely to be incarcerated and **eleven times** more likely to exhibit violent behavior than children from two-parent households.

+ Children without fathers are also **ten times** more likely to abuse chemical substances.

+ Daughters without a father are **711 percent** more likely to have children as teenagers and **92 percent** more likely to get divorced themselves.

+ **Nine out of ten** homeless and runaway children are from fatherless homes, which is **thirty-two times** the national average.

+ Fatherless kids are **five times** more likely to commit suicide, **twenty times** more likely to show behavioral disorders, and **nine times** more likely to drop out of high school.

Thus, it is no surprise that America, with the highest rate of single-parent households of any nation in the world, is also the reigning World Champion of incarceration rate, substance abuse, teen pregnancy, pornography production, and anxiety per capita.[42] *And it all stems from fatherlessness.*[43]

What, then, does such fatherlessness stem from? The very same cancer that enveloped Israel: infidelity to God. Cheat on the Maker of

---

41 While the crude divorce rate has been fairly level, it is a horrible indicator of the percent of marriages ending in divorce, as it only looks at divorces per 1,000 people. Because the marriage rate has gone down so drastically, the crude rate has remained constant, but the divorces per 1000 married women doubled from 1960 to 2020.

42 Every category mentioned has a corresponding citation in the Endnotes to corroborate the claim here that America is the worst nation in the world regarding these issues.

43 The term "fatherlessness" here also includes children who have no real relationship with their father, even though he may live in the same home. To this point, the America First Policy Institute notes that the American school-age boy only spends "about *thirty minutes* per week in one-on-one conversations with his father. For comparison, the same boy on average will spend about *forty-four hours* per week watching television, playing video games, and surfing the internet." For evidence within the book of Hosea itself regarding fathers being held responsible for the trajectory of a nation, see Hosea 4:14.

marriage, and sure enough, marriages (and societies) implode.

For a modern example, consider America once more. Whether you look at the first line of the Declaration of Independence or the back of every dollar, the evidence is overwhelming: America began with God.[44] Back in 1844, the US Supreme Court ruled unanimously (9-0) that the Bible *had* to be taught in school; otherwise, "no man can tell how sudden a catastrophe may overwhelm us and bury all our glory in profound obscurity."[45]

Well, fast forward to the early 1960s, and America goes for the dare. In perhaps the gravest turning point in US history, the Supreme Court declared school-sponsored prayer and Bible readings unconstitutional.[46]

Half a dozen years later, in 1969, no-fault divorce laws opened the door for one spouse to dissolve a marriage for any reason—or no reason at all.[47]

Then in 1973, during the "free love" movement, the Supreme Court ruled that women have the right to end unwanted pregnancies at will, including school girls without parental consent.[48] (Meanwhile in California, ear piercing must have guardian approval.) And since then, with the explosion of erotic media, traditional marriage has been increasingly discarded for more modern, inclusive alternatives—even by much of the church.

One by one, the dominoes have fallen—and what has been the

---

44  This does not mean that the nation always followed well the teachings in Scripture, but merely that the government unashamedly championed the Bible in the public sphere. Horrendous atrocities like slavery did occur while Scripture was in schools. The point is not that requiring the Bible in education will solve all America's problems or create some type of Utopia; rather, that when the Bible got *banned*, America began quickly unraveling and has not turned around since. Also, it should be noted that America did not enforce and has never attempted to enforce a national religion of some sort. When saying the nation "began with God," the phrasing is deliberate: it simply began with the Creator in the spotlight. Some try to argue that this is untrue because the US Constitution never explicitly mentions God, but the individual constitutions of *all fifty states* mention God at least once. As a final note, "In God We Trust" didn't arrive on American coins until 1864, but it still memorializes the foundations of faith upon which the republic was built. (Interestingly, the phrase wasn't put on American paper currency until 1957.)

45  An excerpt of a quote by Daniel Webster, who argued the case in favor of the Bible. For Webster's full quote and others that are similar, check out the short devotion by Ken Boa titled "Daily Encouragement: Day 257" online.

46  This is a reference to the 1962 *Engel v. Vitale* and the 1963 *Abington School District v. Schempp* rulings. America, however, didn't stop there. By 2016, some public school teachers could be axed simply for having a Bible on their desk, receiving directives such as the following from the Henry County School District in Georgia: "You are hereby directed to remove all items which contain religious symbols, such as crosses, printed bibles, angels, bible verses, printed prayers, and biblical quotations from the common areas, hallways, classrooms, and office . . ." (Curiously, there only seems to be only one faith tradition on the Henry County chopping block.)

47  This is a reference to California's Family Law Act of 1969 signed by then-Governor Ronald Reagan, an act that would be progressively adopted by most US states.

48  The year 1973 is a reference to the *Roe v. Wade* Supreme Court decision which was overturned in the summer of 2023, tossing the matter back to the states.

result? What kind of families and what kind of societies have these new "freedoms" created?

*Broken ones.*

While Christ was surely right in declaring, "Seek first the kingdom of God and His righteousness, and all these things will be added to you,"[49] the reverse also holds true: Spurn God, and all will be *subtracted from you.*

This is what happened to Israel. The farther she chased the world, the farther she ran from the God who brought her out of it.[50] Eventually, God's people were so utterly addicted to themselves that self-interest became all they knew. And just like that, Love got traded for lechery.

So, what was God to do? How ought a gracious King treat an arrogant addict? Judgment may be withheld for a time, but sooner or later, mercy must be removed. It wasn't enough to remind Israel of the consequences, to sit her down and express disappointment. The prophets had been doing that for more than a century. **At some point, only suffering will till the soil of a hardened heart,** for humility does not come through prosperity but through humiliation. (Just ask Nebuchadnezzar.[51])

Naturally, humans wince at the thought of being brought down like this—crashing to the ground from our high roosts—but so often it is what we need most. Pride has poisoned us all. Security blankets can stop the shivers, but they can't cure the disease. The only way to be healed is to be humbled; this is the Way of Christ.[52] Not by sword or horse did He save, but on the back of a wobbly donkey.[53] He endured humiliation so that we might embrace our own and rise from

> The only way to be healed is to be humbled; this is the Way of Christ.

---

49   An excerpt of Matthew 6:33 (ESV).

50   Check out connections to passages like Exodus 20:2 and John 15:19.

51   For a full grasp of the reference, read Daniel 4 in its entirety about a man who publicly praises the Lord but still ends up needing severe humiliation to truly embrace faith.

52   "Way" is capitalized not just because Jesus professed to be the Way (John 14:6), but also because the followers of Christ were first identified simply as followers of "the Way" (Acts 22:4 and 24:14, NIV). For more on this concept of being "cured" or "healed" by Christ alone, see Hosea 5:13 and Luke 4:18.

53   The first half of the sentence is a reference to Hosea 1:7, the second half of Lo-Ruhamah's prophecy addressed to Judah. The wobbly donkey is a reference to Mark 11:2, with the "wobbly" description being an allusion to Jesus' specification that the animal would be a donkey on which no one had ever ridden. Thus, the animal would've likely been poor at balancing Him.

it.[54] As His half-brother James put it:

Let the brother of low degree boast in his exaltation, and he who *is* rich, in his humiliation, because he will pass away like a flower of grass.

—JAMES 1:9-10 (BLB)

This is how we become the good soil. In the words of the Almighty, "Plow up the hard ground of your hearts, for now is the time to seek the LORD."[55]

## THE THIRD-BORN: LO-AMMI

When humans desert God, things get ugly. Hosea witnessed this firsthand with the birth of his second and third children.

We aren't told why exactly Gomer broke her vows, but we do know it wasn't an isolated occurrence. In fact, as soon as she was able, Gomer went right back to the street corner, bearing one last child from another man:

Now when she had weaned Lo-Ruhamah, she conceived and gave birth to a son. And the LORD said, "Name him Lo-Ammi, for you are not My people and I am not your God."

—HOSEA 1:9 (ESV)

What a painful verse. Gomer had already betrayed Hosea once. For her to do so again, right after weaning Lo-Ruhamah, must have all but ripped out the prophet's heart. Of course, Hosea knew full well she would cheat on him, but that foreknowledge would've hardly lessened the emotional devastation. Truth be told, that foresight may well have made life worse; his nightmare was becoming his reality, little by little.

Then, on top of that, we have the child's tragic name. The Hebrew here is sharp and straightforward: Lo-Ammi means "Not my people" or "No kin of mine."

Think about calling a child that. The level of heartbreak involved

---

54 Jesus enduring humiliation is a reference to Isaiah 50:6 (NASB95), as well as Acts 8:33. The concept of us rising from our own humiliation pivots on passages like Ezra 9:5-6 (NASB95).

55 An excerpt of Hosea 10:12 (NLT).

in such an utterance cannot be overstated. Even in the movies, only when a parent has been utterly shamed and rejected—when a son has so radically departed from the ways of his father that no family resemblance remains—only then does the father declare, "You're no son of mine."[56] Similarly with Lo-Ammi, God wasn't forsaking His bride; He was expressing just how disfigured she had become.

Still, Scripture paints an even bleaker picture. As if repeat adultery wasn't bad enough, this time around, it seems **Gomer never returned**.[57] See, when Lo-Ruhamah was born, God declared the child's prophetic name *to Hosea*. That means he was present for the birth. But with Lo-Ammi, there's no mention of Hosea at all. For all we know, God spoke Lo-Ammi's name to Gomer in the back of some brothel, wailing all alone.[58] Regardless of the exact timing of Gomer's adulterous departure, Scripture is clear: Eventually, Gomer left for good.

Now while we may not have a record of what set Gomer permanently packing, Scripture doesn't leave us without a hint. Unlike with Jezreel, notice how the Holy Spirit deemed it worthwhile to mention *the weaning of Lo-Ruhamah*. Differences like this should cause us to sit up and listen, for every word in Scripture was hand-selected by God.[59] Indeed, there's a reason He, through the quill of Hosea, includes the weaning of Lo-Ruhamah—a reason that brings the connections to Israel one step deeper.

For nearly two hundred years, God patiently endured Israel's idolatry. So long had they presumed on the riches of God's kindness and forbearance that their hearts had grown into glaciers—cold, hard, and practically immovable. Various judgments came upon them, but not a single one translated into lasting repentance. Thus, the weaning of God's mercy began.

---

56  As a cinematic example, in the film *Harry Potter and the Goblet of Fire*, Bartemius Crouch Sr. declares this to his son, Barty Crouch Jr., after realizing his son has become a follower of evil.

57  The phrase "it seems" here is important, as the Scriptures don't explicitly state when Gomer permanently left. She must've at some point to set the stage for Hosea 3:1-5. Thus, given the changes in phrasing, *it seems* most likely that her severance occurred before Lo-Ammi's birth.

58  If this is the case, Gomer could have easily recounted such to Hosea so that he could record it after they reunited.

59  There is no "fluff" or superfluous detail in Scripture. Some historical particulars may not have any allegorical undertones or christological connections, but they all were, at the minimum, considered significant enough by God Himself to include and thus be examined appropriately. Of course, translations out of the original languages will have various different words, none of which God inspired to the degree He did the authorial manuscripts, but English readers must make due the best we can.

Yes, His mercies are new every morning,[60] but when they don't result in repentance for generations, make no mistake: "'The Lord will judge His people.' [And] it is a terrifying thing to fall into the hands of the living God."[61] In a very real sense, Israel dared God to drop the hammer. After all, what was the worst a loving God would do?

Israel wasn't the only one, either. This twisted expectation of tolerant love has also sunk its teeth deep into modern Western thought. Instead of moral accountability, everything pivots around inclusivity. All lifestyles are to be celebrated, so long as they celebrate everyone else. Even within the church, topics like God's wrath and judgment have become almost taboo.

> In a very real sense, Israel dared God to drop the hammer.

Subsequently, no one is wrong except the person who claims someone is. The modern West says accommodate, accept, and affirm every lifestyle, or you're the problem.

We are witnessing the searing of the conscience for the pursuit of unhindered happiness, the claiming of unalienable rights apart from the Creator who endowed them. Simply put, it's the motto of Outback Steakhouse becoming the battle cry of a hemisphere: "No rules, just right."

This, of course, is nothing new. It was true of ancient Israel, and it was true of Hosea's runaway wife. What began as the supple ground of servanthood eroded into a "Do what you want and who you want!" mudslide. Such selfish ambition set the stage for the "no kin of Mine," Lo-Ammi.

Again, this wasn't God forsaking His covenant but rather Him vocalizing His grief over Israel's unrepentance. It was not her sins that brought such a horrible pronouncement but rather, like Gomer, her refusal to return home.

Undoubtedly, this was the harshest possible slap in the face of God and His prophet. Absolutely nothing is worse than an unrepentant heart. That's why Jesus went so far as to say that if a brother refuses

---

60  Lamentations 3:22 (ESV).
61  An excerpt of Hebrews 10:30-31 (NASB).

the correction of the church, "regard him as you would **a pagan** or a tax collector."[62] Or take the apostle Paul's similar command to the believers in Thessalonica when a church member refuses to submit to God:

> "Take special note of that person and **do not associate with him**, so that he will be ashamed and repent."
>
> —2 Thessalonians 3:14 (AMP)

Without repentance, there's no family resemblance. Martin Luther once said that Jesus "willed the entire life of believers to be one of repentance."[63] In short, refusing to repent is like telling God the Cross wasn't necessary. It's the ultimate diss.

The final line of Lo-Ammi's name declaration is perhaps the most gut-busting of all. We've already unpacked at length the overtones of "not My people." What's left is the blood-curdling phrase, "I am not your God."

First, and quite curiously, the word "God" in this phrase is not found in the most reliable manuscripts. Therefore, the phrase most literally translates to "I am not yours." Let that shake your heart for a moment. Think of how letters to loved ones traditionally finish with the salutation "Yours truly" or even just "Yours."

God is saying, *I can't write that to you anymore. You chose to traffic yourself over sharing life with Me. What could be worse? Your lovers are "Yours" now, not Me.*

The heartache must have been immense. Just from an earthly perspective, few things could cut deeper. And yet God, in His infinite wisdom, would use even this to save the lives of many people.

That said, though Israel's rejection would one day trigger the reconciliation of the world, her adultery still pierced the heart of God.[64] After all, like a bride on her wedding night, Israel used to sing with glee:

---

62  An excerpt from Matthew 18:17 (BSB).

63  This is a quote from the very first of Luther's famous "95 Theses," which he boldly published on the door of the Wittenberg Castle church. It should also be noted that Martin Luther was by no means a perfect man, and his words are not authoritative. All his positions should be weighed and measured against Scripture itself. Doing so for the quote in question yields a high level of accuracy, given the many times Christ (and those in Acts through the Spirit of Christ) commanded the people to repent.

64  For passages that reveal the grief of God's pierced heart, see Isaiah 22:4 and Hosea 11:8.

"The voice of my beloved!
  Behold, he comes,
leaping over the mountains,
    bounding over the hills . . .
**My beloved is mine**, and I am his . . ."[65]

—SONG OF SONGS 2:8, 16A (ESV)

*Not anymore.* In a few short years, Hosea's wife went from promiscuity to adultery to full-blown abandonment. Israel's honeymoon love had long vanished. Like Gomer, she had run off, forgetting who and *whose* she was. In chasing pleasure, she lost everything—including herself.

Even so, this isn't where the story ends. Thankfully, though we relentlessly spurn our Creator, God is forever faithful.

And He has a covenant to keep.[66]

---

65  This is not a direct quote from Israel to God, but many scholars believe Song of Songs parallels the exuberant love between God and His people.

66  The use of present tense "has" here is intentional. As seen in Romans 11 (and throughout the Old Testament prophets), God still has redemptive unfinished business with the "natural branches," the Jews.

# HIDDEN GEMS

## JESUS: OUR CRUSHED CONQUEROR

| | |
|---|---|
| Hosea's firstborn son, Jezreel, bore a name meaning "God will sow." ➞ | Jesus, the firstborn of all creation and seed of Abraham, was sown by God for us. *(Colossians 1:15, Galatians 3:16, Luke 8:11)* |
| Hosea's Jezreel represented the historic blood-stained vineyard of unjust accusation. ➞ | Jesus shed His blood for the Master's vineyard, put to death on unjust accusations. *(1 Kings 21:1-13, Matthew 21:33-39, Matthew 26:60)* |
| Hosea's second-born, Lo-Ruhamah, bore a name meaning "No mercy." ➞ | Jesus was shown no mercy so we could receive mercy. *(Isaiah 53:7-10a, Titus 3:5)* |
| Hosea's Lo-Ruhamah represented those who never knew the Father's love. ➞ | Jesus knew the Father's love before the world began and died so that we might too. *(John 17:24, 1 John 3:16)* |
| Hosea's final child, Lo-Ammi, bore a name meaning "Not my people." ➞ | Jesus was rejected by His people so we could join His family. *(John 1:11-12, John 7:5)* |
| Hosea's Lo-Ammi represented how Israel had become unrecognizable to her Husband. ➞ | Jesus was beaten beyond recognition to become the supreme Husband of His enemies. *(Isaiah 52:14, 2 Corinthians 11:2, Romans 5:10)* |

**BOTTOM LINE:**

Jesus Christ shall one day usher in justice, judgment, and the Gentiles! *(Isaiah 42:1, 2 Corinthians 5:10)*

# WRAP UP: Stirred, Not Shaken

Right from the start, like the rest of mankind, Gomer was addicted to serving herself.[67] This didn't stop Hosea from choosing her; in fact, it's partly why he did.[68]

Likewise, when God chose Israel, she was weak and prone to wander. Nevertheless, He loved her, took her in, and made her flourish, adorning her with beauty and renown.[69] Sadly, it wasn't long before Israel trusted in her beauty rather than the One who bestowed it,[70] giving herself to anyone who came along. And just like that, she went back to slavery—to the world, and to herself.

**It's critical we don't shake our heads at Israel without looking at our own messes.** Hosea's wife had to learn the hard way, but so do we. Rarely is it enough for a child to be told not to touch the stove. Deep inside, we want to test the waters, to feel out the boundaries with our own hands. But then the burns come, and the screaming, and the pain. All this stems from Gomer's great addiction, as well as that of every other human in history: deciding for ourselves what is best.

Still, the story of Gomer's adultery wasn't recorded just so we could learn what not to do. Yes, it serves as a warning in part, but it's also a call to return *ourselves*. **It's meant to stir the spirit**, to bring each wanderer back to the house of the Lord.

Don't be like Ephraim saying, "Ah, but I am rich; I have found wealth for myself; No one has caught me cheating!"[71] Don't stick your neck into that bear trap. As Jesus' half-brother, James, put it, "We all stumble

---

67 Technically, Adam and Eve were not addicted to serving themselves "from the start." The use of "the rest of mankind" here is specifically referring to all humans born of a woman not named Jesus Christ.

68 God told Hosea to marry a woman inclined to infidelity, and so he did. Similarly, God chose the foolish, weak, base, and despised for Himself (1 Corinthians 1:27-28). This doesn't imply, however, that non-believers should pursue foolishness headlong in hopes of somehow increasing their chances of being picked. The "choosing" in 1 Corinthians 1 is past tense.

69 A reference to Ezekiel 16:1-14. Though this is spoken to Jerusalem after the kingdom split, it is surely true of the larger whole as well, for Jerusalem was part of the original inheritance of the Israelites all the way back in Joshua's day (Joshua 18:28).

70 Interestingly, this is curiously similar to the fall of Lucifer who became proud because of his beauty as paralleled in Ezekiel 28:12-19, a passage also pertaining to the king of Tyre.

71 An excerpt from Hosea 12:8. The first half is from the ESV, while the last line is from the NLT.

in many ways."[72] The one who doesn't think he wanders has wandered furthest of all.

God's table is set for a feast, and He wants His beloved present—no matter how long the latest street corner stint.[73] His covenant of peace will not be shaken, nor will those who abide in Him.[74]

Remember, no matter how wretched things get, "The earth is the LORD's, and everything in it. The world and all its people belong to him."[75] All is His, and forever will be.

But is He *Yours?*

---

72  An excerpt of James 3:2 (NIV).

73  The table set for a feast is an allusion to Luke 14:15-23. "His beloved" is a reference to all those who submit to Him, like in Psalm 127:2, not just His beloved Son (Colossians 1:13).

74  God's unshakeable covenant of peace is a reference to Isaiah 54:10. Those in Him being "not shaken" is threaded throughout the psalms, such as in Psalm 21:7, 55:22, 62:2-6, and 112:6. Proverbs 10:30 also speaks to the same.

75  Psalm 24:1 (NLT). To be clear, this verse does not teach universalism, that we all are somehow saved. Rather, it declares that God is the potter of all people and thus has rightful ownership over each of His creations.

# ENGAGE: Group Study 7

**STARTER**   If you were in Hosea's shoes, would you have told your spouse-to-be that he/she was bound to cheat on you, or would you have kept it to yourself?

**TRIVIA**   The three children of Gomer were named by God Himself, but He curiously did so *after* they were born. In all of Scripture, only one other time does the Lord name a baby after birth. Who was he?[76]

**REFLECT**   Do you fit God into your agenda, or do you fit yourself into His? How can you tell?

**PONDER**   Do you think God needs to bring you lower before He can raise you up?

**JOURNAL**   In what ways do you bear God's family resemblance? In what ways do you need to be tilled?

---

**BOIL IT DOWN**   God's mercy is meant to bring us to repentance, but if it doesn't, pain might.

**BRING IT UP**   In what ways do you run away from God most often, and what can prevent this?

**LIVE IT OUT**   Pick a way you need tilling. Then invite a friend to help you pursue change.

---

76  The other baby named by God after birth was Mahershalalhashbaz (Isaiah 8:3, KJV), a Hebrew name meaning "Swift is the booty, speedy is the prey" (Isaiah 8:1, NASB95). The name signified the imminent plundering of Damascus and Samaria by the king of Assyria. Technically, the Lord also renamed baby Solomon "Jedidiah" after birth (2 Samuel 12:24-25), but this isn't included as it is more accurately a name *change*.

# 8

# SALVATION STEPS IN

*"For the time is coming when I*
*will restore the fortunes*
*of My people of Israel and Judah."*
—JEREMIAH 30:3 (NLT)

S OME SAY THAT OUT OF all the phrases in the Bible, two small words are by far the most magnificent.

"These two words," says Desiring God Ministries, "are overflowing with the gospel . . . there may not be two more hopeful words that we could utter." Author Stephen Altrogge agrees, writing, "I would argue that these are the two sweetest words in all of Scripture." As church leader Iain Gordon points out, the phrase "has been loved by countless saints over many millennia."

So, what two small words pack such a punch?

*But God.*

This short phrase is the Bible's ultimate plot twist alert, appearing over forty times in Scripture. "But God" moments represent some of the most stunning turnarounds in history:

+ The flood would have wiped out all life on earth, "**but God** remembered Noah and all the beasts and all the livestock that were with him in the ark."[1]

+ Joseph's brothers meant evil against him, "**but God** meant it for good, in order to bring it about as it is this day, to save many people alive."[2]

+ Even the gospel finds its power in this phrase, for the mob may have "put [Christ] to death by hanging him on a tree, **but God** raised him on the third day."[3]

Well, plain and simple, Hosea's family desperately needed a "But God" moment. The outlook was grim: three kids by multiple dads with a mom hellbent on pleasure. One can just picture the prophet in tears reciting the assurances of the Psalms:

> "Man in his pomp will not remain, **but God** will redeem
> my life.[4] My flesh and my heart may fail, **but God** is the
> strength of my heart and my portion forever."[5]

It was sink or swim time for Hosea's faith. Blame or trust, the choice was his.

"But God" can be the most beautiful words to read in a story, a triumphal entry of sorts, but to the one suffering, it usually comes with a different tone: "B-b-but God, I thought You said You'd do this" or "B-b-but God, how could You allow that?"

> Either we eagerly await the Lord's arrival, or we accuse Him of not showing up.

The point is this: It's not the two words that have power, it's how we use them. Either we eagerly await the Lord's arrival, or we accuse Him of

---

1   Genesis 8:1 (ESV).
2   An excerpt of Genesis 50:20 (NKJV). See Acts 7:9 for another "But God" phrasing regarding Joseph's journey.
3   An excerpt of Acts 10:39-40 (ESV).
4   An excerpt of Psalm 49:12-15. The first half comes from the ESV, while the second half is from the BSB.
5   Psalm 73:26 (ESV).

not showing up. In the dark moments, when the valley of the shadow of death bears down on the soul, intimate encounters with Almighty God can take shape. It's here that the Lord loves to whisper, to comfort the despairing with a reminder of His care. Once hope in what this world offers is at last abandoned, that's when things get good.

So it was with Hosea. Though he was totally obedient, his marriage imploded, and with it, his reputation. Prophesying to Israel was hard enough—a task that got many killed. Now, with his wife as the town prostitute, who would ever listen? And on top of that, imagine having to explain to little Jezreel why Mommy wasn't coming back. Yes, if anyone needed a word from the Lord, it was Hosea—and boy, would he get one.

The final two verses in Hosea 1 usher in a wave of grace so jarring that it almost seems like they don't belong.[6] After a constant barrage of mournful messages, God suddenly flips the script. It's not that all of Hosea's problems would magically disappear. Instead, his heart got what it needed most: a glorious reminder of God's faithfulness.

## THE POWER OF A REMINDER

Amid his darkest sorrow, Hosea's "But God" moment finally arrived. This time, as the word of the Lord came forth, it wouldn't be one of judgment but one of faithfulness. Right after telling Israel, "You are not My people," everything changes. Of all the things God could have followed Lo-Ammi with, check out His very next words:

> "Yet the number of the children of Israel shall be like the
> sand of the sea, which cannot be measured or numbered."
> —HOSEA 1:10A (ESV)

Sound familiar? Surely, it did to Hosea. He may well have read this scripture a thousand times in his scroll of Genesis. It's a piece of God's famous covenant with Abraham, one of the most precious promises in all Jewish history. Most Jewish boys would have memorized it from a

---

6   The original scribes would say these two verses literally don't belong. The Hebrew Bible places them at the beginning of Hosea 2 rather than the end of Hosea 1.

young age. What was the point of God repeating Himself, especially at such a gloomy juncture?

To answer this, we must start by examining the covenant itself.

When first declared, the Abrahamic covenant came as a package deal with God's call to leave everything behind:

> "Go from your country and your kindred and your father's house to the land that I will show you. And I will make of you a great nation . . ."
>
> —GENESIS 12:1A (ESV)

Little did Abram know that this was the first of many echoes. Just one chapter later, after Abram was forced to separate from his beloved cousin Lot, God said to him, "Lift up your eyes . . . I will make your offspring as the dust of the earth, so that if one can count the dust of the earth, your offspring also can be counted."[7]

Then later, when doubt crept in about his ability to have a son, the covenant came forth yet again: "Fear not, Abram, I am your shield; your reward shall be very great . . . Look toward heaven, and number the stars . . . So shall your offspring be."[8] In fact, God declared His covenant to the patriarchs **on ten separate occasions**—six times to Abraham, once to Isaac, and three more to Jacob![9]

Still, the question remains: what connection do these have to Hosea? *More than you might think.*

When we first meet Hosea in Scripture, God calls him to a life of surrender, to obey a hard command involving great sacrifice. Valiantly, Hosea does so, and along the way, a son is born out of wedlock. So it was with Abraham, whose revelation from God began with a command to give up the only home he knew. Just like Hosea, Abraham immediately

---

7   An excerpt of Genesis 13:14-16 (ESV).

8   An excerpt of Genesis 15:1-5 (ESV). This is the first "fear not" in all of Scripture, a phrase God the Father loves to communicate as seen throughout His Word. Jesus also spoke this command quite often, including the final "fear not" in the Bible (Revelation 1:17).

9   The times to Abraham are found in Genesis 12:1-3, 13:14-17, 15:1-6, 17:1-8, 18:18-19, and 22:15-18. The one time with Isaac is recorded in Genesis 26:3-5. To Jacob, the covenant comes forth in Genesis 28:13-15, 35:9-12, and 46:1-4.

obeyed and later found himself with a son out of wedlock.[10]

Both men, amid such familial strife, desperately needed a reminder of God's promise. For Abraham, thirteen years had passed without Sarah conceiving or any affirmation from the Lord.[11] For Hosea, God had just looked upon Israel and mournfully declared, "You are not mine, and I am not yours." Indeed, at the bottom, right when their situations seemed hopeless, that's when their reminders came. Imagine Hosea going back and rereading these words:

> I am God Almighty; walk before me, and be blameless . . .
> And I will establish my covenant between me and you
> and your offspring after you throughout their generations
> for an everlasting covenant, to be God to you and to your
> offspring after you . . . **and I will be their God.**
> —Genesis 17:1b, 7-8 (ESV)

This is why God gave His reminder to Hosea precisely when He did; the very covenant Abraham received was the very counter to Hosea's Lo-Ammi. Though God's family resemblance in Israel had vanished, His promise would forever stand tall. In essence, the Lord was saying, *Israel looks nothing like Me, cares nothing for Me, but take heart, Hosea. I have not forgotten My vow.*

Though Israel grew faithless, the Lord would forever be faithful.

Notice also that God didn't just shout, "Remember the covenant!" No, in His infinite wisdom, the Lord chose a specific line to quote, referencing "the sand of the sea." This was intentional, for out of all ten versions of the Abrahamic covenant, God used this phrase only once—on Mount Moriah.[12] Only after Abraham had endured his most gut-wrenching test, when God had provided the ram instead of Isaac, did the patriarch hear

---

10   It should be noted that the circumstance surrounding the birth of Hosea's son out of wedlock—Lo-Ammi—was decidedly different than that of Abraham's son Ishmael. In Hosea's case, Gomer cheated. Abraham, on the other hand, did the deed with his servant Hagar for lack of trust in God's timing.

11   Saying God didn't affirm Abraham for the thirteen years after Ishmael's birth is to say we have no record of Him doing so. Genesis 16 ends with a declaration that Ishmael was born to eighty-six-year-old Abram. Then Chapter 17 picks up with Abram being ninety-nine. Thus, having no record of significant events in Abram's life over those years, it can be safely suggested that no significant revelation occurred.

12   Technically, it is the angel of the Lord delivering this message to Abraham in Genesis 22, but the "sand of the sea" phrase was also quoted by Jacob back to God in Genesis 32:12.

those precious words. Only after declaring, "Jehovah Jireh" (meaning 'the Lord will provide') did Abraham hear:

> "By myself I have sworn, declares the LORD, because you have done this and have not withheld your son, your only son, I will surely bless you, and I will surely multiply your offspring as the stars of heaven and as **the sand that is on the seashore.**"
>
> —GENESIS 22:16-17A (ESV)

No reminder could have been sweeter to Hosea's ears, no phrase more apt. It was God's way of hugging the prophet's heart, telling him, *Don't worry, child. I provided a substitute for Isaac in his darkest hour, as I always will for My own.*

This wasn't about the Hebrew population increasing. Some two hundred years prior, during King Solomon's reign, "the people of Judah and Israel were as numerous as the sand on the seashore."[13] That part of the covenant had been fulfilled. This was about the *spiritual* children of Israel—all those of faith—being provided a Substitute. Yes, this would include a Jewish remnant, but also the fullness of the Gentiles, who one day will surely comprise "a great multitude that no one could number!"[14]

Finally, after all the doom and gloom, it was time for hope. This was Hosea's "But God" moment, when Light broke through his darkness at last.[15] And yet, what happened that day was only God's preamble. Even more promises were on the way.

## THE PROMISE OF A REVERSAL

After declaring the covenant to Hosea afresh, the Lord released a wave of assurances. What began as a timely reminder turned into a

---

13  An excerpt of 1 Kings 4:20 (NIV).

14  An excerpt of Revelation 7:9 (ESV). Also in this sentence are allusions to Isaiah 10:22, Romans 9:27, 11:25, and Galatians 3:7.

15  The miracle of heaven's Light breaking through the darkness extends far beyond Hosea's personal experience to that of all believers (1 Peter 2:9), and to some extent the whole world (John 1:4-9). Fascinatingly, Isaiah 9:2-3 goes even further, connecting this concept of shining heavenly light to God's nation being "multiplied."

launchpad of redemption. God's first sentence alone could have brought the house down:

> "And it shall come to pass
> In the place where it was said to them,
> 'You are not My people,'
> There it shall be said to them,
> **'You are sons of the living God.'"**
> —HOSEA 1:10B (NKJV)

At a glance, this may seem like a plain reversal of Lo-Ammi, but to Hosea, hearing God's voice like this had to be wildly shocking. "Sons of the living God" was far from a casual term to a Jew. To be a son meant to be an heir, a precious family member, an inheritor in a long line of revered ancestors.

While this may sound normal to a New Testament believer, no Jew would have called himself a "son of God" (or God his own Father) because they saw it as claiming equality with God. That's why when Jesus did so, the

What began as a timely reminder turned into a launchpad of redemption.

religious leaders tried to kill him. And yet, when Jesus asks the disciples who they think He is, how does Peter respond? By saying, "Thou art the Christ, **the Son of the living God.**"[16]

Clearly, such phrasing was sacred. Even the simpler term "sons of God" was reserved for angelic beings in Old Testament times.[17] So what was God communicating to Hosea? Thankfully, the apostle Paul connects the dots for us in his letter to the church in Rome. It wasn't that the Jews

---

16  An excerpt from Matthew 16:16 (KJV). For the primary instance of the Jews seeking to kill Jesus for calling God "My Father," see John 5:18.

17  See Genesis 6:2-4 and Job 1:6, 2:1, 38:7. Some scholars claim that these "sons of God" in Genesis 6 were merely humans in high places. Others—including the oft-lionized Augustine of Hippo—have suggested that these ancient beings were no more than the descendants of Seth. The author of this work, however, sides with true early church fathers like Justin Martyr, Irenaeus, Clement of Alexandria, and Tertullian who all held that these "sons of God" in Genesis 6 were fallen angels. Also backing these venerable sources are the Septuagint renderings to *angelos*, multiple documents among the Dead Sea Scrolls, the writings of Josephus, and even Jude 1:6-7.

were to all become angels,[18] but rather, it was a promise that *the Son of the living God* would gain brothers of all kinds—that the Messiah would welcome fellow heirs conformed to His image.[19]

For a Jew, little could have been more wonderful to imagine.

Still, God wasn't finished. After His global promises, the Lord chose to get personal. In so doing, one by one, each child's name previously pronounced in judgment would be turned upside down. Studying such reversals offers a profound glimpse not only into what God loves but also who He is.

### REVERSAL ONE: THE GATHERING OF JEZREEL

Naturally, the first of the three names redeemed was that of Hosea's firstborn, Jezreel. Remember, Jezreel was known as a place of death and bloodshed. Multiple gruesome slaughters punctuated its history. Surely, if there was a physical valley of the shadow of death, Jezreel would be it. How then would God redeem such a place? With one of the most majestic declarations of all:

> And the children of Judah and the children of Israel shall be **gathered together**, and they shall appoint for themselves one head. And they shall go up from the land, for great shall be the day of Jezreel.
>
> —Hosea 1:11 (ESV)

This was no small promise. After reminding Hosea of the covenant and hinting at a new one, God—in two short sentences—offers a glimpse of how His plan will end. And what a glorious glimpse it was.

For centuries, the Jewish people had been divided. Generations of war and animosity plagued the land—brother against brother, tribe

---

18  Though God's children will by no means become angels, there are peculiar similarities that the elect gain upon spiritual adoption to the heavenly hosts. For example, the Hebrew word מַלְאָךְ (*malak*) that translates to "angel" is also the word for a messenger or representative, which all children of God become (2 Corinthians 5:20). *Malak* is even used of human messengers many times in Scripture (Genesis 32:3, Joshua 7:22, 1 Samuel 19:20). Additionally, just as those who inherit salvation are deemed God's "elect" (Romans 8:33), Paul uses the same Greek word ἐκλεκτός (*eklektos*) to describe "the elect angels" (1 Timothy 5:21) that serve the saved (Hebrews 1:14)!

19  Paul connects the dots in Hosea to spiritual sons of God in Romans 9:25-26. This concept of sonship, as well as co-heirship and conformity to Christ—is unpacked by Paul just prior in Romans 8:14-29.

against tribe. Deep in the hearts of the people resided a certain sadness, a longing for the days of David to return, for the unity and peace they once knew.[20]

It cannot be overstated just how powerful a promise this would have been for Hosea. For Judah and Israel to be *gathered together* meant radical restoration. Imagine a bitterly estranged family enjoying a meal, reunited at last—except on the scale of North and South Korea. No more collusion, no more malice.

O, how desperately Hosea's heart needed such a vision as he grieved his own family's implosion! How he must have pined for the joyous smiles of his kin, the laughter around his table, the snuggles of his runaway wife. Just like Israel, Hosea's family desperately needed heaven's restoration.

How timely, in redeeming the name Jezreel, was God's promise to gather His people. Recall that Jezreel in Hebrew can mean "God will scatter," a repeated warning against idolatry in the Old Testament. Well, amazingly, the reverse of such scattering—for God to gather His people—is even more prevalent.[21] Sometimes it's described as a shepherd gathering his lambs; other times, it's a march home from the four corners of the earth.[22] The key is, as Jeremiah says, "He who scattered Israel will gather them."[23]

> Imagine a bitterly estranged family enjoying a meal, reunited at last— except on the scale of North and South Korea.

This brings us to the aspect of God's unified people **appointing for themselves one head** and **going up from the land**. The Hebrew words here for appoint and head, שׂוּם (*soom*) and ראשׁ (*roshe*), are used in conjunction to describe the appointing of all kinds of leaders, from a replacement

---

20  To be clear, the early days of King David's reign are in view here, before his lust for Bathsheba threw the kingdom into chaos.

21  See the following verses: Deuteronomy 30:3-4; Nehemiah 1:9; Isaiah 27:12, 49:5, 54:7, 56:8; Jeremiah 3:17, 29:14, 31:8-10, 32:37; and John 11:52.

22  The gathering of lambs by a shepherd comes from Isaiah 40:11 and Jeremiah 23:3. The march from the four corners of the earth refers to passages like Isaiah 11:12 and 43:5-6.

23  An excerpt of Jeremiah 31:10 (NIV). This is the ongoing mission of God, to the Jew first and also to the Greek (Isaiah 56:8, Romans 1:16).

for Moses to heads of tribes, commanders of armies, priests, judges, and incoming kings.[24] This one head, however, would embody them all.

As for God's people going "up from the land," that phrase is used twenty times in the Bible, and every single time *except* Hosea 1:11 explicitly refers to liberation from the land of Egypt (to geographically higher Judea).[25] Similarly, in the future described to Hosea, God's people seem to be returning to dwell in the Promised Land under an appointed head.[26] Which leaves us one final question: What makes this "Day of Jezreel" so great?

This answer is not so simple. A few different views exist,[27] but one thing is certain: God's promise to Hosea, like all the others in Scripture, finds its Yes in Christ. When it comes to gathering the children of God, look to Jesus, for as the high priest Caiaphas prophesied, "Jesus would die for the nation, and not for the nation only, but also **to gather into one the children of God who are scattered abroad**."[28]

Bluntly, only in Christ is reunion with God possible. Jesus Himself said, "Whoever is not with me is against me, and whoever does not **gather** with me **scatters**."[29] Likewise, when it comes to unifying a people, look to Jesus, for the Father's ultimate plan is "to bring unity to all things in heaven and on earth under Christ."[30] He is the head of man, the head of the church, the head over all things.[31]

Surely, Jesus is the ultimate *roshe*: the new and greater Moses, the

---

24  In order, these references are Numbers 14:4/Nehemiah 9:17, Deuteronomy 1:13-15, Deuteronomy 20:9, 2 Chronicles 19:8, and 2 Chronicles 11:22.

25  The count of twenty phrase appearances was according to the NASB95. For a smattering of these verses, see Exodus 32:1-8, Deuteronomy 20:1, Judges 19:30, 1 Samuel 12:6, 1 Kings 12:28, 2 Kings 17:7, Psalm 81:10, Jeremiah 11:7, Amos 2:10, and Micah 6:4.

26  Not only is it implied that God would gather His children together in the land associated with His oft-repeated covenant, but plenty of passages explicitly declare this to be true. Perhaps most notable is Isaiah 11:11, which explicitly refers to a second recovery of God's people to the land.

27  It could be, for example, that the promise in question, while surely describing in part the future reign of Christ, is also foreshadowing when all nations will be going up to Jerusalem (see Jeremiah 3:17, Zechariah 8:22, and Micah 4:2). Others who reject a literal reign may say it is purely metaphorical for the church, whose head is Christ (Ephesians 1:22), with the physical land promised to Abraham now being a non-factor. Debating such things falls outside the scope of this work, but the study of such is highly encouraged, as it can drastically affect one's view on the importance of modern-day Israel and Jews in general. A great place to start is Romans 11.

28  An excerpt of John 11:51-52 (ESV). Also note the similarity to Isaiah 49:5.

29  Matthew 12:30 (ESV).

30  An excerpt of Ephesians 1:10 (NIV).

31  These references in order are 1 Corinthians 11:3, Colossians 1:18, Ephesians 1:22, and Colossians 2:10.

Lion of the tribe of Judah, the One with legions of angels on speed dial.[32] He is the Great High Priest, the Supreme Judge, the coming King of Kings.[33] Yes, Jesus of Nazareth is the Light of the world, born in a land of bloodshed to shed His own blood for us.

And that's just name one.

### REVERSAL TWO: THE ACCEPTANCE OF LO-AMMI

The second name God reversed is not the one you would expect.

In birth order, Lo-Ruhamah should have been next in line. And yet, upon finishing his declaration about Jezreel, God skips right to Lo-Ammi. Ending with a bang, the Lord finishes His promise with the line: "**Say to your brothers, 'My people!'** and to your sisters, 'My loved one!'"[34] Granted, He redeems both names in the same sentence, but the order God chose was far from meaningless.

As we've seen in the names, even the tiniest details in Scripture were thoughtfully crafted by the Lord to get His message across. This time, it's all about His magnificent, marvelous, and matchless love.[35] As commentator Albert Barnes deftly wrote, "The words form a climax of the love of God. First, the people scattered, unpitied, and disowned by God, is re-born of God; then it is declared to be in **continued relation** to God, 'My people;' then to be the object of his yearning love."

In other words, when God redeems a human heart, He does so in the same sequence that He redeemed Gomer's children: first by gathering (or drawing) souls to His Son, then adopting them as His own, and finally by keeping them in His compassionate love. It's the story of salvation, unfolding one redeemed name at a time.

As grand as that sounds, this pronouncement may not have been all that shocking to Hosea. Six hundred fifty years prior, in Moses' last days, the great lawgiver gave the people one final address. Throughout

---

32  These references in order are Hebrews 3:3-5, Revelation 5:5, and Matthew 26:53. For more on Jesus being the "new Moses," check out the online article titled, "The Sermon on the Mount and Jesus as the New Moses" by The Bible Project.

33  These references in order are Hebrews 4:14-15, Acts 10:42, and 1 Timothy 6:15. The Lord as king over all the earth can also be seen in Zechariah 14:9.

34  Hosea 2:1 (WEB).

35  A nod to the fantastic song by Keith and Kristyn Getty, "Magnificent, Marvelous, Matchless Love."

his oration, there were various blessings and reminders, even a song. Perhaps most intriguing, however, is the prophecy within. Listen to how strikingly similar this sounds to Hosea:

> And when all these things come upon you, the blessing and the curse, which I have set before you, and you call them to mind among all the nations where the LORD your God has driven you, and return to the LORD your God, you and your children, and obey his voice in all that I command you today, with all your heart and with all your soul, then the LORD your God will restore your fortunes and **have mercy on you**, and **he will gather you** again from all the peoples where the LORD your God has **scattered** you. If your outcasts are in the uttermost parts of heaven, from there the LORD your **God will gather you**, and from there he will take you. And the LORD your God will bring you **into the land** that your fathers possessed, that you may possess it. And he will make you more prosperous and **numerous** than your fathers . . . For the LORD will again **take delight in prospering you**, as he took delight in your fathers.
>
> —Deuteronomy 30:1-5, 9b (ESV)

Now think of Hosea, watching this all play out in the names of his children. In the middle of his nightmare, this had to be a dream come true.

Clearly, one simple sentence from the mouth of the Almighty can pack quite the restorative punch. The reversal of Lo-Ammi must have shot shockwaves of hope through Hosea's pain, as it should ours, because it's a storyline every heart craves—the path from rejection to affection.[36] We're talking about the longing of every bullied child, every estranged spouse, every spurned parent—that rapturous moment when the long-closed door finally opens, when the script flips. Many

---

36  In one sense, God did reject Israel as stated in passages like Isaiah 2:6. But this was not permanent; it was more a rejection of who Israel had become than the nation itself, as Leviticus 26:44 illustrates. Thus, it is not a contradiction to say she went from rejection to affection while also positing that God remained faithful to His bride.

relationships never see this sort of change come full circle, but God's marriage will.

Over and over, Israel had rejected her Husband, just as Gomer did Hosea, running to the world for pleasure and protection.[37] But God, being rich in mercy, because of the great love with which He loved her, even when she was dead in her trespasses, thundered, "My people!" Though she had rejected Him, the Majestic Glory would come for His bride.

If there's one thing to learn from Lo-Ammi's redemption, it's that Jehovah is a covenant-keeping God. He never forgot—nor will He ever forget—the vows He pronounced to the patriarchs. Perhaps no better passage lays this out than one buried at the end of Leviticus, where the Lord predicts Israel's adultery and exile.

> Though she had rejected Him, the Majestic Glory would come for His bride.

In the very same breath, God makes an unwavering promise to *forever be hers.* Hear the Almighty's burning devotion to His bride in His own words as He brings His law to a close:

> For the land will be abandoned by them, and will make up for its sabbaths while it is made desolate without them. They, meanwhile, will be making amends for their iniquity, because they rejected My ordinances and their soul abhorred My statutes. Yet in spite of this, when they are in the land of their enemies, **I will not reject them**, nor will I so abhor them as to destroy them, breaking My covenant with them; for I am the LORD their God. **But I will remember for them the covenant with their ancestors**, whom I brought out of the land of Egypt in the sight of the nations, that I might be **their God**. I am the LORD.
>
> —LEVITICUS 26:43-45 (NASB95)

---

37  A few places that overtly state Israel's rejection of God are Numbers 11:20, 1 Samuel 8:7, and Hosea 4:6.

Israel grieved God more than we'll ever know. Nonetheless, when the Lord claims a people as His beloved bride, He means it. Modern man may come up with a list of exceptions to "till death do us part," but not the Creator. And make no mistake: His reversal of Lo-Ammi wasn't God changing His mind—not even close. It was a declaration of what He had already predicted centuries prior coming to pass, confirming the certainty of this most joyful turn of events.

And still, there's one final reversal to unpack.

## REVERSAL THREE: THE RELIEF OF LO-RUHAMAH

The last name to be restored was the first to be born out of wedlock: little Lo-Ruhamah. Her brothers had already heard their heavenly redemption resound. For Jezreel, the scattered would be gathered; for Lo-Ammi, acceptance was imminent. Now, it was their sister's turn.

Remember, Lo-Ruhamah meant "No mercy" or "She that never knew a father's love," and for good reason. Israel had heinously spat in God's face for generations. More mercy would have only spoiled Israel worse. Thus, to Hosea's daughter came this name, a prophecy of judgment coming home to roost.

> Yes, Israel was headed for exile, but God wouldn't leave her there.

As the Lord put it to Hosea's contemporary, the prophet Amos, "The end has come for My people Israel. I will spare them no longer."[38] And yet, here was a ray of hope. Yes, Israel was headed for exile, *but God* wouldn't leave her there.

Now keep in mind that the reversal of Lo-Ruhamah was a package deal with Lo-Ammi. Don't forget, God made it all one sentence deliberately:

> "Say to your brothers, 'My people!' and to your sisters, 'My loved one!'"
>
> —HOSEA 2:1 (WEB)

Why? Because they are inseparable. To be in God's family is to be His beloved. Even the most rebellious bride, the most obstinate child,

---

38   An excerpt of Amos 8:2 (NASB95).

when embraced by the Almighty, shall be rejoiced over in the end. As the prophet Zephaniah said, a day would come when Israel would finally hear these words:

> "The LORD has taken away his judgments
>> against you . . .
> **The LORD your God** is in your midst,
>> a mighty one who will save;
> he will rejoice over you with gladness;
>> **he will quiet you by his love**;
> he will exult over you with loud singing."
>> —ZEPHANIAH 3:15A, 17 (ESV)

Simply put, only if God is *yours* will you know His love. When you are His and He is yours, "My loved one!" bursts forth from both parties.

Envision a couple reuniting after a long stint apart or a dog at the sight of its beloved owner, home at last. That's the natural response to belonging. It's the way believers greet God because it's how He first greeted them.

Still, as beautiful as that sounds, the opposite also holds true. While God loves the whole world, those who never know Him *never know it.*[39] And without that knowledge, there's no relationship, no joyous greeting, no eternal life.

Everything rides on this.

Just ask Jesus, who said in prayer to His Father, "Now this is eternal life, **that they may know You**, the only true God, and Jesus Christ, whom You have sent."[40] There is no other way to heaven but to know God and His love. Otherwise, we will hear at the throne, "I never knew you. Depart from me."[41]

---

39  Two key verses declaring God's love for the world are John 3:16 and 1 John 2:2. That said, there is disagreement among scholars as to which meaning of "world" [Gk. *kosmos*] is intended in these passages. Some believe, in light of verses like Psalm 5:5 and 11:5, that John does not mean God intimately loves every person on earth, but rather every *type* of person. This view coincides with the use of *kosmos* by John elsewhere, such as John 12:19 (NIV) where the Pharisees say, "Look, *the whole world* has gone after him [Jesus]!" implying a great number of all types of people, not every human on the planet. Others take John's writings to mean God intimately loves every single person but has simultaneously given us the free choice whether or not to return the favor. Either way, the main error to avoid is using these words of John out of context in conjunction with one-liners like Romans 11:32 and 2 Peter 3:9 to claim all people will be saved by God's universal love. This notion is called "Universalism," and it is false.

40  John 17:3 (BSB).

41  An excerpt of Matthew 7:23 (ESV).

Don't be fooled by the world's definition of love, chalking love up to euphoric emotions and celebrated sin. "We know love by this," said John the Apostle, "that He laid down His life for us; and we ought to lay down our lives for the brethren."[42]

**This is the key to cheerful servanthood.** Only if we know the Father's love will we leave our selfishness behind. Only if we see Him as wonderful will our hearts become the same. It all comes down to whether we've been brought near to Him, calling out like Thomas, "My Lord and my God!"[43] Otherwise, our service stinks of fear or pride, trying to show God just how good we are so we can get blessed. Any efforts like that collapse back into selfishness.

> Don't be fooled by the world's definition of love, chalking love up to euphoric emotions and celebrated sin.

This is why the Bible makes the unabashed claim that if you don't know God, you can't be loving.[44] It's not just because you won't know *how* to love; it's because without thankfulness for Love, you're legitimately unable. He who doesn't know Love Himself can only love himself.

Don't let the reversal of Lo-Ruhamah just be one more feel-good statement. It's not. What God declared over Lo-Ruhamah changes everything. Just imagine kneeling before the King of the Universe, and despite all your rebellion, you hear the words, "My loved one!"

Well, for those in Christ, that dream will come true one day. See, while God's final reversal sentence spoke to the names of Hosea's children, it wasn't just for them. God told Hosea to call his *brothers and sisters* these things, not just his kids. Thus, the Lord's words were for the whole nation,

---

42  1 John 3:16 (NASB95).
43  An excerpt of John 20:28 (ESV).
44  A reference to 1 John 4:7-8. Also, it is implied by Galatians 5:22, where love is listed in the fruit of the Spirit. Of course, there are lesser loves than incorruptible *agape* (Ephesians 6:24), of which people are still capable—romantic love for example—regardless of their worldview. The noted sentence refers only to heavenly love, the kind that comes "from a pure heart" (1 Timothy 1:5). To make this clear, the New Testament carefully uses four different Greek words for love: *eros* (romantic), *philia* (friendly), *storge* (familial), and *agape* (divine). These key differences get lost in English translations that merge them under one banner of "love." For instance, when Jesus thrice asks Peter, "Do you love me?" in John 21:15-17, the first two times He uses *agape*, but the final time He switches to *philia*. Meanwhile, Peter responds all three times in the affirmative, but each time he claims *philia* love for Jesus.

Hosea's spiritual family—including all those grafted in.

May this serve as a blessed assurance that, whether ancient Jew or modern Christian, whosoever lives by faith shall be kept in the Father's love.[45] This is the meaning of salvation, to know "the tender mercies of our God, whereby the sunrise shall visit us from on high to give light to those who sit in darkness and in the shadow of death, to guide our feet into the way of peace."[46] Or, as the apostle Peter put it:

> But you are a chosen race, a royal priesthood, a holy nation, a people for his own possession, that you may proclaim the excellencies of Him who called you out of darkness into his marvelous light. Once you were not a people, **but now you are God's people**; once you had not received mercy, **but now you have received mercy**.
>
> —1 PETER 2:9-10 (ESV)

Love comes from a sense of belonging, always. Israel stopped cheerfully serving because she had forgotten the Father's love. *But God*, being rich in mercy, would come for His own.

---

45 The notion of living by faith is found in Romans 1:17, Galatians 3:11, and Hebrews 10:38-39. The language of being "kept" in the love of God can be found most notably in Jude 1:21, but also in Jude 1:1 and John 17:15.

46 An excerpt of Luke 1:78-79 (ESV).

#  HIDDEN GEMS

## JESUS: OUR SCRIPT FLIPPER

The name of Hosea's son Jezreel was met with a promise of united ascent. ➤ Jesus will come in the fullness of time to unite all things to Himself. *(John 17:20-21, Ephesians 1:10)*

The name of Hosea's son Jezreel found redemption in the gathering of God's people. ➤ Jesus is gathering the nations to Himself. *(Matthew 12:30, Matthew 25:31-32)*

The name of Hosea's son Lo-Ammi was met with a promise of precious acceptance. ➤ Jesus accepted rejection to offer acceptance eternally. *(Luke 9:22, Ephesians 1:6)*

The name of Hosea's son Lo-Ammi found redemption in being claimed by God. ➤ Jesus was twice claimed by God's own voice. *(Matthew 3:17, Matthew 17:5)*

The name of Hosea's daughter Lo-Ruhamah was met with a promise of compassionate love. ➤ Jesus showed compassionate love to those being denied it. *(Matthew 9:36, Mark 1:41)*

The name of Hosea's daughter Lo-Ruhamah found redemption in knowing the Father's love. ➤ Jesus knew the Father's love and prayed that we would too. *(John 14:31, John 17:26)*

**BOTTOM LINE:** ─────────────────────────

Jesus flips scripts from tragedy to victory, taking death to give life. *(1 Corinthians 15:20-22, 2 Corinthians 5:21)*

# WRAP UP:
## Never Forget the Future

Sometimes, what the heart needs most is a reminder of the hope it once knew.

Consider what happened when Hosea's family imploded. His wife was missing, his children had scattered, and his reputation was gone with the wind. *But God* wouldn't leave His prophet there. One moment, Hosea was naming his children terms of sharp judgment; the next, he was hearing of hope. For Hosea's family—and the nation they typified—redemption was on the way.

**It's critical in times of despair that we remember the covenants of God.** When everything seems to be collapsing around us, there is no better place to turn. Only with such assurances can we say like the apostle Paul, "I consider that the sufferings of this present time are not worth comparing with the glory that is to be revealed to us."[47]

This is what makes Christian joy invincible. When the heart hopes in eternity, even our gravest hardships can be overcome. Like rain on a windshield, our vision may be muddled and our driving slowed, but inside, we remain unharmed.

Of course, that doesn't mean pain and sorrow evaporate. In this world, tribulation is guaranteed, right up there with death and taxes.[48] But if we hold fast to the hope set before us, instead of drowning in our tears, joy shall bring us home:

> For momentary, light affliction is producing for us an eternal weight of glory far beyond all comparison.
> —2 Corinthians 4:17 (NASB95)

This was what God gave Hosea in his darkest hour—assurance that all would be made right in the end.

---

47  An excerpt of Romans 8:18 (ESV).

48  Guaranteed tribulation is a reference to John 16:33. Death and taxes being certain comes from a quote by Benjamin Franklin, who ironically denounced the 1773 Boston Tea Party as "an act of violent injustice."

That said, God's promises aren't instant fixes. As much as we may long for our problems to spontaneously combust like a pile of oily rags, it rarely works that way. Gomer didn't fling open the door the second God recited His covenant; she was still with her lovers, and Hosea was still estranged.

So how would God bring her back? And who would pay for her despicable crimes?

Someone would.

# ENGAGE: Group Study 8

**STARTER** How can remembering Old Testament covenants benefit someone's faith?

**TRIVIA** In the Protestant Old Testament, there are thirty-nine books. How many are in the Hebrew Bible?[49]

**REFLECT** When you were at your lowest moment, how did your hope revive? In what ways do you feel you've grown as a result?

**PONDER** Is it fair for salvation to come to the disobedient?

**JOURNAL** What are you doing for the helpless? What can you start doing to help others more?

**BOIL IT DOWN** Jesus turns tragedies into testimonies of God's grace.

**BRING IT UP** What's the limit on blessing one's enemies?

**LIVE IT OUT** Write out God's covenant to you. List what He guarantees—and frame it!

---

49 The answer is twenty-four books. In the Hebrew Bible, the twelve "minor prophets" are lumped into a single book, and the books that Christians split into two parts—Samuel, Kings, and Chronicles—are not split either. Interestingly, the books of Ezra and Nehemiah are also joined in the Hebrew Scriptures. These differences account for the fifteen less books in the Hebrew Bible—known as the Tanakh—compared to the Protestant Old Testament.

# 9

# IT'S WHAT SHE SAID

*Israel boasts, "I am rich!*
*I've made a fortune all by myself!*
*No one has caught me cheating!*
*My record is spotless!"*
—Hosea 12:8 (NLT)

F OR HUNDREDS OF YEARS, ISRAEL cheated on God. Like Gomer, she
played the harlot, giving herself to all sorts of nations and idols.
On the one hand, God longed to redeem her, to revive the love she had
at first. But while the King of Creation is love personified, He is also the
Righteous Judge.[1]

Time and again, judgment was foretold, but Israel only ran further
away. How then could God be gracious to her?

When a heinous criminal is caught, a righteous judge doles out
justice, not promises of restoration. We want convicts to be punished, to

---

1   God being love personified is a reference to 1 John 4:8-16. He as the Righteous Judge is found throughout
    the Scriptures, particularly in Genesis 18:25, Psalm 9:8, and Isaiah 30:18.

feel the pain they caused. But what if you could transform their hearts instead—would you still prefer to lock them up?

Of course, transformation often comes *through* discipline, but most penal systems rarely get ex-convicts to stop committing crimes, much less undergo real heart change. The American prison system, for example, sees nearly 80 percent of released inmates back behind bars within six years. So what's the most loving yet just thing to do—especially with a repeat offender?

**This is God's great catch-22:** His mercy calls for forgiveness, but His justice demands a reckoning. Both elements are seen throughout Scripture, curiously coexisting. In the wilderness and the Promised Land, through the time of the Judges and days of the Kings, God's judgment and mercy run together. No better passage recounts this than Nehemiah 9:6-31, the people's confession while under Persian rule.

Take a moment, set this book aside, and give that section of Nehemiah a read. Afterward, compare what you read to the graph below, as the cycle comes up over and over:

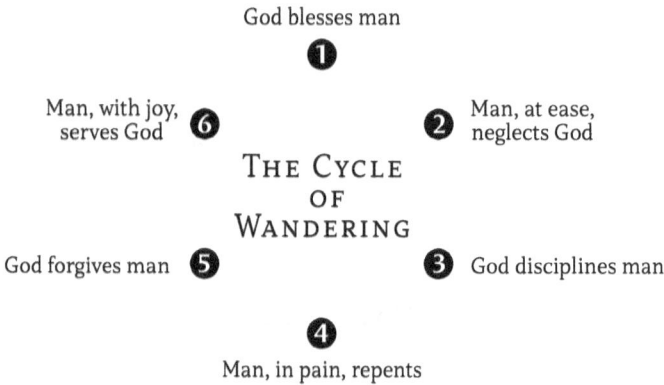

God blesses man
❶

Man, with joy, serves God ❻

Man, at ease, neglects God ❷

THE CYCLE
OF
WANDERING

God forgives man ❺

God disciplines man ❸

❹
Man, in pain, repents

Gomer had wandered far from her husband, and in those days, adultery was a death sentence. Anyone caught was stoned. So, would God administer justice or work redemption? Survey says: both.

Despite mankind's extreme evil, God promises to romance His people, and yet despite His mercy, God promises to judge His creation. Merciful love and resolute justice—two very different virtues that coalesce in the

King. Meditating on such brings the heart to worship, as it did for David, who declared: "I will sing of your **love and justice**; to you, LORD, I will sing praise."[2]

Even Jesus Himself taught His hearers to focus on "the weightier matters of the law: **justice and mercy** and faithfulness."[3] And not only that, God's very name proclaims this reality. Look carefully at how the Father describes Himself when passing by Moses in the cleft of the rock:

> The LORD, the LORD, a God **merciful and gracious**, slow to anger and abounding in steadfast love and faithfulness, keeping steadfast love for thousands, forgiving iniquity and transgression and sin, **but who will by no means clear the guilty**, visiting the iniquity of the fathers on the children and the children's children, to the third and the fourth generation.
>
> —Exodus 34:6-7 (ESV)

God is on a mission to redeem people for Himself, but He can't just let them off scot-free. Sin matters, and it must be paid for. In Israel's situation, before such a sentencing, the nation's crimes had to be laid out, the allegations heard. Indeed, as Hosea 2 vividly illustrates, Israel was headed for heaven's Supreme Court.

## FULLY CHARGED

Picture it: The courtroom is immaculate, every pew aligned. The bailiff stands at attention. Slowly, the seats are filled by those who have heard the rumblings. Tension sits thick on the shoulders of all present, awaiting the looming proceedings. Whispers pierce the air until, at last, the courtroom door opens. As the heads turn, down the aisle walks Israel, a complete reversal of her wedding day. All eyes again are upon her, but this time, it's not admiration they exude—it's disgust. The damsel is

2   An excerpt of Psalm 101:1 (NIV).
3   An excerpt of Matthew 22:23 (ESV).

now the defendant.

"All rise!" booms the bailiff. "The honorable Almighty is presiding."

Suddenly, a sweeping reverence overtakes the room as the Grand Arbiter enters, takes the bench, and sets His eyes on the accused. Israel proceeds to place her hand on the very Book she helped write.[4] Indeed, the Law under her palm was the one she had neglected. After she nervously swears in, the gavel thunders, hushing every lip and thought in the room. **Justice is coming**.

This is the scene we come upon in Hosea 2. After declaring a gracious reversal of the children's names, God Almighty surprisingly turns His attention to exposing the crimes of His beloved Israel. As He stated in pronouncing His name to Moses, though the Lord may be ever merciful, He will by no means clear the guilty. Thus, we find the Judge of the Universe ensconced on the proverbial bench, about to read the charges against His adulterous wife.

Before moving on, it's critical to address just how emotionally charged the situation would have been. God declares Himself to be a jealous God, even going so far as to call His own name "Jealous," and nothing triggers white-hot wrath quite like catching one's spouse in adultery.[5] As Proverbs puts it, "For jealousy arouses a husband's fury, and he will show no mercy when he takes revenge."[6]

To think God Almighty, Love Himself, witnessed His bride in the act for two hundred years straight—it blows the mind. For such heartache, there are no words.

Meanwhile, Israel had become a hideous blend of calloused and terrified. God had done nothing but cherish her, and yet she discarded Him for other lovers. Israel knew full well what she deserved. The Law

---

4    Saying Israel helped write the Bible is a reference to the fact that, though the Spirit of God inspired the various authors to pen the pages of Scripture and didn't need "help," multiple Israelites played a role in its scribing.

5    The Lord's first declaration of being a "jealous God" comes in Exodus 20:5 as He gives the Ten Commandments to Moses. Shortly thereafter, following Israel's worship of the golden calf, He repeats the declaration and adds that His name is literally קַנָּא (*qanna*), the Hebrew word for "Jealous" (Exodus 34:14). Such jealousy is surely different than the sinful covetousness forbidden in the Law. Covetousness is the desire to possess that which belongs to others—but everything belongs to God (Deuteronomy 10:14, Job 41:11, Psalm 24:1). God's jealousy is the ferocity that accompanies love amid betrayal, a brutal grief that rightly arises in the heart of the Almighty when His beloved people spurn Him (Hosea 11:8).

6    Proverbs 6:34 (NIV).

was clear: Anyone caught in adultery was to be stoned to death.[7]

So there Israel stood, fully charged. Her crimes had reached their full measure; her cortisol was shooting through the roof.

Now, to be clear, Hosea 2 never says Gomer (or Israel) appeared before a judge, but the text uses language that paints a similar picture. God calls Israel into account, lists her crimes, and eventually pronounces the verdict.

Even so, there's no semblance of a prosecution or jury in Hosea 2. Visualizing a courtroom may help a modern reader relate to the spectacle, but biblically, such judgment takes place in a *throne room*. God is the great Judge, but He's also the High King, and kings don't resort to randomly selected civilians for a verdict. When you come before a king—especially *the* King—what happens is between you and Him. Everything hinges on that relationship alone.

**Many, like Israel, spend life running from the King**. Even among those who love Him, God often gets the scraps. Yet in the end, no matter how far we run or how near we draw, all of us will find ourselves before the throne of God.[8] And so here we see Israel, standing before the Almighty, the case against her primed and ready.

> When you come before a king—especially *the* King—what happens is between you and Him.

Surely, the nations had witnessed her evils, yet none were called to give an account. In the King's court, only one witness testifies.

To the stand, God calls Himself.

---

7   This law to stone those caught in adultery is found in Leviticus 20:10. Jesus, however, famously stops the mob from such a stoning in John 8:1-11 (though these verses aren't in the earliest manuscripts). Such mercy would have rocked those present, as striking down evil from the congregation in the Old Testament was viewed as admirable (Numbers 25:1-8). This new mercy exemplified by Jesus coincides with His radical reinterpretation of certain scriptures in the Sermon on the Mount, particularly Matthew 5:38-45.

8   All enemies of the Cross (Philippians 3:18) in the end will stand before the great white throne for judgment (Revelation 20:11-15). For those in Christ, however, it will be the throne of grace to which they have come before (Hebrews 4:16), a place not of accusation but reward (1 Corinthians 3:14). Beautiful descriptions of this throne can be found throughout Revelation, particularly in Chapter 4.

# DISORDER IN THE COURT

Imagine the King, with anger and longing, gazing upon His runaway bride. Perhaps after a few heavy seconds, He breaks the silence by quoting from Psalm 50:

> "Hear, O my people, and I will speak;
>> O Israel, **I will testify against you**.
>> I am God, your God . . .
>> What right have you to recite my statues
>> or take my covenant on your lips?
> For you hate discipline,
>> and you cast my words behind you . . .
>> These things you have done, and I have been silent;
>> **you thought that the I AM was one like yourself**.
> But now I rebuke you and lay the charge before you."
>> —Psalm 50:7, 16b-17, 21 (ESV)

Think about being there. The Majestic Glory, after quietly enduring centuries of adultery, was now to testify against His bride. Out of the thousands of offenses He suffered, which ones would He bring up? Just how gory would He get? Those answers—and much more—are waiting in Hosea 2.

**Pause for a moment and read Hosea 2:2-13.**

We soon discover in the prophet's second chapter that out of all the ways God could have recapped Israel's undoing, He recounts three of her most incriminating quotes. These quotations are the crux of the entire trial, the outline of Israel's offenses. Each represents a distinct disgrace that, when unpacked in succession, reveals not only Israel's moral decline but the way the devil has devoured people for millennia.

This is the enemy's three-step guide to spiritual ruin, his all-time bestseller on how *not* to serve: Royalty Refusal, Attempted Exploitation, and in the end, Entitled Prostitution. From these—the three amigos of selfish ambition—comes disorder and every vile practice.

Of course, living by this playbook is lethal, but studying it is vital. After all, if Christians are "to stand against the schemes of the devil," we must know what those schemes are.[9]

And so, the examination begins.

## EXHIBIT A: ROYALTY REFUSAL

The first crime exposed by God is the seed of all sin—a refusal to give God credit. Just listen to the quotation from Israel's lips that the Lord comes to first:

> "Upon her children also I will have no mercy . . .
> For their mother [Israel] has played the whore;
> > she who conceived them has acted shamefully.
> **For she said, 'I will go after my lovers,**
> > **who give me my bread and my water,**
> > **my wool and my flax, my oil and my drink."**
> > > —Hosea 2:4-5 (ESV)

Israel's transgressive trilogy all starts here. Long ago, the Lord had freed her from slavery, built her into a nation, and took her as His own. As God puts it later in Hosea:

> "I led them with cords of kindness,
> > with the bands of love,
> and I became to them as one who eases
> > the yoke on their jaws,
> > and I bent down to them and fed them."
> > > —Hosea 11:4 (ESV)

All along Israel's journey, even through her rebellion, God provided for her. That never changed. What *did* change was her recognition of God's provision.

God's point here is key: At the bottom of it all, Israel ran after her lovers, not because she was greedy or lustful, but because she forgot who gave her all she had. Her downfall didn't begin with an addiction to pleasure or

---

9   The quote is an excerpt of Ephesians 6:11 (ESV). To "stand" here (Gk. *istemi*) means to be publicly opposed to the deceitful pleasure traps of worldliness. Two verses later, in Ephesians 6:13, Paul writes a very similar verse but uses a slightly different Greek word (*anthistemi*) that is often translated "withstand," bringing in the aspect of resisting the temptation to fall away from confident faith (Luke 8:13-15, Hebrews 3:12-14).

thirst for fame. It started as all sin does: with a quiet, nagging suspicion that God wasn't the source of blessing—someone else was.

For some folks, that "someone" is a person with much to offer, be it looks or riches or skill. For others, that "someone" is themselves. Either way, the morality pendulum swings on this single pivot—the question of who deserves the praise for everything we have.

No matter where you turn in society, people compete for praise. From athletes to writers, big companies to little children, practically everyone wants an audience, an admirer, a five-star review. Social media proves it: We want likes.

**This longing is inside every human heart—the longing to feel valued.** As *Lord of the Rings* author J.R.R. Tolkien once said, "The praise of the praiseworthy is above all rewards." Unfortunately, most Westerners spend their lives chasing praise without caring much about where it comes from. In turn, life slowly becomes about numbers instead of nobility, view counts instead of values—and everything snowballs out of control.

So it was with Israel. She had gone down this gutter path for so long that it was nearly all she knew. Everything had become about her: her comfort, her abundance, her survival.

Just look back at the quote in Hosea 2:5. In one brief sentence, what word does she use seven times?

*"My, my, my, my, my, my, my."*

This is what happens when people lose sight of the Praiseworthy. Her selfishness was only a symptom of the root issue: her refusal to give God credit.

Imagine working long and hard on a thoughtful gift for someone you love. Precious hours and dollars are put in, from shopping to crafting to wrapping the present until it looks just right. Eventually, the big moment comes, and you hand over your gift, thinking about all the hard work you put in to make it the best present ever.

Immediately, your special someone loves it! As you take in all the jumps and squeals for joy, excitement electrifies your heart. But suddenly, things take a turn. Your beloved, with tears of appreciation, starts to thank everyone *but you.*

"I'm so glad that the manufacturer makes such quality!" your loved one says. "Look at the gorgeous design! Those machinists must have worked so hard to make this for me. I'm sure the delivery truck driver worked overtime during the holidays too. What a champion! And be sure to tell your boss how much I appreciate his generous pay scale so you could afford this."

How would that feel?

Now imagine how God felt with Israel. The Almighty had not only thoughtfully given His bride all she owned—He had created it. And yet, decade upon decade, generation after generation, she waltzed about claiming everything came from her collection of consorts.

At first blush, this may seem like a petty offense—not acknowledging someone's creativity, effort, and sacrifice—but it stabs far deeper than we realize. Think if you were an author working tirelessly on your first book. After years of penning paragraphs, the glorious day arrives when you save the final edit and ship it off for publication. But somewhere in the process, your sterling manuscript gets stolen and printed under someone else's name.

You'd be outraged. The copyright was supposed to be yours.

Well, if heaven had patents and copyrights, God would own them all. And just like in the legal world, creators deserve payment for their work and the esteem of their audience. Thus, it makes sense why God calls us to honor Him with the firstfruits of all our produce; as the Creator, the royalties belong to Him. Anything less is copyright infringement.

**Put bluntly, not giving back to God is stealing from Him.** That's why God, on the stand, goes on to say:

> "And she did not know
> > that it was I who gave her
> > the grain, the wine, and the oil . . .
> Therefore I will take back
> > **my** grain in its time,
> > and **my** wine in its season."
> —Hosea 2:8-9 (ESV)

By refusing to give God credit for His work, Israel racked up a massive debt. And now, payment was due.

> Simply put, who you credit for creation determines what you will worship.

At the end of the day, it all comes down to what you believe about the origin of life. If you think we're all just accidents—the product of space goop, explosions, and billions of years—then that is all you'll live for: this world. Simply put, who you credit for creation determines what you will worship. What God said through the prophet Jeremiah is telling:

"As a thief is shamed when caught,
    so the house of Israel shall be shamed:
they, their kings, their officials,
    their priests, and their prophets,
who say to a tree, 'You are my father,'
    and to a stone, 'You gave me birth.'
For they have turned their back to me . . ."
        —Jeremiah 27:26-27a (ESV)

Israel started worshipping nature, acting like trees and stones created them. Modern man may be tempted to snicker at such behavior, but that same ideology is pushed in public schools across America. Kids are taught that we all came from astronomical Pop Rocks—that quite literally, the stones gave us birth.[10]

When exchanging the truth about God for a lie, humans withhold from their Creator the thanks He's undoubtedly due. This was Israel's first high crime, and the soil from which the rest of her rebellion grew.

---

10  This is a reference to the Big Bang theory, a postulate that has been tragically taught *as fact* for years in science classes nationwide. For fear of mingling church and state, creationism isn't even an option worthy of debate in American public schools, outlawed by the Supreme Court in 1987. A couple of decades later, in 2005, intelligent design as a whole got expelled by America's highest court, deeming it "unscientific." Instead, we should trust the "real science" that all the matter and energy in the universe began in a dot, that the dot spontaneously exploded, and that 13.7 billion years coincidentally converted the resulting slime into our wildly complex, masterfully precise world. How handy. The important thing is to never challenge such an indisputable *theory*—if you want to keep your teaching job or research grant—because after all, it's dangerous to question a fact. (The author of this book holds a degree in astrophysics and blissfully drank the cultural Kool-Aid for years. Only after personal investigation into the wild assumptions surrounding the Big Bang did clarity come. Meanwhile, in 2015, the force-fed fudge factor called "Inflation" used to explain away massive issues with the Big Bang was disproven so blatantly that Princeton physicist Paul Steinhardt declared it "fundamentally untestable, and hence scientifically meaningless." And yet, there's still no questioning that we came from rocks.)

## EXHIBIT B: ATTEMPTED EXPLOITATION

Right on the coattails of Israel's royalty refusal comes a most curious second quotation. Instead of recounting what Israel had said, God proclaims what she *shall* say. Check it out:

> "She shall pursue her lovers
>     but not overtake them,
> and she shall seek them
>     but shall not find them.
> **Then she shall say,**
>     **'I will go and return to my first husband,**
>     **for it was better for me then than now.'"**
>
> —Hosea 2:7 (ESV)

At first glance, this sounds promising. After all, Israel's "first husband" was the Lord—a fact declared outright by multiple prophets in Scripture. For example, Isaiah quotes God telling His people:

> "For your Maker **is your husband;**
>     the LORD of hosts is His name . . .
> For the LORD has called you
>     like a wife . . ."
>
> —Isaiah 54:5-6a (ESV)

As for God being her *first* husband, the Lord—speaking in the book of Ezekiel—leaves no doubt:

> "I made you grow like a plant of the field. You grew and developed and entered puberty . . . when I looked at you and saw that you were old enough for love, I spread the corner of my garment over you and covered your naked body. I gave you my solemn oath and entered into a covenant with you, declares the Sovereign LORD, and you became mine."
>
> —Ezekiel 16:7a-8 (NIV)

Thus, it initially looks like Israel's second quotation—returning to her first husband—was one of hope, of God's bride finally turning things around. Even some scholars promote such a view, connecting this utterance to that of the prodigal son when he came to his senses and said, "How many of my father's hired servants have more than enough bread, but I perish here with hunger! **I will arise and go to my father** . . ."[11]

Israel's goal wasn't reconciliation; it was exploitation.

Undeniably, these quotes *sound* similar, but there is one massive difference. Israel's announcement ends with a self-centered declaration: "It was better for me back then!" For her, that's the punchline, the takeaway: chase whatever is best for self. Israel's goal wasn't reconciliation; it was exploitation.

The prodigal son, on the other hand, may have started out on a similar path, but that's not where he landed. Listen to the rest of his quote:

> "I will arise and go to my father, **and I will say to him,**
> **'Father, I have sinned against heaven and against you.**
> I am no longer worthy to be called your son. Treat me as one of your hired servants.'"
>
> —LUKE 15:18-19 (ESV)

Talk about a complete 180. Both Israel and the prodigal son came to a point of desperate grief, but only one was *godly grief.* This makes all the difference, for as the apostle Paul wrote, "Godly grief produces a repentance that leads to salvation without regret, whereas worldly grief produces death."[12]

Israel's motivation to return had nothing to do with getting right with God; it was about getting fed. In the words of the *Cambridge Bible for Schools and Colleges,* Israel's second quote was "not so much the expression of penitence, as of a longing to escape from the sense of misery."

In short, Israel just wanted her divine Sugar Daddy back, the One who would make her life comfortable again. But that's not who God is—or ever has been. The King doesn't marry so His wife can go live at the spa;

---

11   An excerpt of Luke 15:17-18 (ESV). The scholars that espouse such a view include Matthew Henry and Albert Barnes, the 17th and 19th century theologians, respectively, who wrote comprehensive Bible commentaries.

12   2 Corinthians 7:10 (ESV).

He marries to have a bride to walk with, to share the kingdom with, and to give Himself to in love.[13]

Israel got this all wrong. When things went south—or more accurately "north" to Assyria—instead of repentance, she sought relief. Like the pagan gods she adopted, Jehovah had merely become someone to appease for personal benefit. *Just do what He says and get what you want*, she thought.

Imagine if your spouse cheated on you for years and then came back with that attitude. Would you welcome your soulmate home? Yet this is so often how God gets treated. Many seek God for what He'll *give* them instead of desiring to serve Him.[14] They want all the benefits with none of the sacrifice because down deep, it isn't about Him; it's about them.

Israel, having credited others for her own creation, became all about herself. She'd stop at nothing to prosper, attempting to exploit Egypt, Assyria, and even God Almighty. But before we stamp her as despicable, we need to check ourselves for evidence of the same attitude.

Caring far more about ease than eternity, Israel's mistakes speak volumes about the human condition: the inclination to put self first. God's design, on the other hand, is the radical opposite: joyful service. Yes, heaven will be the site of eternal rest—from cursed labor and the labor pain of life[15]—but it won't be never-ending naptime! The Bible says those who make up God's bride (the church) will be in charge of many heavenly things, that even in eternity "His servants shall serve Him."[16] What a thought—serving God *forever*.

Nothing of the sort was on Israel's mind. She may have decided to return, but only for the benefits. Perhaps God would have quoted from the book of James at this point:

---

13 The concept of walking with God can be seen throughout Scripture (Genesis 3:8, 5:22-24, 6:9; Leviticus 26:12; and Micah 6:8). God "sharing" His kingdom with His bride is an allusion to Luke 12:32 where the Father is said to "give" His kingdom to Christ's disciples. And for God as a Husband giving Himself, see Ephesians 5:25.

14 To be clear, desiring eternal reward is not wrong. Hebrews 11:6 states that He rewards those who earnestly seek Him. The problem is not the want of gain but the lack of a desire to give which stems from an absence of appreciation.

15 Heaven as eternal rest is described at length in Hebrews 4:1-11. The cursed labor and labor pain of Genesis 3:16-19 will one day be no more as seen in verses like Revelation 14:13, 21:4, and 22:3.

16 An excerpt of Revelation 22:3 (ESV). The concept of Christians being in charge of heavenly things one day is a reference to Matthew 25:21-23.

"You ask and do not receive, because you ask wrongly,
to spend it on your passions. You adulterous people!"[17]
—JAMES 4:3-4A (ESV)

Or maybe He would have gone with the first recorded words of His Son: "Why were you looking for me?"[18] Either way, God wasn't about to reward such a selfish return, causing Israel to spiral and commit her final crime.

It would be the most heinous offense of all.

### EXHIBIT C: ENTITLED PROSTITUTION

Israel's final offense brings the story of Gomer to a head. Not only had she chosen the life of a harlot, but now she was flaunting it. Just look at her last jab—a tiny sentence with massive implications:

"Now I will uncover her lewdness
    in the sight of her lovers,
    and no one shall rescue her out of my hand.
And I will put an end to all her mirth,
    her feasts, her new moons, her Sabbaths,
    and all her appointed feasts.
And I will waste her vines and her fig trees,
    of which **she said,**
    **'These are my wages,**
    **which my lovers have given me.'"**
—HOSEA 2:10-12A (ESV)

How such a small spark can set ablaze a forest![19] It's one thing to commit adultery; it's another to brag about it. Such was Israel in the time of Hosea, a full-blown brazen prostitute. After centuries of cyclical wandering, no semblance of remorse remained. As God later put it to

---

17  An excerpt of James 4:3-4 (ESV).

18  An excerpt of Luke 2:49 (ESV). These are the first recorded words of Jesus on Earth, not accounting for Old Testament quotations from "the Angel of the Lord" or the messianic Servant. Interestingly, Jesus goes on to employ almost the exact same question at the outset of His ministry (John 1:38), on the way to His death (John 18:4), and outside the empty tomb (John 20:15)! Showing up at such pivotal times, one might well deduce that this is the single most important question each human heart must answer.

19  An excerpt of James 3:5 (NIV).

the prophet Jeremiah:

> "Were they ashamed when they committed abomination?
>     No, they were not at all ashamed;
>     **they did not know how to blush.**"[20]
>
> —JEREMIAH 6:15a (ESV)

What began as a simple denial of her Provider had become barefaced debauchery. This is how sin works: wrongdoing grooms the heart not to care. Pleasure addicts aren't made overnight; it's the slow, quiet fermentation of moldy behavior left unchecked. As C.S. Lewis wrote in his eternal classic, *Mere Christianity*, "An apparently trivial indulgence in lust or anger today is the loss of a ridge or railway line or bridgehead from which the enemy may launch an attack otherwise impossible."

This is how sin works: wrongdoing grooms the heart not to care.

Lust is often a war so subtle that only the mind can hear the gunfire. At the beginning, lustful thoughts may be virtually unnoticeable. But there comes a day when what's been growing inside bursts forth. In the words of Jesus' half-brother James:

> Temptation comes from our own desires, which entice us and drag us away. These desires give birth to sinful actions. And when sin is allowed to grow, it gives birth to death.
>
> —JAMES 1:14-15 (NLT)

Israel's quote cuts deeper still. Unlike her first two declarations—which were both statements of resolve—this last remark is literally sin show-and-tell. Imagine not only catching your spouse red-handed in adultery but getting left for an assortment of lovers. Then one day, a

---

20  Again, this is a prophecy of Jerusalem long after the time of Hosea. The claim is not that this verse was spoken directly to Israel but simply that it aptly describes her actions as well.

few weeks later, you pass your spouse on the street corner, working to seduce strangers.[21]

As your eyes meet, a hurricane of emotion whips through your brain, and immediately—to your horror—your spouse approaches you. And in that fateful moment, with a piercing smirk, your life partner proceeds to undo his or her trench coat, pull out a fistful of money, and say, "These are my wages, which my lovers have given me."

What would be your response?

This is but a fraction of what God Almighty experienced with Israel. The oldest profession had become His bride's chosen career, and she kept throwing it back in His face. Israel had forgotten her Husband, and it wasn't the onset of dementia. This was intentional, like children disobeying rules they don't like. Israel had the Law, the prophets, the shrines of the past; reminders were all around. She simply didn't *want* to remember the Lord, so she shut Him out. The psalmist recounts it this way:

> Our fathers, when they were in Egypt,
> **did not consider your wonderous works;**
> they did not remember the abundance of your
> steadfast love...
> Yet he saved them for his name's sake,
> that he might make known his mighty power . . .
> Then they believed his words;
> they sang his praise.
> But they soon forgot his works;
> **they did not wait for his counsel . . .**
> **They forgot God, their Savior,**
> who had done great things . . .
> —PSALM 106:7-13, 21A (ESV)

Oh so often, that's how it goes with sin. It starts with the erosion of thankfulness, not crediting God for creation. Then comes the exploitation,

---

21 Israel's entitled prostitution was far from a knee-jerk reaction. Like much of modern rampant depravity, it was a long time coming. The 27.6 million people being sex-trafficked worldwide aren't the result of just a couple evil kingpins or yesterday's mistakes. The $97 billion-dollar porn industry didn't just suddenly appear. Whether it's international or in the home, sin is always a slow creep.

demanding He proves that He cares. And finally, when the King of the Universe hasn't lived up to *our* expectations, we toss Him aside. No more consideration, no more counsel—just syringes of deadening pleasure.

In the courtroom, all was coming to a close. Three high crimes lingered thick in the air. The defendant and the world stood still. Alas, the decisive moment had arrived; God would now give His verdict.

How would He find His bride? And would Hosea ever find his? With so much at stake and such high-voltage emotion, prepare to be a bit shocked.

The story of Hosea might not end how you think it should.

# HIDDEN GEMS

## JESUS: OUR JUDGED JUDGE

Israel decided everything she had was from her lovers, so to them she went. ⟶ Jesus humbly acknowledged that everything good is from the Father, and to Him, He went. *(John 3:27, John 14:12, John 17:7)*

Israel stubbornly refused to give God the credit He is justly due. ⟶ Jesus personally commanded and completed giving to God what is His. *(Mark 12:17, Luke 23:46)*

Israel declared she would return to the Lord for selfish reasons. ⟶ Jesus returned to be with the Father after leaving Him for selfless reasons. *(John 14:28, Philippians 2:7)*

Israel stewed in worldly grief, refusing to repent of her sin. ⟶ Jesus cried out in godly grief, praying for the repentance of those killing Him. *(Matthew 26:38, Luke 23:34)*

Israel flaunted her gains from whoredom, rejoicing in ungodly wages. ⟶ Jesus cast out temple whoredom, removing the money changers' wages. *(Mark 11:15-16, Romans 6:23)*

Israel rightfully stood in judgment for justice to be served from on high. ⟶ Jesus was taken away by judgment for justice to be satisfied on high. *(Isaiah 53:8, Romans 3:25-26)*

**BOTTOM LINE:**

Jesus lived justly yet was condemned corruptly and shall be the Judge over all. *(John 5:27, Acts 17:31, 2 Corinthians 5:10)*

# WRAP UP: Modern Mayhem

When man discredits his Creator, everything slowly collapses: morals, families, even nations. This was the path Israel took—the path of installing self as sovereign—and things just kept getting worse.

What started as complacency soon became collusion. Lust became adultery; sin became cool. But the story of Israel isn't just some antiquated tragedy, an isolated incident of a people gone mad. It's a warning for anyone who will listen.

**Modern society has much to learn from the crimes of Israel's past.** Especially in the West, there's a growing notion that mankind is somehow beyond all that now—that we are finally sophisticated, advanced, enlightened.

If anything, Western society is showing the opposite trend. In communication, vocabularies are shriveling up. In relationships, families are imploding. Spiritually, we're disconnected. Mentally, we're sicker than ever before. Indeed, if there was ever a time to heed a warning and change course, it would be now.

Unfortunately, the devil is darn good at what he does. (After all, he's had thousands of years to practice.) These days, the same three-step program he put Israel on—thanklessness, exploitation, adultery—is everywhere.

Take marriage, the first institution created by God. Before the vows, the chase is bliss, the hopes sky high. But after entering the promised land of honeymoon happiness, a potent blend of ease and irritation often sets in. Ever so slowly, thankfulness erodes. Demands start erupting rather than praise. As the challenges build (especially with kids), love grows cold. And soon enough, the heart—drunk with disappointment—looks elsewhere for love.

Perhaps that's what happened with Gomer. The nation she epitomized, Israel, definitely walked that route. And now it was coming to an end.

Thankfully, for God's chosen people, He always finishes the good work He starts.

# ENGAGE: Group Study 9

**STARTER**     At what point (if ever) does a reward become an unhealthy motivator?

**TRIVIA**     How many times does the word "judgment" appear in the Gospel of Mark?[22]

**REFLECT**     In what ways do you most commonly offend God, and who might help you overcome those habits?

**PONDER**     Should a Christian apologize to God every time he or she makes a mistake?

**JOURNAL**     Do you care too little about your sin or too much? How does this affect your walk with God?

---

**BOIL IT DOWN**     Heaven takes sin seriously, and so should we.

**BRING IT UP**     What is more important than thankfulness?

**LIVE IT OUT**     Spend three straight minutes in prayer, recounting how merciful God has been.

---

22   The answer is zero. Mark's gospel is the only one that does not contain a single use of "judgment." For comparison, judgment comes up eleven times in Matthew, three times in Luke, and thirteen times in John (using the ESV).

# 10

# A RANSOM FOR RENEWAL

*"Whoever wants to be a leader*
*among you must be your servant . . .*
*for even the Son of Man came*
*not to be served, but to serve,*
*and to give his life as a ransom for many."*
—Mark 10:43b, 45 (NLT)

I N Japan, a curious art form exists where broken ceramics are mended
with gold. This practice, known as *kintsugi*, functions on a seriously
powerful premise: **restoration is worth a precious investment**.

Unlike most repair techniques that aim to hide evidence of breakage,
*kintsugi* creates a brand-new beauty by illuminating the scars of the past.
Each vessel restored in this manner tells a story, silently celebrating its
shatter marks. In fact, so stunning are these golden zigzags that prized
pottery has even been purposely broken just so it may be reborn this way.
But no matter how the vessels come to be broken, the method remains
the same—taking chards of pots destined for landfills and rebuilding

them better than new.

If there is one main theme throughout the Scriptures, it's that God loves to restore. As much as He loves to make new things, God also loves to *make things new.*

With Israel, however, things were complicated. Centuries of sin had hardened her heart to the point where her prostitution was loud and proud. Like Gomer, she had run away from her Husband, giving herself to everyone *except* He who loved her first. The further she went, the more she lost—her morals, her mind, herself. And so, God, after recounting the drama in detail, was set to intervene.

Would He glue the pieces back together?

Before jumping into the verdict itself, one final point must be clarified. Though God surely responds to His creation, He is not *reactionary.* Israel's unfaithfulness did not surprise the Lord or cause Him to act hastily. In fact, nothing does. God is the great Initiator, the "Unmoved Mover" to Aristotle, the "Uncaused Cause" to Aquinas. He is not bound by the law of causality; He invented it.[1] So while the Lord allows Himself to be emotionally "moved" by our actions—whether in grief or pleasure or anger or joy—His will doesn't change.[2] In His own words:

> "Remember this and stand firm,
>     recall it to mind . . .
> for I am God, and there is no other;
>     I am God, and there is none like me,
> declaring the end from the beginning
>     and from ancient times things not yet done,

---

1   As Einstein and others have showed, time is not a separate reality from space, but rather together the two make up a certain interwoven "fabric" of space-time. Especially at velocities near the speed of light or next to extremely massive gravitational bodies, curious interactions between these seemingly separate realms can be readily observed. For example, the speed of time can be affected by the speed of an object. The point here is that while the creation account vividly describes the creation of space and objects therein, it is often forgotten that God also created time itself as the first three words of Scripture suggest: "In the beginning" (Genesis 1:1). To have causality, one must have a time continuum. Thus God, having created such, is above such constraints.

2   God's actions are never knee-jerk reactions to humanity's decision-making. There are certain verses (Genesis 6:6, Jeremiah 8:7-10, Jonah 3:10) that speak of God "relenting" from some course of action, but these must be viewed in light of the whole of Scripture (as well as the original languages). The Bible constantly uses anthropomorphic language to help finite minds better relate to divine realities. Further debate over open theism is outside the scope of this work but can be well examined in articles such as "Does God Change His Mind?" by *Answers in Genesis.*

saying, '**My counsel shall stand,
and I will accomplish all my purpose.**'"[3]

—ISAIAH 46:8-10 (ESV)

This scripture is absolutely paramount to properly unpack the final chapter in Hosea's story. God is not some heavenly FEMA director showing up at disasters to solve problems on the fly, nor is He the pet parent who freaks out when finding a dump on the carpet. Nothing surprises Him— even His own wife's adultery.

With this in mind, we return to the courtroom. God, having laid out the charges against His people, stands poised to deliver His verdict. While testifying, the Lord had already declared a few corrective courses of action (removing Israel from her lovers and taking back His provision), but those were just short-term steps. Now it was time to bring down the gavel for Israel's final fate.

God is not some heavenly FEMA director showing up at disasters to solve problems on the fly, nor is He the pet parent who freaks out when finding a dump on the carpet.

To all in the room, she must have seemed like a goner. After all, adultery was a capital offense, and hers was against the Judge. Just listen to how God finished His testimony:

**"And I will punish her** for the feast days of the Baals
when she burned offerings to them
and adorned herself with her ring and jewelry,
and went after her lovers
and forgot me, declares the LORD."[4]

—HOSEA 2:13 (ESV)

---

3   For more verses to corroborate the concept of God's plan never changing, see Numbers 23:19, Proverbs 19:21, Isaiah 25:1, and Acts 5:38-39.

4   This is considered the end of the Lord's "testimony" against Israel because it ends with "declares the LORD"—a clear break in train of thought.

Tack on her other crimes, and what hope remained? How could God restore such a marriage? And even if He could, *why would He*? The rest of this chapter—and the rest of Hosea's story—deals with these questions.

Long ago, out of all the peoples on the face of the earth, God chose Israel to be His treasured possession. It wasn't because she was strong or impressive that the Lord set His love on Israel; such devotion simply came down to keeping the oath He swore to her forefathers.[5] Just like Hosea, the Lord knew full well His bride would cheat, and yet He loved her anyway.

Surely, the King wasn't about to change His mind now.

## RULING OF HIS LIGHT

The gavel pounds the wood one last time. The moment had arrived. Loud and clear, out came the Judge's ruling, starting with this:

> "Therefore, behold, I will allure her,
>      and bring her into the wilderness,
>      **and speak tenderly to her.**
> And there I will give her her vineyards
>      and make the Valley of Trouble a door of hope.
> And she shall sing there, as in the days of her youth,
>      and as in the day when she came up out of the land
>      of Egypt."[6]
>
> —HOSEA 2:14-15 (ESV, KJV)

If human jaws could unhinge, they probably would have at that moment. What happened to all the condemnation, all the punishment? It's as if the Lord said, "I'll take care of that," and simply moved on. In the blink of an eye, His fury somehow turned to compassion.

What is going on here?

Well, when God makes a covenant, He keeps it. Yes, the circumstances

---

5   This language of Israel being God's "treasured possession" whom He "set His love" on comes directly from Deuteronomy 7:6-8. Curiously, instead of detailing exactly why God chose Israel in this passage, He basically says this: *I decided to love them because I love them.*

6   The first two sentences are Hosea 2:14-15a (ESV), with "Trouble" substituted for "Achor" as the ESV footnote offers. The last sentence is Hosea 2:15b from the KJV.

with Israel were dire, even despicable, but **God's faithfulness is not predicated on our piety**. No matter how ugly things get, a vow is a vow to the Lord. Ages ago, He promised Abram that He would cherish his offspring forever. Thus, while God would surely punish Israel, in the end, He would come back for His bride. It's the classic finish to

> It's the classic finish to countless films: after conquering evil and saving the world, the hero goes back for the girl.

countless films: after conquering evil and saving the world, the hero goes back for the girl. Those movies, however, are all spinoffs; God's plan is the original release.

Try to imagine just how bonkers this would be to behold. Picture a freshly convicted serial felon hearing from the Judge:

> "How can I give you up, O Ephraim?
>      How can I hand you over, O Israel? . . .
> My heart recoils within me;
>      **my compassion grows warm and tender**."
> —Hosea 11:8 (ESV)

Only God Almighty has this level of patience and dogged goodwill. Cheated on for centuries, His heart still pines for the good of His wife. Even her punishment comes back to His love: "For the LORD disciplines those he loves, and he punishes each one he accepts as his child."[7] That's why He started His verdict with "therefore." To be disciplined by God is to be on the road of redemption. As David wrote in the Psalms:

> For His anger lasts only a moment,
>      but His favor lasts a lifetime!
> Weeping may last through the night,
>      but joy comes with the morning.
> —Psalm 30:5 (ESV)

---

7   Hebrews 12:6 (NLT).

Then, returning to his verdict, God follows up His shock introduction with an even wilder announcement—He is planning a renewal of their vows:

> "And in that day, declares the LORD, you will call me
> 'My Husband' . . . and **I will betroth you to me forever**.
> I will betroth you to me in righteousness and in justice,
> in steadfast love and in mercy. I will betroth you to me
> in faithfulness. And you shall know the LORD."
> —HOSEA 2:16A, 19-20 (ESV)

It is difficult to express just how absurd this would have sounded to God's chosen people. Instead of the guillotine, Israel was getting the golden glue of *kintsugi*. Her shattered pot of a marriage was to be restored even better than before. The descriptors are astounding: *righteousness, justice, love, mercy, faithfulness*. This was no ordinary repair job; God was proclaiming that a masterpiece was (and still is) in the making. And then, just when it seems too good to be true, God drops perhaps His most stunning punchline yet: "And you shall know the LORD."

To the untrained eye, this may not seem like much. After all, people preparing to recite lifelong vows usually know one another well. But, as is often the case, the English here doesn't tell the whole story. The Hebrew word being translated, יָדַע (*yada*), can mean to simply be acquainted with someone. However, in the context of marriage, Scripture frequently uses *yada* to describe consummation—becoming intimately and fully "known."[8]

Of course, with God this is spiritual, not sexual, but the imagery is startling nonetheless. Picture it: The God of the Universe on the throne, promising a prolific adulteress that He and she will soon become one.[9] Jesus literally defined salvation this way:

---

8   Ten separate times in Scripture, *yada* is used to denote the act of being physical intimate with someone, from Adam and Eve (Genesis 4:1) to Elkanah and Hannah (1 Samuel 1:19). This enriches the profound New Testament concept of being "fully known" by God in 1 Corinthians 13:12, as well as Christ's definition of eternal life in John 17:3. Of course, this does not mean saved souls participate in physical intimacy with the divine, but it does heighten one's excitement for the level of "knowing" that followers of Christ will experience for all eternity.

9   See Ephesians 5:31. This isn't to say that Israel (or anyone else) will become God. Rather, it's an allusion to Jesus' prayer in John 17:22-23 in which He prays for His followers to be one in Him, just as He is one with the Father. It is the language of intimate unity, not deification.

"This is eternal life, that they **know** You, the only true
God, and Jesus Christ whom You have sent."[10]

—JOHN 17:3 (NASB95)

Everything rides on knowing the Lord. (And one day, all of Israel will!)[11]

Finally, as if that all wasn't enough, God ends His verdict with a bang.
In one fell swoop, He brings the whole case full circle, reiterating His
promise to reverse each child's name:

"And in that day I will answer, declares the LORD,
I will answer the heavens,
and they shall answer the earth,
and the earth shall answer the grain, the wine, and the oil,
and they shall answer **Jezreel**,
and I will sow her for myself in the land.
And I will have mercy on **No Mercy**,
and I will say to **Not My People**, 'You are my people';
and he shall say, 'You are my God.'"

—HOSEA 2:21-23 (ESV)

This marks the end of God's verdict and the beginning of something
new. Back in the day, "Israel was holy to the LORD, the firstfruits of His
harvest."[12] Now, one could hardly tell that was ever the case.

Certainly, great was her fall, but so would be her return.

---

10  Interestingly, this is the only time in Scripture that Jesus calls Himself "Jesus Christ." As an aside, because
the New Testament was written in Greek, the word here is not the Hebrew *yada* but the Greek *ginosko*
(though these can function in a similar way). For more, see Strong's G1097 at BlueLetterBible.org.

11  For more on this concept, see Jeremiah 31:33-34 and Romans 11:26. Scholars debate whether this "Israel"
mentioned in Romans 11:26 refers literally to ethnic Jews (who one day will welcome their Messiah) or
figuratively to all "children of the promise" who follow Jesus as in Romans 9:6-8. While argumentation
surrounding this dispute falls outside the scope of the current work, it should at least be noted that the
immediate context of Romans 11:26—namely, the previous verse—states that "a partial hardening has come
upon Israel, until the fullness of the Gentiles has come in" (Romans 11:25, ESV). Hence, by contrasting Israel
with the Gentiles and mentioning the hardening of Jewish hearts toward their Messiah (Romans 11:7-8,
2 Corinthians 3:12-16), we know that Paul was at least referring to ethnic Israel right before declaring "all
Israel will be saved." One's interpretation of this passage is no small deal, as it nudges the heart toward
(or against) personally supporting modern-day Jews and the land of Israel. For Paul's thoughts on how
Gentile Christians are to financially bless messianic Jews, see Romans 15:27.

12  An excerpt of Jeremiah 2:3 (ESV).

# GOING FOR GOMER

After the courtroom scene comes the final act in Hosea's story.

God, having drawn out His blueprint for redeeming Israel, now tells Hosea to follow suit. Already, the prophet had displayed more cheerful servanthood than most do in a lifetime, yet God commanded Him to take one giant last leap.

Honestly, one must feel for the guy. Hosea had faithfully obeyed the Lord for years—and what had it got him? His family had imploded; his name lay in disgrace. Whatever influence he had on the nation was long gone. Put it this way: If there were an Old Testament Olympic event to see who lost the most while serving God, Hosea would at least make the podium.[13]

Just pause for a moment and consider life in his sandals. How natural it would have been for Hosea to shake a fist at God in the wake of such loss and pain. How many hearts, when asked to keep giving sacrificially, clam up unless they're immediately repaid? Hosea easily could have grumbled against God, but in one of the most brilliant displays of cheerful service in history, Hosea chose the narrow road.

He, like the Lord, would redeem his wife.

### PART I: HE SHALL SEARCH THE STREETS

At the end of Hosea's story, everything happens so fast. One moment, the Lord pronounces Israel's redemption; the next, He calls for Gomer's. Just think of how wrenched Hosea's heart must have been when receiving His final mission:

> The LORD said to me, "Go, show love to your wife again, **even though she loves another man and continually commits adultery.** Likewise, the LORD loves the Israelites

---

13  Assuming suffering is even comparable, the case can be made that Job and Jeremiah suffered more than Hosea. Outside of those characters, however, one is hard-pressed to find an obedient Old Testament follower of God who lost more than Hosea. Joseph was thrown into prison for remaining pure, but he quickly was shown favor and put in charge of Pharoah's empire. Perhaps Moses could contend given the sheer amount of grumbling he endured, but then again, He was meeting with God as one speaks with a friend (Exodus 33:11), which might more than balance out. Elijah is another frontrunner, navigating death threats and long-term life in the desert for obeying the word of the Lord, but alas, it's a bit like apples versus oranges in the end.

although they turn to other gods and love to offer raisin cakes to idols."

—HOSEA 3:1 (NET)

It's hard to overstate the level of strength and courage God was asking of His prophet. Hosea had spent years grieving the gross unfaithfulness of his wife. His heart was gutted, his children traumatized as their mommy went door to door. Never once from Gomer was there even an ounce of remorse, yet Hosea was told to go love her again.

Of all the commands to "go" in Scripture, this one may be the hardest. Noah was told to go out of the ark to be fruitful and multiply the earth. Abram's first word from God was "go," but the Lord packaged it with a huge promise. In fact, practically every time God commands someone to go in the Bible, He guarantees that blessing will follow, be it freedom or land or victory.[14]

> It's hard to overstate the level of strength and courage God was asking of His prophet.

This wasn't the case for Hosea. God basically said, "Go and be radically selfless, even though your wife enjoys cheating on you." That's all the prophet gets—a reminder of how poorly he's been treated.

And yet, *he goes.*

Consider for a moment just how utterly humiliating Hosea's task would have been. Unsure which man was his wife's latest lover, the prophet would have been out searching the streets, asking strangers if they had seen Gomer. Imagine the looks of derision on their faces, the sneers of disapproval, and all the sarcastic responses he endured.

Just think what it would be like if a pastor showed up at your door in search of his runaway wife. The humiliation would be off the charts. In Hosea's situation, the prophet may have ran into one of Gomer's lovers, being mocked with graphic details of how they made love. Each door would have been a fresh knife to the heart.

---

14  A few examples of this are Exodus 3:16 to Moses, Judges 1:2 to Judah, and Judges 4:6 to Barak (through Deborah).

Little did Hosea know, however, that God was teaching him *kintsugi*. Each small step of obedience was one more drop of golden glue; the art of redemption was underway. During his mission to redeem his wife, all had to be laid aside for the sake of seeking the lost, just like the One to come. Gomer had practically cost him everything, and yet somehow, she was worth it—just like Israel was to God.

Frankly, few—if any—stories in the Old Testament come close to the pound-for-pound gospel foreshadowing of Hosea.[15] Seven hundred years after Hosea searched the streets, the Messiah would do the same. Sent on a mission to "the lost sheep of the house of Israel," Jesus laid aside a life set apart to come for heaven's adulterous bride.[16]

Indeed, to the ultimate Servant came the command, "Go out quickly to the streets and lanes of the city, and bring in the poor and crippled and blind and lame."[17] It was Christ who came to seek the lost: to the sheep who knew His voice but had wandered, to the son in the proverbial pigsty. He endured the shame for our guilt, making Himself "of no reputation."[18] Yes, Jesus came humbly to reach the world—and now, so should we.

**The sins of the world must not disgust Christians to the point where we stop reaching out:**

> "For we ourselves were once foolish, disobedient, led astray . . . but when the goodness and loving kindness of God our Savior appeared, He saved us, not because of works done by us in righteousness, but according to His own mercy . . ."
>
> —Titus 3:3-5a (ESV)

---

15 The only exception would be the story of Joseph, which is absolutely jam packed with pointers to Christ. That said, the matchup is a bit unfair given that Joseph's life comprises some 419 verses in Genesis, compared to Hosea's meager thirty-nine verses in Hosea 1-3.

16 The quote is an excerpt of Matthew 15:24 (ESV). A strong emphasis on the Jews in Christ's ministry can also be seen in Matthew 10:5-6, as well as the apostle Paul's in Romans 9:1-5. For more on laying aside, see John 13:4 (ESV) and Philippians 2:7 in *The Living Bible*. As for heaven's bride, the language is intentionally vague. Traditionally, the bride of the Father in the Old Testament is Israel, and the bride of Christ is the church (Ephesians 5:23). But Jesus, being God, can accurately be considered the husband of both. (Whether or not the church is the fulfillment of Old Testament Israel or a distinct entity comes down to one's view of covenantal theology.)

17 An excerpt of Luke 14:21 (ESV). Admittedly, this quote is in a parable of Jesus, not a quote directly to the Son; however, as He is the Father's "holy servant" (Acts 4:27 and 4:30) sent to preach the good news (Isaiah 61:1), the connection to Christ is appropriately made.

18 An excerpt of Philippians 2:7 (KJV).

This is why we strive to become all things to all people, that by all means, some may be saved—because that's what He did for us! Hosea was told to go, and so are we, as made clear by Jesus' last words in Matthew:

> **"Go, therefore**, and make disciples of all nations, baptizing them in the name of the Father and of the Son and of the Holy Spirit, teaching them to observe all that I have commanded you. And behold, I am with you always, to the end of the age."
>
> —MATTHEW 28:19-20 (ESV)

Christ's redemptive work is complete, but we are still to bear much fruit. As Proverbs says, "he who wins souls is wise."[19]

So, to the lost sheep of Israel: Go!

To the unreached people groups: Go!

And to those near and dear who have wandered from the truth: Go, tell it on the mountain![20]

The Ultimate Hosea has, is, and yet will come.

### PART II: HE SHALL PAY THE PRICE

Of course, Hosea didn't just go looking for Gomer. Eventually, the floozy was found.

The Bible doesn't explicitly record how or where he discovered her, but it can be inferred from what happened next. For the prophet himself recounted in his own words:

> **"So I bought her for myself** for fifteen shekels of silver and a homer and a half of barley."
>
> —HOSEA 3:2 (NASB95)

This was no normal purchase, far too meager an amount for the price of a bride. In those days, there was only one place where humans were

---

19  An excerpt of Proverbs 11:30 (ESV).

20  For more on going to the Jews, see Romans 1:16, as well as the article "To the Jew First: The Meaning of Romans 1:16" by *Fellowship of Israel Related Ministries.* For verses on going to the unreached, see Matthew 24:14, Acts 1:8, Romans 10:14-15, and Romans 15:20-21. For a passage about reaching those who have wandered from the truth, see James 5:19-20. And regarding telling the gospel on the mountain, see Isaiah 40:9 and 52:7.

bought and sold like this: the slave auction block.

The scene is almost unthinkable. Hosea the prophet, after years of being mocked and neglected, goes out in search of his runaway wife. Upon interviewing the townspeople—potentially for days—he finally gets a lead.

*Gomer, you say? Yeah, that's the prostitute up for auction tomorrow. Couldn't get enough business to pay her keep, that one. So the ol' boss is puttin' her up for sale. Why, I might have a crack at her myself—could use a pretty little slave like that.*[21]

A long, sleepless night follows as horrors flood Hosea's mind. The shame would be colossal, but there was no turning back.

Day eventually breaks, and Hosea heads to the auction. The public square is bustling with people eager to see who buys who and for what amount. One by one, the slaves get dragged out, naked and bound with ropes. Countless stares pierce the prophet as he waits for his bride to be up.

And then, out walks Gomer. For the first time in years, Hosea lays eyes on his wife as he feels the townspeople's eyes on him. Unfortunately, Scripture doesn't give details of the auction itself. Perhaps there were multiple bidders; perhaps just one. All we are told is at the end of the chaos, Hosea comes out on top with a bid of **"fifteen shekels of silver and a homer and a half of barley."** But why, out of all the possible particulars, did the Holy Spirit choose *this* to point out?

To answer this question, let's break down the two items in Hosea's bid separately. Up first, the fifteen silver shekels.

Throughout Scripture, silver is used to illustrate the process of refinement or purification. For example, Psalm 66 includes the line, "For you have tried us, O God; You have refined us as silver is refined."[22] King David also sang a similar line:

> The words of the LORD are pure words,
> like silver refined in a furnace on the ground,
> purified seven times.
>
> —PSALM 12:6 (ESV)

---

21 Such detestable phrasing is used here because of the extremely perverse state of Israel at the time. In reality, the quotes could have been far more gruesome.

22 Psalm 66:10 (ESV). Note also the concept of being "tried" here, connecting to the courtroom analogy of Hosea. For another silver refinement passage, see Isaiah 48:10.

Already, connections are afoot, but this barely scratches the surface. Remember, Hosea didn't just pay with silver; He bid silver *shekels*. These common Jewish coins pop up throughout the Bible, especially in the Law of Moses.

For instance, when a census was taken, every numbered person was to donate half a shekel as **"a ransom for his life** to the LORD."[23] In another place, God declares the reparations for a lost slave to be exactly thirty shekels.[24] And as a last example, in Leviticus 27, the Lord tells Moses the cost for a woman to be redeemed from certain vows she could not fulfill: thirty silver shekels.[25] Keep this amount in mind.

Then we come to the homer and a half of barley. In ancient Israel, barley was a common resource for food and trading, but only once does Scripture give this grain direct spiritual significance.[26] In the book of Numbers, God lays out a test for adultery if a man suspects his wife of unfaithfulness, part of which requires the man to bring his wife to the priest with an offering "of barley flour on her behalf . . . a grain offering of jealousy, a grain offering of memorial, a reminder of iniquity."[27]

Because of this, barley to an Israelite evoked the idea of an adulteress on trial—quite the link to Gomer. And here's the kicker: in Hosea's day, **a homer and a half of barley sold for fifteen shekels.**[28] Thus, the total

---

23  An excerpt of Exodus 30:11-13 (ESV). Interestingly, such donations were then used to build the sanctuary of the tabernacle (Exodus 38:25-28).

24  A reference to Exodus 21:32. Some versions use "servant" instead of "slave", but the point holds. It's also worth noting that such servanthood was poles apart from the wicked enslavement of African Americans and much more akin to people in massive credit card debt. Furthermore, all slaves were set free at the year of Jubilee and often were so favorably treated that even when they gained legal opportunities to be free, they decided to stay with their masters. For more on this, see Exodus 21:6 and Leviticus 25:10.

25  A reference to Leviticus 27:2. For more information on this somewhat controversial verse, see *Matthew Poole's Commentary* or the *Jamieson-Fausset-Brown Bible Commentary*.

26  Some might argue that it was also used in the grain offering (Leviticus 2:1-16) or the Feast of Unleavened Bread (Exodus 12:15-20), but Scripture does not command that the bread must be made of barley flour; wheat was perfectly acceptable. Some also might point to Leviticus 27:16 for the consecration of property to the LORD through barley seed valuation, but this is specifically the *seed* of the plant. Barley itself is not in view.

27  An excerpt of Numbers 5:15. The first phrase is from the NIV; the second from the NASB95.

28  Here's the math for the value of Hosea's barley: In 2 Kings 7:1, we are told that the fair market price for barley is two "seahs" for a shekel. (Though this isn't written exactly in Hosea's day, it is within a few decades.) According to the NASB95 and *NET Bible* footnotes in 2 Kings 7:16, a seah was a dry measure equivalent to about 11 liters. Thus, 22 liters of barley (two seahs) was worth one shekel. This is the first step. Next, as seen in the ESV footnote for Hosea 3:2, the definition of one homer is a dry volume of 220 liters, meaning a homer and a half equals 330 liters. Finally, dividing 330 liters (1.5 homer) by 22 liters per shekel, we see that 1.5 homer of barley would have cost fifteen shekels. Therefore, adding this to Hosea's original fifteen shekels yields a total bid worth thirty shekels—a stance taken by many biblical scholars, including Dr. Claude Mariottini and Charles Ellicott.

price Hosea paid to redeem Gomer was thirty shekels!

Here's where it all comes together: **Hosea's bid was far more meaningful than what he happened to have in his pockets that day.** The silver hinted at a coming refinement, the shekels at a ransom for life. Reparations were made for a lost female slave, redemption from vows she couldn't keep. In front of all those people and their skeptical glances, Hosea bought back his wife.

Can you think of someone else who was sold for thirty shekels of silver and put on trial for unfaithfulness to God—someone who came "not be served but to serve, and to give His life as a ransom for many"?[29]

Yes, indeed, it all points to Christ yet again. Jesus was sold for thirty shekels of silver, just as the prophet Zechariah predicted.[30] Though perfect, He was still put on trial, stripped naked, and paraded before crowds. And yet, at the very same time, the Lord became Hosea to us:

> I will ransom them from the power of the grave; I will redeem them from death.
>
> —HOSEA 13:14A (KJV)

What better cheerful Servant than Immanuel.

## PART III: HE SHALL VOICE THE VOW

One final moment concludes Hosea's story—one of dogged, breathtaking grace. The prophet had just bought back his wife, naked and ashamed, from the slave block in the town square. He had been cheated on, humiliated, defamed—all because of her.

If anything, the onlookers would have expected Hosea to at least scourge her. Legally, he had the right to get even. Some might even have started picking up stones, hoping to end Gomer's life of filth. Hosea totally could have cast the first stone; it would have been completely lawful for him to launch her execution. Perhaps even Gomer thought she

---

29  An excerpt of Mark 10:45 (ESV).

30  A reference to Matthew 26:15, 27:3, 27:9, and Zechariah 11:12-13. Note that Matthew 27:9 declares Jeremiah as the originator of the prophecy, while the prediction itself is recorded in Zechariah. Scholars have various theories to explain this, most persuasively that Jeremiah may have "spoken" the prophecy as Matthew declares but just didn't write it down. In this view, verbal tradition would have then passed the saying down to the time of Zechariah, who decided (by inspiration of the Holy Spirit) to include it in his writings.

was meeting her death, like Mephibosheth before the throne of David. Whatever the case, all eyes were on Hosea and his crucial next move. And that's when he turned the world on its head.

Amid such tension and warranted dread, Hosea erupts with a mouthful of mercy:

> And I said to her, "You must **dwell as mine for many days**. You shall not play the whore, or belong to another man; so will I also be to you."
>
> —HOSEA 3:3 (ESV)

Think if you were Gomer, hearing those words. Right when the gavel of judgment should have crushed her, she was redeemed by the man who loved her unconditionally.

Few moments in Scripture are as eye-opening, scandalous, and upside-down as this. Gomer had done nothing to deserve restoration; indeed, she had done everything to escape it. But Hosea, being rich in mercy because of the great love with which he loved her—even when she was dead in her trespasses—made her alive together with him![31]

Gomer had gone about scattering her love, and yet Hosea planted her back in his house. She hardly knew the love of the Father, and yet she was shown it afresh. "You are mine," said the prophet with compassion, "and forever, I will be yours."

For Hosea, this was the perfect reversal of all the kids' names in a single explosion of grace. Around every turn, behind every word, the power of the gospel was on display. Freedom came to Gomer by the mouth of a prophet and the price he cheerfully paid. So too, Christ, the ultimate Prophet to come, preached peace and paid dearly for us. One can indeed picture many of

> Gomer had done nothing to deserve restoration; indeed, she had done everything to escape it.

---

31  A parallel repurposing of Ephesians 2:4-5 (ESV) to emphasize Hosea's typification of Christ. This, of course, is not meant to imply that Hosea was divine or that he somehow saved Gomer's soul.

Christ's quotes being said by Hosea to his bride:

+ "Come to me . . . and I will give you rest."[32]

+ "You did not choose Me, but I chose you."[33]

+ "I have come that [you] may have life, and have it in all its fulness."[34]

+ "Come, follow me."[35]

+ "As the Father has loved me, so have I loved you. Now remain in my love."[36]

+ "Let's go off by ourselves to a quiet place . . ."[37]

+ "Rise! Let us go!"[38]

The story of Hosea shines a light on the gospel like few other narratives in history. God initiated a covenant with mankind even though He knew we would cheat. Full of ourselves, we each go our own way, rejecting His comfort and care. Slowly, we become so enslaved to selfish desires that, over time, we forget God altogether.

> God initiated a covenant with mankind even though He knew we would cheat.

But one glorious day, God came down to our auction block and paid to redeem us. Like with Hosea, faithful love triumphed. And yet, as divine as that sounds, it's not quite the happily-ever-after it seems. Sure, Hosea voiced a vow to his wife, but notice: *there's no record of Gomer's response.*

**This omission on Gomer's behalf isn't some accident; it's a wakeup call.** The Holy Spirit is asking, *What should be Gomer's response? And*

---

32  An excerpt of Matthew 11:28 (NASB95).

33  An excerpt of John 15:16 (ESV).

34  An excerpt of John 10:10 (BSB).

35  An excerpt of Mark 10:2 (NASB95).

36  John 15:9 (NIV).

37  An excerpt of Mark 6:31 (NLT).

38  An excerpt of Mark 14:42 (NIV).

*more importantly, what will be yours?*

Don't walk away from studying Hosea without responding to God's call to come home. Be clothed in His humility and refined by His grace. Give God Almighty your cheerful service, not just some dutiful ritual: "Beloved, if God so loved us, we also ought to love one another."[39]

If there's one call to latch onto, may it be this:

> Therefore, as God's chosen people, holy and dearly loved, clothe yourselves with compassion, kindness, humility, gentleness and patience. Bear with each other and forgive one another if any of you has a grievance against someone. **Forgive as the Lord forgave you.** And over all these virtues put on love, which binds them all together in perfect unity. Let the peace of Christ rule in your hearts, since as members of one body you were called to peace. **And be thankful.**
>
> —COLOSSIANS 3:12-15 (NIV)

May the story of Hosea remind us all of the kneeling we desperately need—in our world, in our churches, in our hearts.

A true hero cheerfully serves.

---

39  1 John 4:11 (ESV).

# HIDDEN GEMS

## JESUS: OUR MERCIFUL MENDER

Israel was allured by sin, turning brazenly to prostitution. ➞ Jesus allured sinners, speaking tenderly to prostitutes. *(Matthew 21:31, Luke 7:37-50, John 4:7-26)*

Israel left her first love, the Lord. ➞ Jesus will bring back His "first love," Israel. *(Hosea 11:1-11, Romans 11:1-27)*

Israel leveraged her inheritance to share it with other gods. ➞ Jesus secured an inheritance to share it with His brothers. *(Isaiah 53:12, Ephesians 1:11)*

Hosea walked humbly, searching the streets to redeem his wife. ➞ Jesus walked humbly, searching the streets to redeem the lost. *(Matthew 18:11, Luke 14:21-23)*

Hosea suffered willingly, paying the price to ransom his beloved back from a life of slavery. ➞ Jesus suffered willingly, paying the price to ransom His beloved back from a life of slavery. *(1 Corinthians 6:19-20, 1 Corinthians 7:23, 1 Peter 1:18-19)*

Hosea forgave gladly, voicing the vow to be with his wife always. ➞ Jesus forgives gladly, voicing the vow to be with His own always. *(Ephesians 4:32, Matthew 28:20)*

**BOTTOM LINE:**

Jesus, even if we are faithless, loves us back to health in Himself. *(John 13:1, 2 Timothy 2:13, Revelation 19:11)*

# WRAP UP:
# More Than Conquerors

When people envision heroes, they usually don't think of people like Hosea. They picture ironclad armor and death-defying feats, vanquishing foes and preserving justice. Accepting humiliation to redeem an adulteress just doesn't fit the category. As a result, many hear of stories like Hosea and write them off as witless romance. But which is harder for a man to do: risk his life for a cause he believes in, or lay it down daily for those causing him pain?[40]

When Hosea came for Gomer, no red carpet was laid out before him—just a gauntlet of derision and shame. There wasn't a medal waiting for him at the finish line or even a promise of reward should he prevail. Still, he humbly went forth, obeying the Father and redeeming his wayward wife off the streets.

So it is with Jesus. Born amongst dung and slobbery hay, God came to mankind as a servant. He could have descended in power, but the King knelt down instead, choosing to wash our dirt-crusted feet. Sure, some people placed their cloaks on the road, waving palm branches as He rode into Zion, but less than a week later, they screamed for His demise. Why? *Because He wasn't the hero they envisioned.*

**If we want to give God the honor He deserves, we must value the virtues of His Son.** Being gentle and lowly might not always be cool, but the God of heaven assuredly digs it.[41] Heroes don't always need capes and cannons; all it takes is a heart of sacrifice.

Cheerful servanthood may not seem like much, but it's the most effective heart surgery in the world. No bypass can cure the selfishness of man; only the supreme Servant who made him. In the end, it comes down to knowing Christ Jesus—the One who came to save us Gomers. Nothing is better than life with Him, and nothing really changes without it:

---

40 Of course, this is not meant to devalue the sacrifice of those who have given their lives for others. Such people should still be reverently honored.

41 An excerpt of Matthew 11:29 (ESV), the only verse in Scripture where Jesus describes His own heart.

So let us know, let us press on to know the LORD.
His going forth is as certain as the dawn;
And He will come to us like the rain,
Like the spring rain watering the earth.

—Hosea 6:3 (NASB95)

Yes, indeed, He will come.

# ENGAGE: Group Study 10

**STARTER** What would be the appropriate response of Gomer to being redeemed by Hosea? How do you think she lived as a result?

**TRIVIA** Hosea 3 contains only five verses. There are six chapters in the Bible with even fewer verses—five of those being in Psalms. What is the other tiny chapter?[42]

**REFLECT** What is something God is calling you to cheerfully sacrifice for the sake of those around you?

**PONDER** Besides turning from personal sin, what does God command us to do that He has never done Himself?

**JOURNAL** In what ways do you most commonly wander from God? From this study of Hosea, what might help?

**BOIL IT DOWN** God has taken the initiative to save us and is calling the world to respond.

**BRING IT UP** What are ways to best prevent becoming unfaithful to God?

**LIVE IT OUT** Assess what you have and give more than you're used to—with joy!

---

42 The five psalms in the Bible with four or less verses are Psalm 117, 123, 131, 133, and 134. The only other chapter in Scripture with less than five verses is Esther 10, which only has three.

# EPILOGUE

J OURNEYING THROUGH THE OLD TESTAMENT has been no small endeavor, but stopping now would be a great shame. The wealth of promises and prophecies studied are but a fraction of the pointers to Christ. Around every historical corner and character, there have been signposts aimed at the Messiah. Now we have the treasure map to find Him—and the key of servanthood to read it. But merely knowing where the gold is buried doesn't make a scavenger rich. Metal detectors are only worth buying if you're willing to dig at the beep.

This is the adventure ahead—exploring and adoring the life of the Christ. For centuries, many prophets and righteous people longed to see the supreme Servant, to hear the word from His lips.[1] Generation after generation died in faith, "not having received the things promised, but having seen them and greeted them from afar."[2] Even the angels eagerly awaited the fulfillment of Immanuel, how God would dwell with us.[3]

And then, He came.

So, while we praise the Lord for the Old Testament, it's time to open His long-awaited sequel: The Life and Times of Yeshua.[4] In the gospels, accounts of Jesus' life are unpacked directly. If the prophetic shadows of the Messiah seem vivid, just wait for the Man Himself. After all, seeing a

---

1    This is confirmed verbatim by Jesus' words in Matthew 13:17.
2    An excerpt of Hebrews 11:13 (ESV).
3    A reference to 1 Peter 1:12, speaking on both the mystery of the gospel and the sending of the Holy Spirit.
4    Yeshua is the original Hebrew name by which the Messiah was called. The name "Jesus" is the product of the precious name of God's Son being transliterated numerous times through multiple languages (Hebrew to Greek to Latin to English).

sketch of a man's figure is quite different than hearing his voice.

Hence, while this Old Testament study has come to a close, the journey has certainly not. All the servants we've met thus far were, as the apostle Paul would say, "only shadows of the reality yet to come. And Christ himself is that reality."[5]

Hosea's narrative may be finished, but an even better covenant unfolds.[6] Just as the Lord married Israel at Sinai, so the church prepares for her heavenly Husband. Just as Gomer's name means "complete," so too we are being completed. The fullness of the Gentiles is being brought in. Broken hearts are being made whole. And each new day, God Almighty works in those who love His Son, bringing about the fulfillment of what He has spoken.

One by one, His promises are coming true.

✦

*"And I am sure of this,*
*that he who began a good work*
*in you will bring it to completion*
*at the day of Jesus Christ."*
—PHILIPPIANS 1:6 (ESV)

---

5   An excerpt of Colossians 2:17 (NLT). The "shadows" referenced by Paul are Old Testament Jewish customs, but the biblical characters function similarly as historical harbingers, detailed at length in this work.

6   The biblical concept of a "better covenant" can be seen in Hebrews 7:22 and 8:6.

# ACKNOWLEDGMENTS

My utmost appreciation also goes out to the following people,
for by no means could this have been completed
without their steadfast support:

To my beloved wife Kendra,
for all the thoughtful encouragement and patient companionship.

To the team at Developing Great Relationships,
for the opportunity to unpack Scripture as a full-time vocation,
including the writing of this very book.

To Mike Yorkey, my incredible editor and comrade,
for all the brilliant revisions, refreshing laughs, and selfless help.

To Emily Morelli, my excellent graphic designer,
for the countless hours spent perfecting every last page.

To Kurt, Eric, Logan, Griff, Jac, and all my fellow Bible miners,
for the rich brotherhood and shared love of God's Word
that keeps my fire burning.

To these and all others
who put up with me all these years,
I love you all.

And finally, to Stanley J. Vermeer,
whose passion for a revival of cheerful servanthood in the church
triggered the necessary curiosity and determination
to pursue this project and others yet to come.

# ABOUT THE AUTHOR

RAISED IN SMALL TOWN ILLINOIS, Alex W. Foley began his adventures by acquiring a bachelor's in astrophysics from the University of Illinois. Meanwhile, his side gigs included everything from coaching tennis to writing poetry to roofing. Eventually, after surrendering to Christ in 2014, Alex completed his master's in theological studies and spent time in South Asia equipping the persecuted church.

Now residing in Iowa, Alex writes as the research director for Developing Great Relationships, a nonprofit that organizes biblical retreats and conferences to fortify marriages. Even outside of work, Alex loves to study the Word of God and share it with others, bringing his passion for the Scriptures to an increasing number of church pulpits, college ministries, and youth events.

In his free time, Alex relishes time spent in the great outdoors with his amazing wife and young daughter, as well as playing chess, conquering new disc golf courses, and singing in a barbershop quartet.

**To invite Alex to speak at your next event, contact him at:**
AlexWFoley@daretokneel.org

# ENDNOTES

## INTRODUCTION: *WHAT GIVES?*

"In the timeless words of C.S. Lewis, 'There must be a real giving up of the self . . .'"
   C.S. Lewis, *Mere Christianity*, William Collins, 2017, 227.

"John Piper echoes this sentiment, preaching, 'The problem with the world . . .'"
   Louie Giglio, et al., *Passion: The Bright Light of Glory*, W Publishing Group, an imprint of Thomas Nelson, 2014, 107.

"Aristotle spoke of our misguided pleasure-quest some 2,300 years ago: 'The problem . . .'"
   The quote is traditionally attributed to Aristotle, though no surviving piece of his writing contains this phrase.

"C.S. Lewis went so far as to describe hell as 'the ruthless, sleepless, unsmiling . . .'"
   The first half of the quote is from the original preface to Lewis' *The Screwtape Letters*. The second half of the quote is from page 232 of the same.

"In the words of pastor Rich Wilkerson Jr., 'You can always give without loving . . .'"
   Rich Wilkerson Jr., "What Are You Washing?" Vous Church. The sermon can be found at the following: https://www.youtube.com/watch?v=v1yrse21OXU.

## CHAPTER 1: FROM EDEN TO EXODUS

"The '80s hit song by the rock band Loverboy says it well: 'Everybody's working . . .'"
   A lyric from *Working for the Weekend* by Loverboy.

"According to *National Geographic*, rhinos charge at 30 mph . . ."
   Rhino statistics cited were found at https://www.lasikmd.com/blog/5-animals-worst-vision.

## CHAPTER 2: MOSES THE ADVOCATE

"As one scholar, T.D. Alexander, put it, 'Worship, to be true . . .'"

Alexander, T. D. (1994). *Exodus*. In D. A. Carson, R. T. France, J. A. Motyer, & G. J. Wenham (Eds.), *New Bible Commentary: 21st Century Edition* (4th ed., p. 116). Leicester, England; Downers Grove, IL: InterVarsity Press.

"As Franklin D. Roosevelt put it, 'A smooth sea . . .'"

Roosevelt, Franklin. Fireside Chat, April 14, 1938.

## CHAPTER 3: DAVID THE REDEEMER

"In essence, it gave Mephibosheth a new set of ABCs . . ."

Adapted from a lesson on Bible.org by Steven J. Cole entitled, "The Beauty of God's Grace."

"Judging the Lord to be a selfish tyrant, Adam and Eve took matters . . ."

This connection was largely inspired by a Charles Stanley manuscript on the following webpage: https://biblecentre.org/content.php?mode=7&item=830.

## CHAPTER 4: ISRAEL THE WANDERER

"As one Hebrew dictionary puts it, 'The meaning of Israel is . . .'"

"Israel Meaning," *Abarim Publications*, https://www.abarim-publications.com/Meaning/Israel.html.

"When it comes to America, as Ronald Reagan once declared, 'If we ever forget . . .'"

Reagan, Ronald. Ecumenical Prayer Breakfast, August 23, 1984, Dallas, Texas.

"It was a recurring sound heard in the heart through a stethoscope . . ."

This is the medical definition of "murmur" stated by *Oxford Languages*.

## CHAPTER 5: THE ONE TO COME

As the late pastor Tim Keller put it, "Crown Him or kill Him. Nothing in between."

A quote from Timothy Keller's sermon, "The King Is Come."

## CHAPTER 6: BROKEN PROMISE LAND

"As one expositor put it, 'It is his heart that speaks . . .'"

J. Robertson, *Hosea*; J. L. Nuelsen, E. Y. Mullins, & M. O. Evans (editors), *The International Standard Bible Encyclopaedia* (Vol. 1–5), Chicago: The Howard-Severance Company, p. 1426.

"Others have dubbed Hosea the second greatest love story ever told, 'second only to the . . .'

Steve Weaver, "The Second Greatest Love Story Ever" (Exposition of Hosea 3:1-5), *Historian*, July 18, 2006, pastorhistorian.com/2006/07/18/the-second-greatest-love-story-ever-exposition-of-hosea-31-5/.

"In Hebrew, the word 'Diblaim' comes from a doubling . . ."

"The Amazing Name Diblaim: Meaning and Etymology." *Abarim Publications*, May 5, 2014, www.abarim-publications.com/Meaning/Diblaim.html#.Xt1bT2hKhPY.

"Fascinatingly, the word translated 'comfort' here is the Hebrew נחם (*nâcham*), which can mean both 'to pity, console . . .'"

James Strong, *The New Strong's Exhaustive Concordance of the Bible: With Main Concordance, Appendix to the Main Concordance, Topical Index to the Bible, Dictionary of the Greek Testament*, Thomas Nelson, 1990, H5162.

"Thousands of years later, martyred missionary Jim Elliot would say, 'He is no fool . . .'"

Jim Elliot and Elisabeth Elliot. *The Journals of Jim Elliot*. F.H. Revell Co., 2002, p. 174.

"Not all scholars agree on the identity of said queen, but as one encyclopedia puts it, 'It is generally believed . . .'"

From the page titled, "Queen of Heaven" in *The Cyclopedia of Biblical, Theological, and Ecclesiastical Literature*. James Strong and John McClintock; Harper and Brothers; NY; 1880.

"As C.S. Lewis said, 'I believe in Christianity . . .'"

"Reflections: Christianity Makes Sense of the World." *C.S. Lewis Institute*, December 1, 2013, www.cslewisinstitute.org/resources/reflections-december-2013/.

## CHAPTER 7: SOME KIND OF FAMILY

"In the words of The Bible Project, 'Sometimes people need strange. . .'"

Whitney Woollard, "Sign Acts: The Weird, Wonderful World of Prophetic Communication by Whitney Woollard: BibleProject," April 30, 2020, bibleproject.com/blog/sign-acts wonderful-world-prophetic-communication.

"Briefly, we examined how the Hebrew name גֹּמֶר (transliterated 'Gomer') most nearly . . ."

Mike Campbell, "Meaning, Origin and History of the Name Gomer," *Behind the Name* www.behindthename.com/name/gomer#:~:text=Meaning%20%26%20History,wife%20of%20the%20prophet%20Hosea.

"For example, in 1963, the percent of American births to unmarried mothers was 6.3 percent. By 2020, that number grew to 40.5 percent—a 543 percent increase . . ."

These figures on births to unmarried women come from two CDC reports. The 2020 rate can be found on *National Vital Statistics Reports, Volume 70, Number 17*, on page 5. The 1963 rate is found in an archived table at the following address: cdc.gov/nchs/data/statab/t991x17.pdf.

"Subsequently, the rate of American kids living only with their mom more than tripled . . ."

This statistic comes from https://fathers.com/statistics-and-research/the-extent-of-fatherlessness/.

"These days, a fourth of all children in the United States, some 18.4 million, live without a full-time father . . ."

This statistic is for 2021 and comes from https://www.fatherhood.org/father-absence-statistic.

"Fatherless kids are twenty times more likely . . ."

This statistic comes from Voice for the Voiceless as cited by https://americafirstpolicy.com/latest/20220215-fatherlessness-and-its-effects-on-american-society.

"Children without fathers are also ten times more likely to abuse chemical substances . . ."

This statistic comes from the National Center for Fathering as cited by https://americafirstpolicy.com/latest/20220215-fatherlessness-and-its-effects-on-american-society.

"Daughters without a father are 711 percent more likely to have children as teenagers and 92 percent more likely to get divorced themselves . . ."

This statistic comes from https://thefatherlessgeneration.wordpress.com/statistics/.

"Nine out of ten homeless and runaway children are from fatherless homes, which is thirty-two times the average . . ."

This statistic comes from the Rochester Area Fatherhood Network as cited on https://thefatherlessgeneration.wordpress.com/statistics/.

"Fatherless kids are five times more likely to commit suicide, twenty times more likely to show behavioral disorders, and nine times more likely to drop out of high school . . ."

These statistics come from the US Dept. of Health, the US Center for Disease Control, and the National Principals Association Report, respectively, as cited on https://thefatherlessgeneration.wordpress.com/statistics/.

"Thus, it is no surprise that America, with the highest rate of single-parent households of any nation in the world, is also the reigning World Champion of incarceration rates, substance abuse, teen pregnancy, pornography production, and anxiety per capita . . ."

The incarceration rate comes from https://www.nytimes.com/2008/04/23/world/americas/23iht-23prison.12253738.html.

The substance abuse statistic comes from https://worldpopulationreview.com/country-rankings/drug-use-by-country.

The teen pregnancy statistic is only for the "developed world" and comes from the Guttmacher Institute as cited on https://www.guttmacher.org/fact-sheet/adolescent-pregnancy-and-its-outcomes-across-countries.

The pornography statistic comes from https://techcrunch.com/2007/05/12/internet-pornography-stats/?guccounter=1. The anxiety per capita statistic comes from https://www.statista.com/statistics/1115900/adults-with-anxiety-disorders-in-countries-worldwide-by-gender/.

The anxiety per capita statistic comes from https://www.statista.com/statistics/1115900/adults-with-anxiety-disorders-in-countries-worldwide-by-gender/.

"By 2016, public school teachers could be axed simply for having a Bible on their desk . . ."

Skinner, Victor. "Parents Slam School's Ban on Religious Symbols in the Classroom." *EAGnews.org*, 2 June 2020, www.eagnews.org/2016/10/parents-slam-schools-ban-on-religious-symbols-in-the-classroom/.

## CHAPTER 8: SALVATION STEPS IN

"'These two words,' says Desiring God Ministries, 'are overflowing with the gospel . . .'"

A quote from Jon Bloom's article, *But God,* found at https://www.desiringgod.org/articles/but-god.

"Author Stephen Altrogge agrees, writing, 'I would argue that these . . .'"

A quote from Stephen Altrogge's article, *Why "But God" Are the BEST Words in the WHOLE Bible!* found at https://theblazingcenter.com/2019/08/but-god.html.

"In fact, as church leader Iain Gordon points out, the phrase 'has been loved . . .'"

A quote from Iain Gordon's article, *But God in the Storms of Life,* found at https://jesusplusnothing.com/series/post/but-god-bible-verses-storms-trials-life.

"As commentator Albert Barnes deftly wrote, 'The words form . . .'"

A quote from *Barnes' Notes on the Bible* as found at https://biblehub.com/commentaries/hosea/2-1.htm. Bold added.

## CHAPTER 9: IT'S WHAT SHE SAID

"The American prison system, for instance, sees nearly 80 percent of the inmates . . ."

This statistic was found in the following article on *Prison Legal News*: https://www.prisonlegalnews.org/news/2019/may/3/long-term-recidivism-studies-show-high-arrest-rates/.

"As *Lord of the Rings* author J.R.R. Tolkien once said, 'The praise of the praiseworthy . . .'"

Tolkien, J.R.R. *The Two Towers*, Harper Collins UK, 2022.

"In the words of the *Cambridge Bible for Schools and Colleges*, Israel's second quote was 'not so much . . .'"

This quote is from the *Cambridge Bible for Schools and Colleges* and can be found at https://biblehub.com/commentaries/hosea/2-7.htm.

"As C.S. Lewis wrote in his eternal classic, *Mere Christianity*, 'An apparently trivial . . .'"

Lewis, *Mere Christianity*, p. 117.

## CHAPTER 10: A RANSOM FOR RENEWAL

"In fact, so stunning are these golden zigzags . . ."

A report of said intentional breakage can be found at the following: https://www.washingtonpost.com/wp-dyn/content/article/2009/03/02/AR2009030202723.html.